ECONOMIC COMMISSION FOR EUROPE
Committee on Environmental Policy

ENVIRONMENTAL PERFORMANCE REVIEWS

GEORGIA

UNITED NATIONS
New York and Geneva, 2003

Environmental Performance Reviews Series No.18

NOTE

Symbols of United Nations documents are composed of capital letters combined with figures. Mention of such a symbol indicates a reference to a United Nations document.

The designations employed and the presentation of the material in this publication do not imply the expression of any opinion whatsoever on the part of the Secretariat of the United Nations concerning the legal status of any country, territory, city or area, or of its authorities, or concerning the delimitation of its frontiers or boundaries.

UNITED NATIONS PUBLICATION
Sales No. E.03.II.E.35
ISBN 92-1-116851-1
ISSN 1020-4563

Foreword

The Environmental Performance Reviews are intended to assist countries in transition to improve their management of the environment by establishing baseline conditions and making concrete recommendations for better policy implementation and performance, and to integrate environmental policies into sectoral policies at the national level. Through the Peer Review process, they also promote dialogue among UNECE member countries and harmonization of environmental conditions and policies throughout the region.

This work was initiated by Environment Ministers at the second "Environment for Europe" Conference in Lucerne, Switzerland, in 1993. At the request of the Ministers, the UNECE Committee on Environmental Policy, meeting in special session in January 1994, decided to make the Environmental Performance Reviews a part of its regular programme. As a voluntary exercise, the Environmental Performance Review is undertaken only at the request of the country itself.

The studies are carried out by international teams of experts from the region, working closely with national experts from the reviewed country. Through a process of broad consultations, the experts comprehensively assess a wide range of issues related to the environment, covering three broad themes: the framework for environmental policy and management, the management of pollution and natural resources, and economic and sectoral integration. The team's final report contains recommendations for further improvement, taking into consideration the country's progress in the current transition period.

The teams also benefit from close cooperation with other organizations in the United Nations system, including the United Nations Development Programme, the United Nations Environment Programme, the World Bank and the World Health Organization.

This Environmental Performance Review is the eighteenth in the series published by the United Nations Economic Commission for Europe. I hope that this Review will be useful to all countries in the region, to intergovernmental and non-governmental organizations alike and, especially, to Georgia, its Government and its people.

Brigita Schmögnerova
Executive Secretary

Preface

The Environmental Performance Review (EPR) of Georgia began in December 2001, with the first preparatory mission, during which the final structure of the report was established. Thereafter, the review team of international experts was constituted. It included experts from Canada, Finland, France, the former Yugoslav Republic of Macedonia, Poland, the Russian Federation and the United States of America, together with experts from the secretariat of the United Nations Economic Commission for Europe (UNECE) and the European Centre for Environment and Health of the World Health Organization (WHO/ECEH).

The review mission took place from 16 to 28 November 2002. A draft of the conclusions and recommendations as well the draft EPR report were submitted to Georgia for comment in January 2003. In February 2003, the draft was submitted for consideration to the Ad Hoc Expert Group on Environmental Performance. During this meeting, the Expert Group discussed the report in detail with representatives of the Georgian Government, including the Minister of Environment and Natural Resources Protection, focusing in particular on the conclusions and recommendations.

The EPR report, with suggested amendments from the Expert Group, was then submitted for peer review to the UNECE Committee on Environmental Policy at its special session in Geneva on 18 February 2003. A high-level delegation from the Government of Georgia, including the Minister of Environment and Natural Resources Protection, participated in the peer review. The Committee adopted the recommendations as set out in this report. The review of Georgia's environmental performance is evidence of the efforts that the Government is making to improve environmental management, including the drafting and implementation of national legislation adapted to world standards. However, this process is constrained by the country's difficult economic situation as it attempts to move towards a market economy. Special attention was given during the reviews to the quality, use and supply of water resources, including drinking water, air and waste management, economic instruments, international cooperation, integration of environmental consideration into economic development, the policy framework, the implementation of national and international legislation, agriculture, energy and transport. The report stresses that the environment should become a priority, and an area of fruitful cooperation among all ministries and other key partners that have national or international competencies and responsibilities for environmental protection and management.

The UNECE Committee on Environmental Policy and the UNECE review team would like to thank both the Government of Georgia and the many excellent national experts who worked with the international experts and contributed with their knowledge and assistance. UNECE wishes the Government of Georgia success in carrying out the tasks before it to meet its environmental objectives and policy, including the implementation of the recommendations to support and promote environmental protection, and to improve overall living standards in Georgia.

UNECE would also like to express its deep appreciation to the Governments of Denmark, Germany, the Netherlands and the United Kingdom and to the European Commission for their support to the Environmental Performance Review Programme, to the European Centre for Environment and Health of the World Health Organization for its participation in the Review, and to the United Nations Development Programme, the World Bank and WHO for their contributions to the work in Georgia and the preparation of this report.

LIST OF TEAM MEMBERS

Ms. Mary Pat SILVEIRA	(ECE secretariat)	Team Leader
Mr. Ivan NARKEVITCH	(ECE secretariat)	Project Coordinator
Mr. Jyrki HIRVONEN	(ECE secretariat)	Introduction
Mrs. Irina KRASNOVA	Russian Federation	Chapter 1
Ms. Mijke HERTOGHS	(ECE secretariat)	Chapter 2
Mr. Antoine NUNES	(ECE secretariat)	Chapter 3
Ms. Helle HUSUM	Denmark	Chapter 4
Mr. Janusz ZUREK	Poland	Chapter 5
Mr. Ivan NARKEVITCH	(ECE secretariat)	Chapter 6
Mr. Ron HOFFER	United States of America	Chapter 7
Mr. Ljubco MELOVSKI	The former Yugoslav Republic of Macedonia	Chapter 8
Ms. Karin BURNOD-REQUIA	France	Chapter 9
Mr. Rene NIJENHUIS	(ECE secretariat)	Chapter 10
Mr. Bo LIBERT	(ECE secretariat)	Chapter 11
Mr. Guennadi VINOGRADOV	(ECE secretariat)	Chapter 12
Ms. Louise GRENIER	Canada	Chapter 13
Mr. Jouni J.K. JAAKKOLA Mr. Andrey I. EGOROV	(WHO/ECEH)	Chapter 14

UNECE Information Unit
Palais des Nations
Ch-1211 Geneva 10
Switzerland

Phone: +41 (0)22 917 44 44
Fax: +41 (0)22 917 05 05
E-mail: info.ece@unece.org
Website: http://www.unece.org

The mission for the project took place from 15 to 28 November 2002.

LIST OF NATIONAL CONTRIBUTORS

Mrs. Nino Chkhobadze Minister	Ministry of Environment and Natural Resources Protection
Mr. Zurab Tavartkiladze The first Deputy Minister	Ministry of Environment and Natural Resources Protection
Mr. Zaal Lomtadze Deputy Minister	Ministry of Environment and Natural Resources Protection
Mr. George Kolbin, Coordinator	Ministry of Environment and Natural Resources Protection
Mrs. Khatuna Akhalaia	Ministry of Environment and Natural Resources Protection
Mrs. Mariam Bakhtadze	Ministry of Environment and Natural Resources Protection
Ms. Nino Chikovani	Ministry of Environment and Natural Resources Protection
Ms. Keti Chubabria	Ministry of Environment and Natural Resources Protection
Ms. Tamar Gobejishvili	Ministry of Environment and Natural Resources Protection
Mr. Janri Karchava	Ministry of Environment and Natural Resources Protection
Mr. Anuri Kopilashvili	Ministry of Environment and Natural Resources Protection
Mrs. Marina Makarova	Ministry of Environment and Natural Resources Protection
Ms. Maya Metreveli	Ministry of Environment and Natural Resources Protection
Mr. George Nabakhtiani	Ministry of Environment and Natural Resources Protection
Mr. Irakli Oshoridze	Ministry of Environment and Natural Resources Protection
Ms. Tinatin Tetvadze	Ministry of Environment and Natural Resources Protection
Ms. Nino Tkhilava	Ministry of Environment and Natural Resources Protection
Mr. Ivane (Vano) Tsiklauri	Ministry of Environment and Natural Resources Protection
Mr. David Gzirishvili	National Agency of Climate Change
Mrs. Maka Tsereteli	Ministry of Environment and Natural Resources Protection
Mr. Devi Khichineishvili	NGO "Partnership for Social Iniciatives

TABLE OF CONTENTS

LIST OF FIGURES

LIST OF TABLES

LIST OF BOXES

ACRONYMS AND ABBREVIATIONS

BAT	Best available techniques
BOD	Biological oxygen demand
CEEN	Caucasus environmental NGO network
CFCs	Chlorofluorocarbons
CIS	Commonwealth of Independent States
CITES	Convention on International Trade in Endangered Species of Wild Fauna and Flora
COD	Chemical oxygen demand
CPI	Consumer price index
DDT	dichlorodiphenyltrichloroethane
EBRD	European Bank for Reconstruction and Development
EC	European Commission
EECCA	Eastern Europe, the Caucasus and Central Asia
EIA	Environmental impact assessment
EIB	European Investment Bank
EMEP	Cooperative Programme for Monitoring and Evaluation of the Long-range Transmission of Air Pollutants in Europe
EPR	Environmental Performance Review
EU	European Union
FAO	Food and Agriculture Organization of the United Nations
FDI	Foreign direct investment
GDP	Gross domestic product
GEF	Global Environment Facility
GHG	Greenhouse gas
GIS	Geographic information system
HCFCs	Hydrochlorofluorocarbons
HDI	Human Development Index
HMs	Heavy metals
IAEA	International Atomic Energy Agency
ICZM	Integrated Coastal Zone Management
IFIs	International financing institutions
IMF	International Monetary Fund
IPCC	Intergovernmental panel on Climate Change
IPPC	Integrated pollution prevention and control
ISO	International Standardization Organization
IUCN	World Conservation Union
JICA	Japan International Cooperation Agency
MAB	Man and Biosphere Programme of UNESCO
MAC	Maximum allowable concentration
MARPOL	International Convention for the Prevention of Pollution from Ships
MEAs	Multilateral environmental agreements
NATO	North Atlantic Treaty Organisation
NEAP	National Environmental Action Plan
NEHAP	National Environment and Health Action Plan
NGO	Non–governmental organization
NMVOC	Non-methane volatile organic compounds
ODP	Ozone depletion potential
ODS	Ozone-depleting substances
OECD	Organisation for Economic Co-operation and Development
OSCE	Organization for Security and Co-operation in Europe
PAH	Polyaromatic hydrocarbon
PCB	Polychlorinated biphenyl
PIC	Prior informed consent
POP	Persistent organic pollutant

PPP	Purchasing power parity
REC	Regional Environmental Center for Central and Eastern Europe
RON	Research octane number
SEE	State ecological expertise
TACIS	Technical Assistance to the Commonwealth of Independent States
TRACECA	Transport Corridor Europe–Caucasus–Asia
UNDP	United Nations Development Programme
UNECE	United Nations Economic Commission for Europe
UNEP	United Nations Environment Programme
UNESCO	United Nations Educational, Scientific and Cultural Organization
USAID	United States Agency for International Development
VAT	Value-added tax
VOC	Volatile organic compound
WHO	World Health Organization
WWF	World Wide Fund for Nature

SIGNS AND MEASURES

..	not available
-	nil or negligible
.	decimal point
ha	hectare
kt	kiloton
g	gram
kg	kilogram
mg	milligram
mm	millimetre
cm^2	square centimetre
m^3	cubic metre
km	kilometre
km^2	square kilometre
toe	ton oil equivalent
l	litre
ml	millilitre
min	minute
s	second
m	metre
°C	degree Celsius
GJ	gigajoule
kW_{el}	kilowatt (electric)
KWh	kilowatt-hour
kW_{th}	kilowatt (thermal)
MW_{el}	megawatt (electric)
MW_{th}	megawatt (thermal)
MWh	megawatt-hour
GWh	gigawatt-hour
TWh	terawatt-hour
Bq	becquerel
Ci	curie
MSv	millisievert
Cap	capita
Eq	equivalent
H	hour
kv	kilovolt
MW	megawatt
Gcal	gigacalorie
Hz	hertz

Currency

Monetary unit: Georgian Lari

Exchange rates: IM F

Year	Lari/US $	Lari/Euro
1995	..	..
1996	1.26	1.60
1997	1.30	1.47
1998	1.39	1.56
1999	2.02	2.16
2000	1.98	1.83
2001	2.07	1.86

Source: IM F. International Financial
Statistics, September 2002.
Note: Values are annual averages. Lari/Euro
rate is calculated using U S$/Euro rates from
the IM F IFS September 2002.

INTRODUCTION

I.1   The physical context

Georgia is the westernmost country of the South Caucasus, situated on the eastern coast of the Black Sea. The Greater Caucasus, the main ridge of the Caucasus Mountains, forms the northern border of the country and the Lesser Caucasus Mountains occupy the southern part of the country. These two mountain systems are connected by the Liakhvi mountain range that bisects the country from northeast to southwest. To the west of this divider is the Kolhhida lowland area up to the coast of the Black Sea. To the east of the Liakhvi range is the Kartalinia Plain, a high plateau that extends along the Kura river to the border with Azerbaijan.

The country has 310 kilometres of Black Sea coastline and it is bounded by four countries: the Russian Federation to the north (border length 723 km) and Turkey to the south-west (border 252 km), Armenia to the south (164 km) and Azerbaijan (322 km) to the south-east. The rugged Caucasus Mountains constitute about 85% of the land's total area of 69,700 km^2.

The highest elevations, including Georgia's highest peak Mount Shkhara (5,069 m) and Mount Kazbek (5,037 m), are situated at the Greater Caucasus with several other peaks higher than 4,500 m. In the Lesser Caucasus Mountains in the south, the altitude rarely exceeds 3,000 m. Along the coast of the Black Sea and the river valleys of the Kolkhida lowlands the elevations are generally below 100 m.

Georgia has thousands of rivers (about 25,000, most of them less than 25 km long) either draining into the Black Sea to the west or through Azerbaijan to the Caspian Sea to the east. The two largest rivers, the Kura (or Mtkvari) (384 km long) and the Rioni (327 km long), flow in opposite directions. The Kura rises in Turkey and runs eastwards across the plains of eastern Georgia and Azerbaijan into the Caspian Sea, while the Rioni (rising in the Greater Caucasus) and the smaller Inguri and Kodori rivers run through the fertile Kolkhida Lowlands into the Black Sea to the west.

Georgia's climate is quite varied ranging from year-round subtropical conditions on the Black Sea coast to continental, cold winters and hot summers in the east. The Greater Caucasus range forms a barrier against cold air from the north, while warm, moist air from the Black Sea moves easily into the coastal lowlands from the west. Along the Black Sea coast the region's subtropical Mediterranean climate allows palm trees to grow. The area is very humid and receives 1,000 to 2,000 mm of precipitation per year, often exceeding 2,000 mm in the coastal areas. The midwinter average temperature is 5° C and the midsummer average is 22° C.

The plains of eastern Georgia, shielded from the influence of the Black Sea by mountains, have a more continental climate. Humidity is lower than in the west and rainfall averages 500 to 800 mm per year. Winter temperatures average between 2° C to 4° C, while average summer temperatures range from 20° C to 24° C. Alpine and highland regions in the east and west, and the semiarid region on the Iori Plateau to the southeast have their own distinct microclimates.

At higher altitudes, precipitation is sometimes twice as heavy as in the eastern plains. In the west, the climate is subtropical to about 650 m; above that altitude is a band of moist and moderately warm weather, then a band of cool and wet conditions. Alpine conditions begin at about 2,100 m, and above 3,600 m mountains are covered by snow and ice year-round.

Land at lower altitudes has been extensively transformed for agricultural purposes and little of its native wildlife remains. Dense forests and woodlands cover 41% of the country mostly in the western and mountainous regions. In the sparsely wooded eastern uplands, underbrush and grasses predominate. Almost a third (28%) of the land is meadows and pastures, 11% is arable land and 4% is under permanent crops. Use of the remaining land (16%) is undefined (see figure I.1).

Georgia has one of the most diverse agricultural sectors of any of the former Soviet republics. The share of GDP from agricultural production has been diminishing during the past years, but it still stood at 22% in 2001. The long growing season allows the cultivation of almost any crop. The main agricultural crops are corn and winter wheat. Georgia has a long winemaking tradition and wine is its most important agricultural product. Other important crops are tea, citrus fruits and non-citrus fruits. The cultivation of tea and citrus fruit is confined to the western coastal area. Animal husbandry, mainly raising of cattle, pigs and sheep, is also important (figure I.2).

The country has abundant mineral resources, including gold, copper, lead, manganese, iron ore, coal, marble, and alabaster. Manganese, of which Georgia has one of the richest deposits in the world, was an important export commodity until 1990; construction materials such as marble and alabaster

are used domestically. However, at the moment only small amounts of any of the minerals are mined.

Georgia's potential oil reserves are estimated at 580 million tons, of which 200 million tons are in offshore fields of the Black Sea. The proven gas reserves stand at 8.5 million m^3, and estimated reserves at 125 million m^3. Georgia also has around 1 billion tons of coal reserves but the coal is not of good quality.

Almost 80% of Georgia's electricity in 1999 was produced by hydropower. Although hydroelectricity is abundant, production dropped from 14,421 million kWh in 1990 to 7,232 million kWh in 1996. Currently, only 1,300 MWs, less than half the total hydropower production capacity of 2,700 MWs, is used.

Figure I.1: Land use, 1996

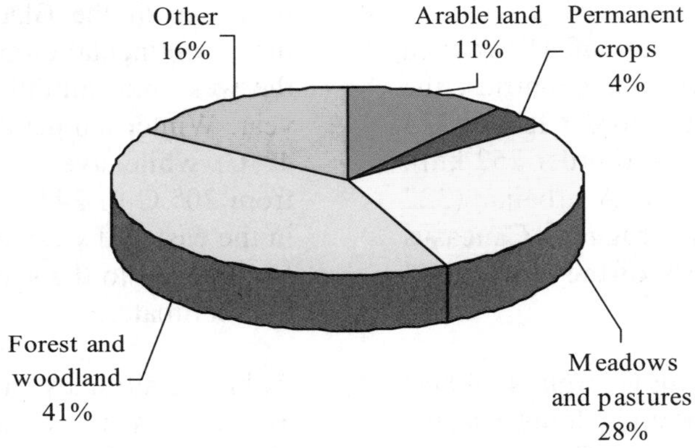

Other
16%

Arable land
11%

Permanent
crops
4%

Forest and
woodland
41%

Meadows
and pastures
28%

Source: http://www.parliament.ge/GENERAL/stat/emain.htm, 2002.

Figure I.2: GDP – composition by sector (per cent of total GDP)

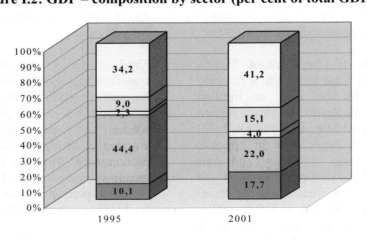

Source: UNECE common statistical database, 2002.

I.2 The human context

In 2001 the total population of Georgia stood at 4,945,000. The average population density of 71 persons/km^2 is quite low, but local population densities vary significantly due to Georgia's mountainous topography and urbanized population. The population is mainly concentrated along the river valleys and the coast of the Black Sea. The Kura river valley, where the capital Tbilisi (pop. 1,272,000) is located, is heavily and densely populated. Other important urban centres are Kutaisi (pop. 224,300), the second largest city located on the Rioni river, and Rustavi (pop. 159,000), situated downstream from Tbilisi on the Kura river. Both Batumi (pop 137,000), the capital of Ajaria, and Sokhumi (pop 59,000), the capital of Abkhazia, are on the Black Sea coast.

Georgians comprise the largest ethnic group, making up 70.1% of the population. The biggest minority groups are Armenians (8.1%), Russians (6.3%) and Azerbaijanis (5.7%). Other minority groups include Ossetians (3.0%), Greeks (1.89%), Abkhazians (1.8%), Ukrainians (0.97%), Kurds (0.62%), and Jews (0.46%).

The country's fertility rate decreased from 2.2 in 1990 to 1.1 in 2000, which is lower than the European Union average of 1.5 in 2000. The birth rate fell sharply from 17.1 (per 1000) in 1990 to 8.2 in 2001. The infant mortality rate fluctuated wildly during the 1990s, but the long-term trend has been decreasing, the rate falling from 15.8 (per 1000) in 1990 to 11.8 in 2001. Average life expectancy increased from 72.9 years in 1990 to 76.4 years (78.8 years for women and 74.0 years for men) in 2001 (table I.2).

In 1997, Georgia's Human Development Index (HDI) as calculated by the United Nations Development Programme (UNDP) stood at 0.729 (on a scale of 0.0 to 1.0) and the country ranked 85th. Georgia's ranking improved to 70th place in 1998 when its HDI was 0.726. Since then, Georgia's ranking has dropped to 81st place, with an HDI of 0.748 in 2000.

The country's literacy rate in 2000 was 99% and the attainment quotient of post secondary or tertiary education for adults aged 25 and older is 11.85%. The official language of the country is Georgian, but at least 11 other languages, including Abkhaz, Mingrelian and Ossetin, are spoken.

The dominant religion is Georgian Orthodox Christianity, to which 65% of the population belong, and an additional 18% belong to other Orthodox churches (Russian Orthodox and Armenian Apostolic). In Ajaria, the majority of Georgians are Sunni Muslims, and there are Shi'ah Muslims among the Azeri population. The total Muslim population is about 11%.

Table I.1: Living standard indicators

	1990	1991	1992	1993	1994	1995	1996	1997	1998	1999	2000
Passenger cars (per 1000 inhabitants)	..	88,9	88,0	86,3	81,5	65,4	59,7	48,8	47,8	..	..
Basic telephone lines (per 1000 inhabitants)	99	102	105	105	97	102	105	113	116	123	..
Mobile telephone subscribers (per 1000 inhabitants)	..	..	..	..	..	..	0	6	11	19	..
Internet hosts	..	..	..	..	..	57	212	413	738	898	..
Estimated Internet users (in thousands)	..	..	..	..	..	600	2 000	3 000	5 000	20 000	..

Source: ITU. Yearbook of Statistics 2001 and UNECE Transport Division, 2002.

Table I.2: Demography and health indices

	1990	1991	1992	1993	1994	1995	1996	1997	1998	1999	2000	2001
Birth rate (per 1000)	17,1	16,4	13,4	11,3	10,6	10,4	10,0	9,6	8,9	7,8	8,0	8,2
Fertility rate	2,2	2,1	1,8	..	..	..	1,4	1,3	1,2	1,1	1,1	..
Mortality rate (per 1000)	8,5	8,6	8,6	9,0	7,7	7,0	6,4	7,0	7,5	7,7	8,2	8,0
Infant mortality rate (per 1000)	15,8	13,8	12,6	18,3	16,7	13,1	17,4	..	15,2	17,6	14,9	11,8
Female life expectancy at birth (years)	76,4	76,7	76,8	..	..	..	..	..	77,9	81,2	79,3	78,8
Male life expectancy at birth (years)	68,9	68,9	69,0	..	..	..	..	..	71,0	73,8	73,5	74,0
Life expectancy at birth (years)	72,9	73,0	73,1	..	..	..	..	..	74,7	77,7	76,4	76,4
Population aged 1-14 in total (%)	24,6	24,5	24,2	..	..	..	..	..	..	20,4	20,4	20,4
Population aged 65 or over in total (%)	9,3	9,7	10,2	..	..	..	..	..	8,3	13,3	13,4	13,6

Sources: UNECE. PAU webpage on 24.1.2003.

I.3   The historical and economic context

History

The independence movement resurfaced in Georgia after the collapse of the Communist regimes in Eastern Europe in the late 1980s. In elections for the Georgian Supreme Soviet, in November 1990, the majority of votes went to the coalition of pro-independence parties. Mr. Zviad Gamsakhurdia, the leader of the coalition, became the Chairperson of the new legislature and Georgia's de facto head of State. In April 1991 the Georgian Supreme Soviet declared the republic independent from the Soviet Union.

In May 1991 Mr. Gamsakhurdia was elected as Georgia's first President but in December 1991 opposition forces besieged him in the Government's headquarters. Mr. Gamsakhurdia fled the capital in January 1992, and the opposition declared him deposed. In March 1992, Mr. Eduard Shevardnadze was chosen to lead the country as acting Chairperson of the State Council. Later that year he was elected to the post by popular vote.

Tensions between different national groups had been growing within the country before independence. In 1989 fighting broke out in South Ossetia between Ossetian separatists and Georgians. Hostilities ended with a ceasefire agreement in 1992 and a joint Georgian-Russian peacekeeping force was deployed in the region. After the leaders of Abkhazia declared their republic independent, fighting broke out in Abkhazia in July 1992. Georgian troops were sent into the area, but by October 1993 the Georgian militia was expelled and more than 200,000 ethnic Georgians fled from the area.

Georgia joined the United Nations in July 1992, becoming its 179th Member State. It joined the Commonwealth of Independent States (CIS) in October 1993. The following year Georgia and the Russian Federation negotiated an agreement that allowed the latter to maintain three military bases on Georgian territory in exchange for military training and supplies, but it was not ratified by the Georgian Parliament. The same year, Georgia joined the Partnership for Peace programme, which provides for limited military cooperation with the North Atlantic Treaty Organisation (NATO).

A United Nations-sponsored agreement, backed by peacekeeping troops from the Russian Federation, established a ceasefire in Abkhazia in April 1994.

Under the agreement, Abkhazia was to remain part of Georgia with a high degree of autonomy. In February 1995 the Abkhazian leadership announced that the republic was abandoning its demands for complete secession from Georgia and would instead insist upon a confederal structure of two sovereign States.

In August 1995 the Georgian legislature approved a new constitution, which restored the office of the presidency and established a 235-member legislature. In November 1995, presidential and legislative elections took place. Mr. Shevardnadze, who had survived an assassination attempt in August 1995, was overwhelmingly elected as president with more than 70% of the vote. His party, the Citizens' Union of Georgia, also became the largest party in the new legislature.

The 1995 Constitution did not define the territorial status of Abkhazia and South Ossetia, where sporadic clashes continued to occur. In January 1996 CIS leaders agreed to impose economic sanctions against Abkhazia until it agreed to rejoin Georgia. By the end of 1996, the governments of Georgia and South Ossetia reached an agreement to avoid the use of force against one another, and Georgia pledged not to impose sanctions against South Ossetia.

In February 1998, President Shevardnadze survived a second assassination attempt, and, in May, fighting was renewed between separatist and pro-Georgian forces in Abkhazia, causing more than 30,000 people to flee their homes. And finally, Gamsakhurdia supporters in the military led a one-day revolt in October 1998, fighting with government troops but surrendering after talks with government negotiators.

The political status of the provinces of Abkhazia and South Ossetia is unresolved and outbreaks of violence continue to erupt in Abkhazia. Currently, peacekeepers from the Russian Federation, under CIS authority, along with United Nations observers, are stationed in Abkhazia. The Georgian Government has offered the region considerable autonomy in order to encourage a settlement, which would allow the displaced to return home. Fighting in neighbouring Chechnya (Russian Federation) has generated fears that the conflict will spill over into Georgia. Several thousand Chechen refugees moved into Georgia's Pankisi Gorge in late 1999, causing tensions between the Governments of Georgia and the Russian Federation.

In legislative elections in October 1999, the Citizens' Union of Georgia won a majority of the seats. Mr. Shevardnadze was re-elected President in April 2000.

Economic context

The break-up of the Soviet Union disrupted established trade patterns but armed conflicts and several years of political instability created even more serious damage to the economy. Between 1990 and 1995 Georgia's GDP declined more than that of any other former Soviet republic. In 1994 GDP was only 23.4% of its 1989 level. This economic hardship led Georgia to become dependent upon foreign financial and humanitarian aid, but the increasing political stability in the mid-1990s enabled its economy to recover.

The GDP contraction bottomed out in 1995, when Georgia tightened its monetary and fiscal policies with support from the International Monetary Fund (IMF). The Georgian economy began to recover, and since 1995 it has grown steadily. Growth was especially strong in 1996 and 1997, when GDP grew 11.2% and 10.6% respectively. After 1997 growth was moderate at 2 to 4.5% a year. Part of the growth was attributable to the stabilizing effect of the new national currency, the lari, introduced in September 1995 to replace the provisional currency, the Georgian coupon (table I.4).

Annual inflation as measured by the consumer price index (CPI) was a staggering 22,470% in 1995, but fell to 39% in 1996 and further still to 6.9% in 1997. In 1998 the economic and financial crises in the Russian Federation and in Asia, drought and political events (such as outbreak of hostilities in Abkhazia and an assassination attempt against the President) curbed GDP growth to 2.9%. Delayed effects of the crisis were felt in 1999, when GDP growth was 3% and CPI inflation rose sharply to 19.2%.

After the introduction of the lari, foreign direct investment (FDI) also began to increase. From a modest US$ 6 million in 1995, FDI grew to US$ 265 million in 1998. The Baku-Supsa oil pipeline, the first major infrastructure investment project, was completed in April 1999. Since then, the FDI level has fallen, amounting to US$ 109.9 million in 2001. In the future the construction of the Baku-Tbilisi-Ceyhan oil pipeline and the Shah-Deniz gas pipeline will offer opportunities for investments in the energy sector and in related infrastructure.

In a very difficult economic-political climate, the Georgian Government has recorded some remarkable achievements. Hyperinflation was tamed, the country qualified for IMF economic structural adjustment facility credit status, a new stable national currency was introduced, prices were freed to follow market prices, currency controls and investment obstacles were removed, accession to the World Trade Organization was prepared and agreements were signed for the development of a pipeline to transport Caspian oil across Georgia to the Black Sea.

Shortly after independence the Government adopted a law on privatization but delayed its implementation until the return of political stability in the mid-1990s, when privatization began in earnest. By mid-2001 more than 15,500 small enterprises, 1,300 medium- and large-sized enterprises, and 789,000 hectares of agricultural land had been privatized. The privatization of the large companies has been slow and difficult, since they need substantial capital investments.

Energy shortages continue to hinder Georgia's economic development. Electricity production is in a critical condition, and the country is able to meet its electricity needs only by importing energy from neighbouring countries. Hydroelectric power accounted for 79.6% of power generation in 1999, and its share rose as plants burning fossil fuels stood idle because the country was unable to pay for gas and oil imports. The electricity shortages and rationing have resulted in public unrest (especially in the winter 2000/2001). In 1998, Georgia privatized Tbilisi's energy distribution system to generate the capital needed to rehabilitate the sector.

Corruption in Georgia is a persistent obstacle to investments and to economic development. It has stunted economic growth and undermined the credibility of the Government and its reforms. In 2000 the Government created an Anti-corruption Commission. It issued a report, and the Anti-corruption Coordinating Council was created in the summer of 2001 to implement its recommendations.

Problems with fiscal policy have affected macroeconomic conditions and international lending to Georgia in recent years. An IMF programme initiated in 1996 was put on hold in 1999 due to Georgia's failure to meet its budgetary targets. Improved macroeconomic performance and a more realistic budget in 2000 paved the way for

IMF approval of a new programme for Georgia in January 2001. Georgia's fiscal performance since then has been uneven, and the IMF programme was halted repeatedly in 2001-02, following Georgia's continued difficulty in reaching targets and complying with IMF requirements.

Georgia's economic performance is slowly improving. With a 4.5% increase in 2001, GDP grew for the seventh consecutive year, although it was still only 33.3% of its 1989 level. When GDP per capita is measured according to purchasing power parity (PPP), the change is more visible. In 1994 GDP per capita (at PPP) was only US$ 1,784 but in 2001 it had grown to US$ 3,545. Inflation is under 5%, and the current account balance deficit is diminishing.

I.4   The institutions

Georgia is a multiparty democratic republic with a strong executive presidency. All citizens aged 18 or older are eligible to vote. The country has 11 administrative units, including two autonomous republics: Ajaria and Abkhazia. Environmental responsibilities are distributed among 15 regional environmental bodies, including the Ministry of Environment in Ajaria and the State Committee of Ecology in Abkhazia.

According to the 1995 Constitution, the president is the head of State and directly elected to a maximum of two five-year terms. The president appoints a council of ministers headed by a minister of State. The council of ministers is accountable to the president. The 1995 Constitution also created a new legislature to replace the former State Council. The new parliament is unicameral with 235 members elected for a four-year term. One hundred and fifty of the members are elected on a proportional basis and 85 are elected in single-member constituencies.

The autonomous republics of Ajaria and Abkhazia and the region of South Ossetia have their own locally elected governments, consisting of a legislature and a local leader. Ajaria does not seek secession from Georgia, and its local government cooperates with Georgia's central Government and recognizes the country's Constitution. The local governments of separatist Abkhazia and South Ossetia are not recognized by Georgia's central Government.

Table I.3: List of Ministries and Departments

Ministry of Labour, Health and Social Affairs
Ministry of Urbanization and Construction
Ministry of Transport and Communication
Ministry of Food and Agriculture
Ministry of Economy, Industry and Trade
Ministry of Environment and Natural Resources Protection
Ministry of Fuel and Energy
Ministry of Justice
Ministry of Finance
Ministry of Refugees Affairs
Ministry of Defence
Ministry of the Interior
Ministry of State Property Management
Ministry of State Security

Departments
State Department of Forestry
State Department of Geology
State Department of Land Management
State Department for the Management of Reserves, Protected Areas and Hunting Farms
State Department of Hydrometeorology
State Department of State Border Control
State Department of Geodesy and Cartography
State Department of Standardization, Metrology and Certification
State Department of Social and Economic Information

Source: Ministry of Environment and Natural Resources Protection, 2002.

Georgia's judiciary is based on a civil-law system. The Supreme Court is the highest court. Its judges are elected by the legislature, on the recommendation of the president, for a term of ten years. Georgia also has a Constitutional Court, which rules on the constitutionality of new legislation. The president, the legislature and the Supreme Court each appoint three of the nine judges of the Constitutional Court, who serve for ten years.

I.5 Environmental context

The diminishing economic activity of the 1990s eased the impact of industrial production on the environment. At the same time, hardship among the population led to more exploitation of natural resources (such as firewood). Lack of investment in infrastructure led to its deterioration, increasing the impact of non-industrial sectors on the environment. According to the National Environmental Action Plan (NEAP 2000):

- Reduced economic activity has significantly reduced surface water pollution caused by industrial and agricultural emissions.
- The central and regional authorities lack the funds to maintain, restore or repair outdated water-supply systems or waste-water treatment facilities.
- Municipal waste is disposed of in poorly designed and managed landfills.
- The exploitation of natural resources without authorization is leading to environmental degradation, a reduction in habitats and a decline in biodiversity.
- Significant agricultural land is lost to erosion.
- The degradation of the environment leads to a deterioration in public health and a reduction in labour.

Table I.4: Selected economic indicators

	1990	1991	1992	1993	1994	1995	1996	1997	1998	1999	2000	2001
GDP (change, 1989=100)	84.9	67.0	36.9	26.1	23.4	24.0	26.7	29.5	30.3	31.2	31.8	33.3
GDP (% change over previous year)	-15.1	-21.1	-44.9	-29.3	-10.4	2.6	11.2	10.6	2.9	3.0	1.9	4.5
GDP in current prices (million lari)	0.2	0.2	1.5	27.6	1,807	3,693	3,847	4,639	5,041	5,666	6,016	6,617
GDP in current prices (million US$)	..	..	..	..	1,088	2,860.4	3,046.7	3,575.5	3,626.8	2,796.9	3,044.2	3,192.9
GDP per capita (US$ PPP per capita)	5,801	4,738	2,679	1,945	1,784	1,873	2,122	2,487	2,811	3,061	3,245	3,544
Share of agriculture in GDP (%)	31.5	28.6	55.1	69.7	65.1	44.4	34.1	30.7	27.8	26.0	21.3	22.0
Industrial output (% change over previous year)	-5.7	-22.6	-45.8	-36.7	-39.1	-13.5	6.8	8.2	-1.8	7.4	10.8	-5.0
Agricultural output (% change over previous year)	6.8	-36.0	-13.4	-11.9	11.5	13.4	6.0	6.5	-10.0	8.0	-15.0	6.0
Labour productivity in industry (% change over previous year)	-4.3	-23.7	-43.7	-27.1	-33.8	-4.5	11.2	22.7	0.2	7.3	17.2	1.6
CPI (% change over the preceding year, annual average)	4.2	78.7	1,176.9	4,084.9	22,470.0	163.0	39.0	6.9	3.6	19.0	4.0	4.7
PPI (% change over the preceding year, annual average)	..	..	..	..	..	..	..	..	2.3	15.7	5.8	3.6
Registered unemployment (% of labour force, end of period)	..	..	0.3	2.0	3.8	3.4	3.2	8.0	4.2	5.6	..	..
Balance of trade in goods and non-factor services (million US$)	..	..	-378.0	-448.0	-365.0	-337.4	-350.9	-558.9	-760.4	-533.9	-506.1	-549.4
Current account balance (million US$)	..	..	-248.0	-354.0	-277.2	-215.6	-274.9	-374.9	-416.5	-195.1	-261.9	-211.4
"　　　　(as % of GDP)	..	..	..	..	-25.5	-7.5	-9.0	-10.5	-11.5	-7.0	-8.6	-6.6
Net FDI inflows (million US$)	..	..	0.0	0.0	8.0	6.0	40.0	203.0	265.3	81.2	131.7	109.9
Net FDI flows (as % of GDP)	..	..	..	..	0.7	0.2	1.3	5.7	7.3	2.9	4.3	3.4
Cumulative FDI (million US$)	0.0	0.0	0.0	0.0	8.0	14.0	54.0	257.0	522.3	604.5	735.7	845.6
Foreign exchange reserves (million US$)	..	..	0.7	1.0	41.4	194.0	188.9	199.8	123.0	132.4	109.4	160.3
(as months of imports)	..	..	0.01	0.01	0.67	3.33	2.95	2.28	1.39	1.84	1.36	1.84
Total net external debt (million US$)	..	..	94.1	596.0	962.5	1,022.7	1,168.1	1,312.6	1,506.4	1,568.8	1,500.3	1,439.7
Exports of goods (million US$)	..	..	267.0	457.0	380.7	362.7	417.0	493.5	300.0	329.6	459.4	496.1
Imports of goods (million US$)	..	..	645.0	905.0	745.7	700.1	767.9	1052.4	1060.4	863.4	965.5	1045.6
Ratio of net debt to exports (%) (calc)	..	..	283.7	76.7	39.6	35.5	35.7	37.6	19.9	21.0	30.6	34.5
Ratio of gross debt to GDP (%)	..	..	..	..	92.3	42.5	44.5	42.3	44.9	60.8	52.9	50.1
Exchange rates: annual averages (NC/US$)	..	..	..	..	1.7	1.3	1.3	1.3	1.4	2.0	2.0	2.1
Population (1000)	5,417.6	5,417.9	5,409.4	5,438.3	5,418.4	5,416.9	5,382.6	5,403.2	5,259.6	5,251.3	5,023.0	4,945.6

Source: UNECE Common statistical database and National Statistics.

Figure I.3:   Map of Georgia

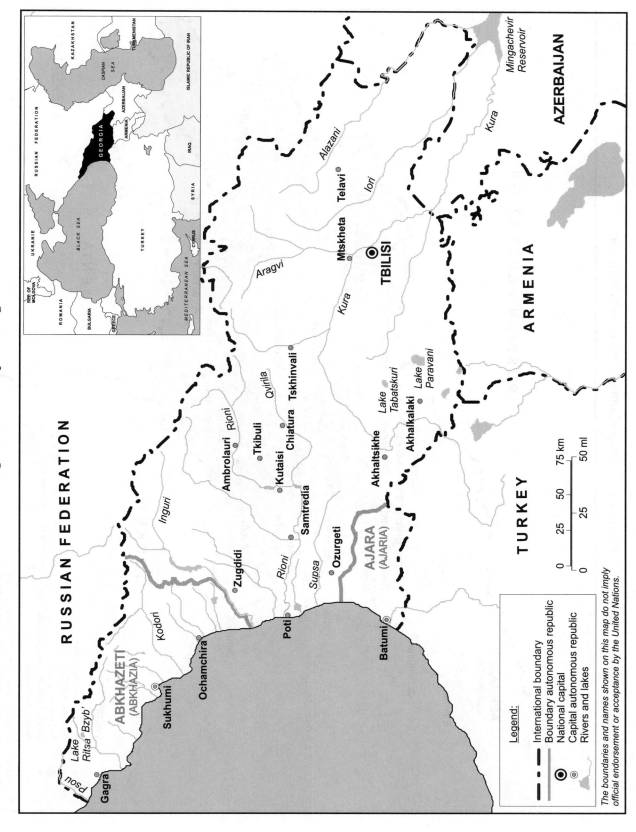

Figure I.4:   Map of administrative units in Georgia

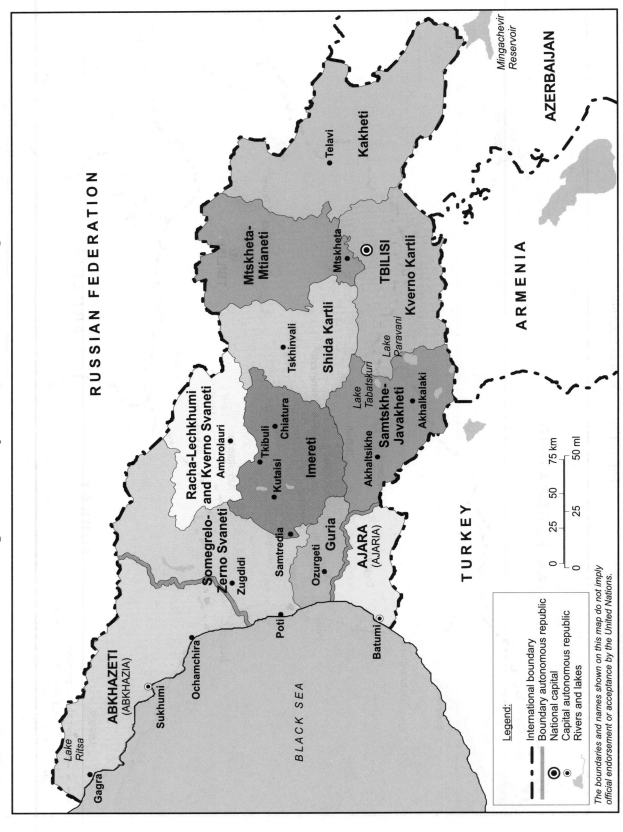

PART I: THE FRAMEWORK FOR ENVIRONMENTAL POLICY AND MANAGEMENT

Chapter 1

POLICY, LEGAL AND INSTITUTIONAL FRAMEWORK AND SECTORAL INTEGRATION

1.1   Environmental policies

Context

Since it proclaimed its independence from the former Soviet Union on 9 April 1991, Georgia has been taking steps to establish a legislative system to match the changed political conditions and emerging problems, including environmental ones. Among the most serious of these are: a dangerous increase in air pollution, particularly in cities; water pollution, especially from untreated waste-water discharges, and a degradation of the drinking-water-supply sources; waste caused by poor waste and hazardous chemical management; land degradation; and degradation of the Black Sea owing to pollution.

To address these challenges, efforts have been made to develop a suitable body of environmental legislation.

Policy objectives and priorities

The National Environmental Action Plan (NEAP), adopted in 2000, sets out six priorities among the actions aimed to address environmental problems. These include:
- The rehabilitation and improvement of water-supply and sewage systems;
- An increase in the share of municipal transport and monitoring of fuel quality;
- A policy to prevent pollution by encouraging the introduction of best available techniques (BAT) and cleaner production methods;
- The improvement of waste management through the application of economic instruments;
- The introduction of integrated coastal zone management to address the environmental problems of the Black Sea;
- The preservation of biodiversity, including that of forest ecosystems.

The NEAP is the most up-to-date environmental policy statement. Under the Law on Environmental Protection, the Ministry of Environment and Natural Resources Protection, in cooperation with other ministries, is mandated to develop a strategy for sustainable development. A National Commission for Sustainable Development was therefore established in 1996 by presidential order, but it has so far failed to develop a strategy, and no practical work is being done on it. The principal reasons appear to be a lack of common vision for the priority directions of the country's development, weak inter-institutional cooperation, the poor representation of stakeholders, and the unavailability of a methodological basis for the preparation of the strategy. The Law on Environmental Protection also stipulates that national environmental action plans should be based on the strategy for sustainable development, but this has obviously not been possible.

The State's environmental policy objectives for specific activities are further detailed in numerous planning documents that are already in force. Among these are:
- The Programme for social and economic recovery and economic growth approved by Presidential Decree No. 89 on 10 March 2001, and the Interim paper on the national plan for poverty reduction and economic growth approved by Resolution No. 1282 of the President of Georgia on 30 November 2000;
- The National Environmental Action Plan adopted in May 2000 by Presidential Decree No. 191.

A number of planning documents that address specific environmental issues are being prepared, including:

- The national programme and action plan on climate change;
- The national programme and action plan for phasing out ozone-depleting substances;

- The forestry development strategy;
- The integrated coastal zone management programme;
- The national Black Sea strategic action plan;
- The biodiversity strategy and action plan;
- The State programme and action plan on environmental education;
- The strategy (concept) of the State programme for improving fuel quality;
- The national action programme to combat desertification.

Environmental programmes, strategies and plans are nearly always prepared with the financial support of international organizations – predominantly the Global Environment Facility (GEF) and the World Bank. The Ministry of Environment and Natural Resources Protection is mostly charged with coordinating the drafting work that is often done by NGOs or mixed working groups without significant involvement of the Ministry, while implementation is predominantly an obligation of the Ministry and other State bodies.

Although there are many political documents on environmental protection, its impact should be measured in terms of implementing measures and actual results. However, there is no procedure for reporting on the state of implementation, and no official statements have been made on this issue. In general and in comparison with economic and social issues, environmental protection is not viewed as a priority. Regular cuts in budgetary funding prove that environmental protection receives little attention. It should also be noted that the proliferation of planning and strategic documents, each with their own priorities and objectives, is likely to lead to more confusion rather than to a clear concept of the necessary actions and the genuine priorities.

Although the established priorities correspond to the country's principal environmental problems, government bodies should outline implementing measures with clear time frames and a sequence of actions so that government activity can focus on the priorities. In addition, the strategy for sustainable development should be developed, as required by the Law on Environmental Protection. It should establish a nationwide environmental policy, integrating sectoral priorities, and provide for better coordination of environmental protection activities by the ministries.

1.2 The legal framework for environmental protection

The legal framework

The Constitution is supreme. No other regulatory document can contradict it. Parliament enacts laws. Environmental legislation for Parliament's consideration is drafted by the Parliamentary Committee for Environmental Protection and Natural Resources. It consists of 16 deputies and 5 staff members. The President of Georgia is both head of State and head of Government, and according to the Constitution is responsible for formulating and ensuring implementation of domestic policy. The President adopts decrees and orders, which may establish rules lacking in laws or ensure implementation of legislative requirements. Ministries and agencies within the executive branch of the State power adopt orders and decrees in accordance with their mandates. International treaties signed by the President and ratified by Parliament are part of the national legal system and take precedence over national laws.

The Constitution of Georgia establishes basic rules on environmental protection and natural resource use. Its article 37 proclaims that everyone is entitled to live in a healthy environment and to use natural and cultural resources, and is obliged to protect them. The Georgian Government is responsible for ensuring the rational use of natural resources and the protection of the environment in the interest of present and future generations. The same article also grants the right to everyone to have access to complete, objective and timely information on his or her working and living conditions.

The Law on Environmental Protection, adopted on 10 December 1996, establishes the general legal framework for comprehensive environmental protection and for the use of natural resources. It covers a wide range of issues, including environmental standard setting, licensing of activities connected with natural resource use, environmental permitting, keeping State registers of environmental information, and monitoring. It outlines general environmental requirements for the production of goods and the generation of waste, and establishes procedures for the State ecological expertise of economic projects. The Law proceeds from the "polluter pays" principle and provides for an obligation on nature users and polluting sources to pays taxes, and to insure against environmental risks. Provision is also made for establishing tax privileges to those who use best available techniques and low-waste technologies or produce ecologically friendly products.

Article 6 of the Law lists citizens' environmental rights, including the right to live in a healthy environment, to use natural resources, to obtain full, true and timely information on the state of the environment, to join public environmental protection organizations, to take part in decision-making, to receive compensation for environmental damage, and to challenge decisions on new projects, or the construction, reconstruction and use of facilities that create a risk to the environment.

The Law contains framework rules on State ecological expertise, environmental permits and standard setting that are further developed in specific laws and governmental regulations.

The Law on Ambient Air Protection (1999) is clearly meant to follow the European legislation. It contains direct references to certain EU directives and other acts without transposing or incorporating their provisions. So implementation of the Law requires direct application of such directives, although it is not clear how this should be done as the directives are addressed to EU member States, and not to executive bodies or other persons in Georgia.

As to its contents, the Law establishes a framework for the regulation of air pollution, including such measures as the establishment of air quality standards (values) and monitoring.

The Law on the Transit and Import of Wastes Into and Out of the Territory of Georgia adopted in 1995 and further amended in 1997 is aimed to implement the Basel Convention. It restricts the import and export of hazardous and non-hazardous waste. The Law contains many references to European regulations on waste. Although, generally, harmonization with international practices is positive, in technical terms, direct application of EU rules to Georgia's governmental bodies without any adaptation complicates implementation. It would be better to take certain provisions from EU directives and to incorporate them into Georgian law.

The 1998 Law on Pesticides and Agrochemicals provides for the registration of pesticides and agrochemicals. Only registered pesticides can be used, exported, imported and traded. Prohibited and restricted pesticides may be used or traded with a special permit from the Ministry of Agriculture. In exceptional cases such as agricultural emergencies, the Ministry of Agriculture after coordination with the Ministry of the Environment and the Ministry of Health may issue permits for the import, trade and use of prohibited or restricted pesticides. Lists of permitted pesticides are reviewed every five years. Controlling agencies are allowed to suspend and ban the use of pesticides. All new pesticides are subject to tests.

The 1998 Law on Hazardous Chemical Substances covers the handling of hazardous chemicals and provides for various procedural restrictions to ensure their safe use, including classification, registration, permitting and labelling. Enterprises handling chemicals are obliged to set up emergency response teams and prepare contingency plans. It is prohibited to locate such plants near cities, densely populated areas or facilities producing food. Chemicals should be classified and the Ministry of Health should establish classification rules. However, no such rules have been adopted. Registration and State expertise are also within the competence of the Ministry of Health. Provision is made for access to information about chemicals. Certain competences in relation to chemicals are delegated to the Ministry of Agriculture, including keeping the State register in cooperation with the Ministry of Health.

The 1999 Forest Code comprehensively regulates all forest use and protection, including ownership rights, institutional arrangements, procedures for leasing forests and inspection measures.

The protection of valuable ecosystems is regulated by the Law on Specially Protected Areas adopted in 1996, which established a system of natural reserves, national parks, protected landscapes, biosphere reserves and others, and determines a regime for their use and protection. The types of protected areas explicitly follow the World Conservation Union (IUCN) classification and the Law contains references to IUCN categories.

Box 1.1:   Selected environmental legislation

- Law on Soil Protection (1994)
- Law on Plant Protection (1994)
- Law on the Transit and Import of Hazardous Wastes (1995)
- Law on Protected Areas System (1996)
- Law on Mineral Resources (1996)
- Law on State Ecological Expertise (1996)
- Law on Environmental Permits (1996)
- Law on Environmental Protection (1996)
- Law on Wildlife (1996)
- Law on Self-Government (1997)
- Law on Water (1997)
- Law on Forest Use (1998)
- Law on Hazardous Chemical Substances (1998)
- Law on Nuclear and Radiation Safety (1998)
- Law on Pesticides and Agrochemicals (1998)
- Law on the Sea Area of Georgia (1998)
- Law on the Creation and Management of Kolheti Protected Areas (1998)
- Law on Compensation for Damage from Hazardous Substances (1999)
- Forest Code (1999)
- Law on Ambient Air Protection (1999)

Generally, these laws establish a legal framework for addressing the principal environmental issues and their scope is broad. The following draft laws now before Parliament are aimed at filling the gaps and further improving the environmental legislation:

- Amendments to the Forest Code;
- Amendments to the Law on Protected Area Systems;
- The draft law on the red data lists and red data book;
- The draft law on waste; and
- The draft law on public access to environmental information and decision-making.

The laws regulating environmental protection determine general legal norms that are not sufficiently developed in regulatory acts. For instance, the Forest Code contains a list of ministerial regulations to be adopted to ensure its implementation. Only few have been adopted. The lack of implementing rules reduces the efficiency of environmental policy and laws.

Licensing of natural resource use and environmental permitting

According to the Law on Environmental Protection, there is a combined system of licences and permits. There are three kinds of environmental licences: licences for environmental protection activities, licences for environmental pollution and licences for the use of natural resources. The first two are issued at the discretion of the Ministry of Environment and Natural Resources Protection, in accordance with criteria established by law; the third is decided by intersectoral councils under the Ministry of Environment and Natural Resources Protection. Environmental permits, which may only be given after an environmental licence has been issued and both an environmental impact assessment and a State ecological expertise have been carried out, are also under the sole responsibility of the Ministry of Environment and Natural Resources Protection.

The licence for environmental protection activities covers environmental audits, hydrometeorological studies and other environmental protection activities that require specific skills. The licence for environmental pollution concerns emissions and discharges of harmful waste or any negative physical impact on the environment. The licence for the use of natural resources covers water use, the extraction of minerals, land use, forest cutting, fauna and flora. The licence sets fixed quotas for the use of the natural resources.

There are four interdepartmental councils responsible for licensing the use of natural resources: one for minerals; a second for surface water; a third for flora; and a fourth for fauna. In conformity with the decision of the respective interdepartmental council, the competent ministry or its local representative issues licences. Licences allow the licensee to take a definite type and volume of natural resources within an established period of time. Licences are not always sufficient for using natural resources. For instance, the use of forests also requires a contract for forest use and a forest-cutting permit from the local representative of the State Forestry Department.

In addition to the licences, a person wishing to begin an economic activity must also apply for an environmental permit from the Ministry of Environment and Natural Resources Protection or its regional bodies. Such permits are issued only if the outcome of the State ecological expertise is positive. Entrepreneurs need to obtain several permits, but only one is specific to the environment. The 1996 Law on Environmental Permits outlines the permitting procedure. The applicant has to submit a feasibility study of the project and an environmental impact assessment (EIA) to the Ministry of Environment and Natural Resources Protection, and must provide the Ministry with other related information (e.g. information about the applicant, intended impacts on the environment, contingency plans).

The Law lists four categories of activities. The first two concern activities with a potential for causing a serious or significant and irrevocable impact on the environment and health. They require an environmental permit from the Ministry. The third category concerns activities that should not have a serious impact on the environment; they require a permit from the regional offices of the Ministry, and from the Ministry of Environment and Natural Resources Protection of the autonomous republics of Ajaria and Abkhazia. For the fourth category, defined as activities with an insignificant impact on the environment, the regional offices and the local bodies of the Ministry issue permits.

The Law on Environmental Permits defines "environmental permits" and states that they allow an operator to emit and discharge pollutants; however, according to the Law on Water and the Law on Ambient Air Protection, pollutants may be discharged into water and air only if a separate permit has been obtained for each. So formally this means that for one and the same impact (discharge of effluents) an operator has to obtain a water discharge permit and an environmental permit.

In practice, a person wishing to build a new facility or start an economic activity connected with the use of certain natural resources, or wishing to modify significantly his company's production process, has to obtain several licences and an environmental permit, and conclude the necessary agreements for nature use. These procedures are not integrated and decisions are taken separately for each type of use and environmental impact, without duly considering the interconnection among all natural objects and natural resources within one ecosystem. Besides, it makes the whole procedure very heavy and inefficient.

EIA and State Ecological Expertise

Economic activities that could have a significant impact on the environment or are connected with the use of natural resources are permitted only after conducting an EIA and if the State ecological expertise is positive. EIA and State ecological expertise (SEE) are two interconnected procedures of State decision-making that are regulated by four different instruments: the Law on Environmental Protection, the Law on State Ecological Expertise, the Regulations on Environmental Impact Assessment and on Procedures for Conducting the State Ecological Expertise approved by the Ministry of Environment and Natural Resources Protection. Activities subject to EIA and SEE are listed in the Law on State Ecological Expertise (art. 5) and the Law on Environmental Permits (art. 4). In general, all projects that require an environmental permit also require a positive State ecological expertise.

According to these regulatory acts, before applying to State bodies for a natural resource licence and an environmental permit, the applicant has to conduct an EIA on his own initiative and at his own expense. The aim of EIA is to reveal all the potential effects of the intended activities, including environmental, social and economic ones. EIA is mandatory for the activities listed in the Law on Environmental Permits and voluntary for others. The operator has to submit the results together with other documentation for environmental review by the Ministry of Environment and Natural Resources Protection (State ecological expertise).

The Ministry of Environment and Natural Resources Protection's Department for State environmental assessment, which is authorized to carry out State ecological expertise, conducts on average 65 to 68 a year. The Department keeps a list of experts, including scientists, and lawyers, who actually conduct the ecological expertise. On the basis of the expert opinions, the Department prepares an environmental summary with either a negative or a positive assessment. The respective licences and permits are issued, and the project is allowed to go ahead only with a positive assessment. With this tool the Ministry manages to control new economic projects; however, the provision of the Law (art. 5) that requires State ecological expertise of various programmes and plans is not fully complied with.

Georgia's EIA and State ecological expertise procedures generally conform to international practice. At the same time, the Law on State Ecological Expertise does not provide for draft laws, long-term plans and economic development strategies to be assessed, although strategic impact assessment, as such an assessment is called, is now internationally accepted practice. Besides, the Law does not require the long-term, cumulative or transboundary effects of planned actions to be studied.

1.3   Enforcement and compliance mechanisms

Inspection rules and procedures

Environmental inspection is carried out by several State bodies, which have special inspectorates. The State Ecological Police has a special role. It was created in 1992 within the Ministry of the Interior as the successor to the former fishing inspectorate. The Police enforce legislation on poaching, illegal mining, illegal forest use and food safety. In total, 458 policemen are engaged in inspection work. They are equipped with vehicles, arms and other means to find and detain offenders. Police authority is decentralized; inspection powers are assigned to police units in 67 districts with 3-4 policemen each.

The Ministry of Environment and Natural Resources Protection also plays a significant role in inspecting industrial facilities that emit and discharge pollutants, use water, biological resources or minerals (except oil and gas). Its regional offices are also authorized to carry out inspections. Inspectors are empowered to visit facilities, ask for environmentally relevant documents, carry out tests and check technological equipment if they have permission from the court. They may also file administrative cases with the courts.

Inspection is under-funded. For instance, the Ministry's regional environmental bodies do not have the means to respond immediately to information about offences. Although the Ecological Police is better equipped, it also suffers from a shortage of material, professional staff and technical capacity.

The duplication of enforcement functions undermines the efficiency of inspections. In many instances the law directly assigns enforcement functions to several State bodies simultaneously, thus creating a basis for administrative duplication. For instance, the Law on Pesticides and Agrochemicals provides that enforcement shall be carried out by the Ministries of Agriculture, Environment and Health. The State Forestry Department, the State Ecological Police and the Ministry of Environment and Natural Resources Protection are responsible for inspecting forestry activities and enforcing the Forestry Code. In practice, it causes inter-agency rivalry and conflicts and places an extra burden on companies that have to deal with several inspectors with the same competence.

Under the 2001 Law on the Control of Production Activities, an inspection may be conducted only with a court order. Although provision is also made for such court orders to be issued within 24 hours, this procedural requirement, in fact, prevents enforcement officers from taking immediate action against offenders. In addition, the courts have wide discretionary powers, as the Law does not lay down the criteria that the courts should follow in taking decisions. For instance, in Tbilisi, of 10 applications from State bodies for court orders on the same grounds, the courts issue orders permitting inspections to only half of them, without legal reasons. Conceptually, the Law was adopted as a measure to prevent corruption, avoid duplication of inspection competence and optimize the regime of inspections. It was adopted in response to claims that numerous environmental inspections hampered facilities and inspections were inefficient because many inspectors visited facilities to verify compliance with the same legislative provisions, but failed to achieve tangible results – the improvement of environmental performance of the facilities. For instance, in Tbilisi despite the broad inspection powers granted to many environmental State bodies and the numerous inspections that take place, petrol stations still avoid equipping themselves with oil waste treatment devices as required by law. It may be presumed that such non-compliance is caused by corruption.

Liability for environmental damage

Action taken in violation of the legal requirements is subject to administrative and criminal sanctions under the Administrative Violation and Criminal Codes. Any environmental damage caused must be compensated in full. Compensation is regulated by the Civil Code and the Law on Pollution by Hazardous Substances. Under the Law, polluters are obligated to rehabilitate polluted sites. To date, there have been six cases of enforcement, all in connection with land pollution from oil. Administrative sanctions comprise fines, suspension or closure of operations. Criminal sanctions are applied for more serious actions that cause significant harm. Irrespective of the administrative or criminal sanctions, individuals causing damage must pay for it.

According to the State Ecological Police, in the first 10 months of 2002, enforcement officers have uncovered 11,420 environmental violations and taken 593 cases to court. At the same time, they claim that many environmental violations go undetected or unpunished, for several reasons, including legal deficiencies. For instance, enforcement officers lack sufficient powers to apply adequate sanctions, or even to inspect companies or other natural resource users properly.

Certain contradictions between the Administrative Violation and Criminal Codes create another barrier to efficient enforcement of environmental rules. For instance, the Criminal Code envisages that criminal action may be taken only after administrative sanction for the same offence, while the Administrative Violation Code does not have a compatible provision that may be recognized as one preceding the right to take criminal action. This concerns, for instance, illegal fishing. Under the Criminal Code, criminal sanctions may be applied for the violation of rules for mineral resources use only if the damage caused is significant, but does not determine the threshold above which the damage is deemed significant. In this case, no criminal sanctions may be imposed at all.

1.4   Institutional arrangements

Environmental   institutions   and   their mandates

The Ministry of Environment and Natural Resources Protection is the key agency in charge of environmental policy implementation. It consists of a central office, 12 regional departments in the principal cities, scientific institutes, an inspectorate and monitoring laboratories with a total staff of 522, of whom 196 work in the central office in

Tbilisi. It also has three units with a special status of double subordination, which report both to the Ministry's central office and to the local administrations. They include the Ministry of Environment of Ajaria, the State Committee of Ecology of Abkhazia and the Tbilisi Committee for the Protection of the Environment and Regulation of Natural Resource Use.

The Ministry also operates several institutes, centres and laboratories dealing with scientific research in marine ecology, fisheries and others.

The Ministry's competences and powers are outlined in the Law on Environmental Protection. They comprise inter-sectoral coordination, administering the monitoring system, and natural resource management. The Ministry is responsible for controlling pollution, preparing the annual State-of-the-Environment report, maintaining natural resources registers (cadastres), regularly developing sustainable development strategies and action plans. It sets limits (quotas) on the use of such natural resources as water, minerals (except oil and gas) and fauna and flora (except forests), and on this basis issues licences. It also promulgates environmental quality standards and every five years sets maximum permissible emissions, discharges and other impacts for individual sources. As mentioned above, the Ministry carries out State ecological expertise.

The other institutions involved in environmental protection and regulation of natural resource use are:
- The Ministry of Labour, Health and Social Affairs
- The Ministry of Urbanization and Construction
- The Ministry of Food and Agriculture
- The State Department of Geology
- The State Department for the Management of Reserves, Protected Areas and Hunting Farms
- The State Department of Land Management
- The State Department of Social and Economic Information
- The State Department of Forestry
- The State Department of Geodesy and Cartography
- The Main Department of Ecological Police of the Ministry of the Interior
- The State Department of Standardization, Metrology and Certification

Figure 1.1: Administrative Structure of the Ministry of Environment and Natural Resources Protection of Georgia

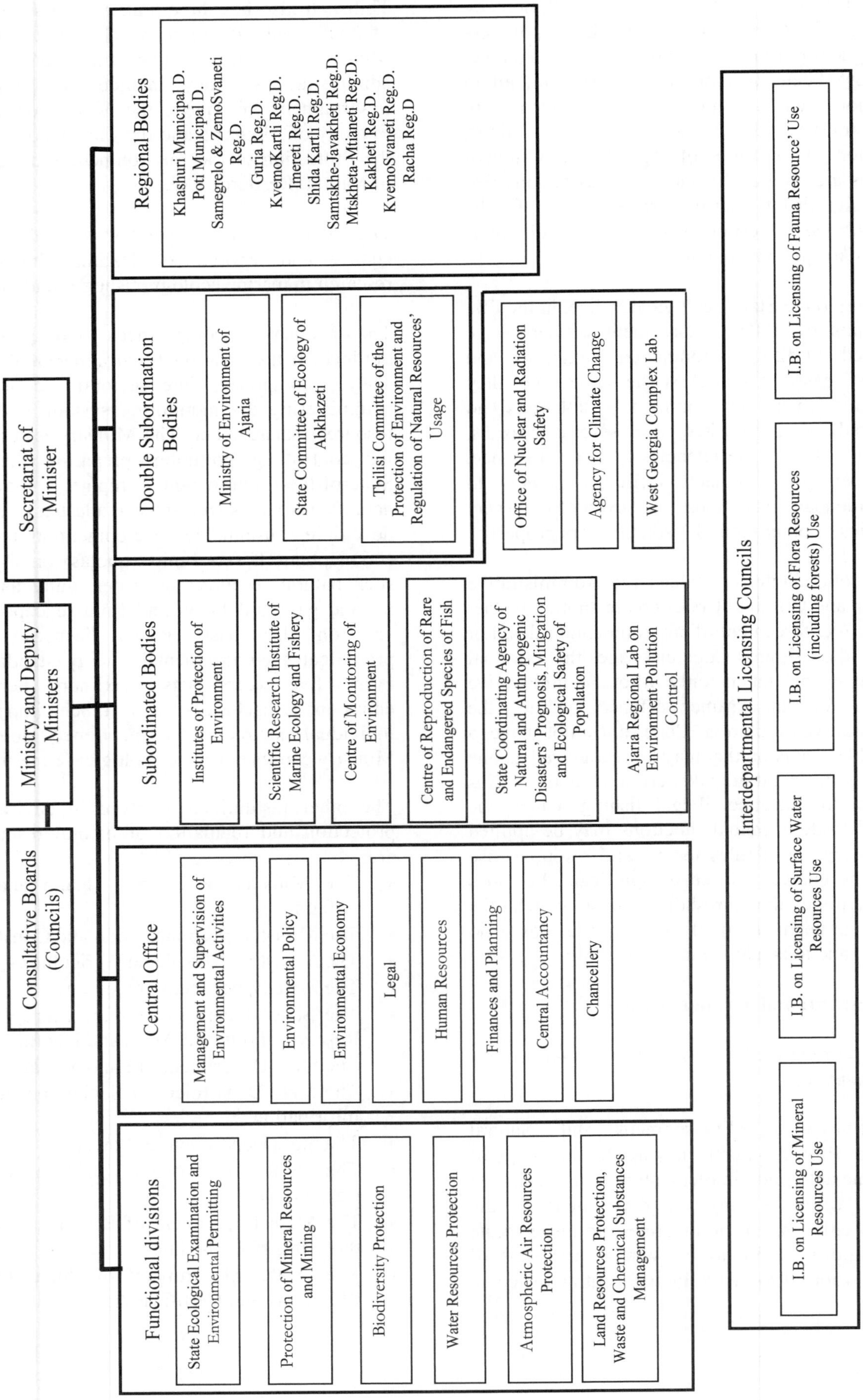

Secretariat of Minister

Ministry and Deputy Ministers

Consultative Boards (Councils)

Regional Bodies
- Khashuri Municipal D.
- Poti Municipal D.
- Samegrelo & ZemoSvaneti Reg.D.
- Guria Reg.D.
- KvemoKartli Reg.D.
- Imereti Reg.D.
- Shida Kartli Reg.D.
- Samtskhe-Javakheti Reg.D.
- Mtskheta-Mtianeti Reg.D.
- Kakheti Reg.D.
- KvemoSvaneti Reg.D.
- Racha Reg.D

Double Subordination Bodies
- Ministry of Environment of Ajaria
- State Committee of Ecology of Abkhazeti
- Tbilisi Committee of the Protection of Environment and Regulation of Natural Resources' Usage
- Office of Nuclear and Radiation Safety
- Agency for Climate Change
- West Georgia Complex Lab.

Subordinated Bodies
- Institutes of Protection of Environment
- Scientific Research Institute of Marine Ecology and Fishery
- Centre of Monitoring of Environment
- Centre of Reproduction of Rare and Endangered Species of Fish
- State Coordinating Agency of Natural and Anthropogenic Disasters' Prognosis, Mitigation and Ecological Safety of Population
- Ajaria Regional Lab on Environment Pollution Control

Central Office
- Management and Supervision of Environmental Activities
- Environmental Policy
- Environmental Economy
- Legal
- Human Resources
- Finances and Planning
- Central Accountancy
- Chancellery

Functional divisions
- State Ecological Examination and Environmental Permitting
- Protection of Mineral Resources and Mining
- Biodiversity Protection
- Water Resources Protection
- Atmospheric Air Resources Protection
- Land Resources Protection, Waste and Chemical Substances Management

Interdepartmental Licensing Councils
- I.B. on Licensing of Fauna Resource' Use
- I.B. on Licensing of Flora Resources (including forests) Use
- I.B. on Licensing of Surface Water Resources Use
- I.B. on Licensing of Mineral Resources Use

Source: Ministry of Environment and Natural Resources Protection

1.5 Integration of environmental concerns into economic and social policies

Sustainable development policies

Sustainable development, in the sense that environmental protection should become an integral part of the process of economic revival and economic growth, is proclaimed in many political and legislative documents as the main principle and objective of the country's policy.

As stated in the National Assessment Report for Sustainable Development submitted to the World Summit for Sustainable Development in Johannesburg (South Africa), integrated planning is considered to be one of the principal legal mechanisms to ensure adequate integration of environmental concerns in economic and social policies. The basic rules are laid down in the Law on Environmental Protection, which states that the planning system comprises long-term strategic plans (strategy for sustainable development), and environmental management plans for enterprises. Unfortunately, none of these plans has yet been developed, although efforts to draft such plans have been made. This is despite Presidential Order No. 763, adopted in 1996, which provided for the establishment of the National Commission for Sustainable Development with a mandate to develop a strategy for sustainable development. Although established, it has failed to fulfil its mandate.

The recent Programme for social and economic recovery and economic growth and the Interim paper on the national plan for poverty reduction and economic growth confirm that in Georgia environmental aspects are rarely taken into account in socio-economic development planning. This could be explained by the lack of experience in strategic planning, the absence of a unified vision for the country's development and institutional weakness.

Integrated planning remains inefficient because of a common legal barrier: the lack of governmental regulatory acts necessary for implementing legislative requirements. As in other cases, implementing legislation related to planning, including sustainable development, is lacking and this, in turn, impedes the adoption of the necessary plans.

Environmental concerns have become part of sectoral policies and strategies to be implemented by ministries that set up environmental units responsible for ensuring environmental protection in agriculture, forestry, oil and gas exploration and exploitation or in the interest of public health. Their strategies lay down objectives and measures to be taken to reach such objectives. In addition, environmental concerns are integrated into sectoral activities through the licensing procedures, when interdepartmental boards bring together representatives of different ministries.

Coordination framework

Coordination among the State bodies that share responsibility for regulating the use of natural resources takes place through the mechanism for making joint decisions on licences for the use of natural resources. As mentioned above, four interdepartmental councils take such decisions.

The Ministry of Environment and Natural Resources Protection is the main coordinator of environmental measures by ministries and agencies. It also plays a coordinating role in the development of Georgia's Integrated Coastal Management Project by the Ministry of Urbanization and Construction, the State Department for the Management of Protected Areas, the Ministry of Labour, Health and Social Affairs, the Ministry of Transport and Communication and other agencies.

The National Consultative Commission for Integrated Coastal Zone Management established by Presidential Decree No. 608 of 25 October 1998 forms a coordination framework for ensuring the sustainable development of the Black Sea region. The Commission is co-chaired by the Ministry of Environment and Natural Resources Protection and the Ministry of Urbanization and Construction and comprises representatives of various governmental bodies and the public.

In practical terms, coordination is not well-developed. According to the National Assessment Report for Sustainable Development, cooperation between central governmental bodies and local agencies remains weak. The competences assigned to these agencies are vaguely defined and overlap. Environmental protection enjoys formal support from politicians; however, aspects related to the environment are often neglected during decision-making processes.

Framework for decentralization

Georgia is a unitary State with a regional level playing a significant role in governing social affairs. There are 11 administrative units including two autonomous republics – Abkhazia and Ajaria – that have certain legislative and implementation competence in environmental protection. According to article 3 of the Constitution of Georgia, the central authorities have exclusive competence over land, minerals and natural resource legislation, the environmental monitoring system and the meteorological service. This means that governmental bodies in the regions may not take independent legislative action in these areas.

At the regional level, units of the Ministry of Environment and Natural Resources Protection have executive powers in environmental protection. These regional units fulfil certain environmental permitting functions and are entirely responsible for enforcement. In certain areas regional units play a leading role. Thus, they are principally responsible for identifying sources of pollution and investigating cases of pollution emissions and discharges. In spite of these significant mandates, regional offices suffer from a lack of capacity. In many cases, because of the low salaries that they offer they have to hire underqualified staff. Capacity-building efforts are often counterproductive, as employees leave for better jobs once they gain a qualification. Besides, regional offices are poorly funded and are not sufficiently equipped to conduct inspections and other work.

In addition to the regional units of the central executive bodies, each district has its own administration headed by a governor, who enjoys the status of presidential representative. However, environmental protection is not within the governor's purview.

1.6   Conclusions and recommendations

Georgia is strongly committed to environmental protection. Over the past decade, the country has created firm legal and political groundwork for activities in this area, including environmental legislation and numerous planning documents. The legislation attempts to follow advanced international practices and provides for the application of widespread legal mechanisms and standards, including environmental impact assessment, economic instruments, inspection and monitoring, and permitting. At the same time,

several laws, like the Law on Air Protection or the Law on State Ecological Expertise, make explicit reference to EU legislation without adapting this legislation to the specific needs of the Georgian legislative system. This leads to the odd situation where a law can call for the implementation of another law that proceeds from rules that are not valid in the country. Furthermore, most of the EU legal documents, such as the directives, provide a framework and set objectives for certain activities but give EU member States discretion in providing for the ways and means of reaching them.

Recommendation 1.1:
The Ministry of Environment and Natural Resources Protection and other relevant ministries, in attempting to converge their legislation with EU directives, should adapt the objectives and standards to national legal practice.

To follow best European experience in the legal regulation of environmental protection, drafters of national laws may also borrow mechanisms or procedures from EU directives or other legislative acts and adapt them to the country's legal system.

Overall, the environment-related legislation is comprehensive, but, in many instances, it lacks the necessary implementation mechanisms. Among the most important are regulations that clearly translate framework provisions of laws into competences, functions, obligations, practical measures and procedures.

Recommendation 1.2:
The Ministry of Environment and Natural Resources Protection and other relevant State bodies should:
(a) Prepare the necessary regulations and other appropriate instruments for government decision or adoption;
(b) Amend existing laws that do not conform to the appropriate criteria.

Licensing and environmental permitting are widely recognized tools for environmental protection. They allow the State to control activities that use natural resources and to prevent or mitigate adverse environmental impact. At the same time, licensing and permitting procedures in Georgia appear to be unduly complicated and lack integration. According to the Law on Environmental Protection, there is a combined system of licences and permits. There are three kinds of environmental licences: licences for environmental protection activities, licences for environmental pollution and licences for the use of natural resources. The first two are issued at the discretion of the Ministry of Environment and Natural Resources Protection, in accordance with criteria established by law; the third is decided by intersectoral councils under the Ministry of Environment and Natural Resources Protection. Environmental permits, which may only be given after an environmental licence has been issued and both an environmental impact assessment and a State ecological expertise have been carried out, are also under the sole responsibility of the Ministry of Environment and Natural Resources Protection.

However, the Law on Water and the Law on Ambient Air Protection require additional permits for the discharge of emissions into water and air. Under this system, an entrepreneur may have to obtain several licences for a single project, requiring applications to different interdepartmental councils for licences and then to the respective ministries for permits. The procedure is costly and time-consuming for the applicant and inefficient for the administration.

Recommendation 1.3:
The Ministry of Environment and Natural Resources Protection should:
(a) Streamline the licensing procedures so that all environment-related licensing decisions are taken by a single body;
(b) Redraft the Law on Environmental Permits and streamline permitting procedures to ensure that only one environment-related permit is required. In this regard, the respective provisions of the Law on Water and the Law on Ambient Air Protection should be harmonized with the Law on Environmental Permits.

The prevention of environmental impact and a comprehensive approach to environmental protection are ensured through State ecological expertise and environmental impact assessment. Although these mechanisms have already been successful, further improvement is needed. The legal rules are too general. Among other things, they do not take into consideration specific features of various economic and other projects, do not provide for scoping, and do not require long-term, cumulative and transboundary effects to be assessed.

Recommendation 1.4:
(a) The Ministry of Environment and Natural Resources Protection should develop detailed regulations for conducting State ecological expertise and environmental impact assessment that would provide for the comprehensive assessment of all impacts, including long-term, cumulative and transboundary effects. The requirements for scoping as an integral part of the EIA procedure should be introduced too;
(b) The Government is encouraged not to approve projects subject to EIA before the assessment and the State ecological expertise have been completed and the environmental permit issued by the Ministry of Environment and Natural Resources Protection, as stipulated in the law.

Inspection and enforcement by State bodies remain an important tool for ensuring compliance with legal requirements. The legislation for this has been developed, but significant institutional questions have not been addressed. These are generally of two kinds: duplication of functions and unclear functional boundaries on the one hand, and lack of capacity, on the other.

Recommendation 1.5:
(a) The Government should consider proposing legislative amendments to provisions, in particular, of the Forest Code and the Law on Pesticides and Agrochemicals that cause duplication of enforcement competences. The rights and obligations of each inspection unit should be clearly specified and differentiated, and due cooperation among them should be provided for. The Government should initiate the harmonization of the Administrative and Criminal Codes to allow enforcement bodies to take adequate action against offenders;
(b) The Ministry of Environment and Natural Resources Protection should establish an environmental State inspectorate with full inspection powers for environmental enforcement. Companies should also be encouraged to carry out self-monitoring and reporting, as is now required in the Law on Ambient Air Protection. To support self-monitoring, the Ministry of Environment and Natural Resources Protection should encourage the establishment of accredited laboratories and accrediting agents.

Chapter 2

ECONOMIC INSTRUMENTS, FINANCING AND PRIVATIZATION

2.1 Introduction

Georgia has made some significant progress in moving towards macroeconomic and financial stability, but the process remains partial and vulnerable. Growth has, however, remained modest for a number of reasons including drought, interruptions in the energy supply, and a lack of industrial and agricultural restructuring. Fiscal performance remains a problem, with tax revenues remaining amongst the lowest in the region. This is primarily due to institutional weakness, the large shadow economy and widespread corruption. During 2001, Georgia's GDP grew by 4.5% and GDP per capita was US$ 588. The country faces many challenges. It is struggling to improve living standards, to reduce poverty, to fight corruption, to resolve territorial conflicts and to impose law and order. The Government has made progress in developing a poverty reduction strategy, which focuses on improving the business environment with a view to fostering private sector development and stimulating economic growth. The privatization of State property is an important part of Georgia's economic reforms. The privatization process has progressed well in the small and medium-sized enterprises and is continuing in large-companies. The low level of foreign investment will hinder the further development of the private sector in the near future.

2.2 Economic instruments for environmental protection

Background and policy objectives

Economic instruments for the environment were rarely used in Georgia before independence. The broader introduction of economic instruments for environmental protection and natural resource use coincided with the beginning of the political reform and the transition to a market economy. Taxes on environmental pollution with harmful substances were introduced in 1993 (Government Resolution No. 1010, 1992) and taxes on the use of natural resources in 1994 (Government Resolution No. 725, 1993). When Georgia adopted a single tax code in January 1998, these taxes were incorporated in that Tax Code, in sections XI and X, respectively.

Chapter 5 of the Law on Environmental Protection of 12 October 1996 provides the basic principles for environmental taxes: the polluter pays and the user pays principles. More specifically, the pollution tax was aimed at moving to market-based methods in environmental management, and protecting and improving the environment by raising revenue for the State budget. The tax on the use of natural resources was intended to be levied according to the user pays principle, although this principle was not defined in the resolution introducing this tax.

The pollution and natural resource taxes were modelled on systems that were in force in other countries in the subregion, with some modifications to take Georgia's specific conditions into account. One important difference is that Georgia's system does not include charges on solid waste. Furthermore, no environmental fund to support environmental investments has ever been established. The Ministry of Environment and Natural Resources Protection has made several attempts to establish an environmental fund to channel the revenues from environmental taxes to environmental projects. For several reasons (including opposition from the Ministry of Finance, the Parliamentary Committee on Financing and Budgeting and the International Monetary Fund), such a proposal has not received wide political backing.

The economic instruments in force in Georgia today include:

- Taxes on environmental pollution, i.e. on air emissions and waste-water discharges;
- Taxes on the extraction and use of natural resources;
- User charges for municipal services;

- Product charges on certain environmentally harmful products, e.g. on petrol;
- Penalties and fines for non-compliance;
- Financial incentives such as grants and soft loans.

Since 1998, the Ministry of Environment and Natural Resources Protection has launched several studies to evaluate the effectiveness and efficiency of the economic instruments used in its environmental policy. The studies were conducted in cooperation with donor organizations. The reviews all indicated that the number of substances covered by the pollution tax is very high, making monitoring and enforcement difficult and expensive even in a well functioning enforcement system; payment is based on permitted emissions, not on actual emissions; the number of enterprises liable to pay tax is theoretically very high; and revenues are not used for environmental protection.

The studies formed the basis of relevant sections in the 2000 National Environmental Action Plan (NEAP). The NEAP highlights the main problems, and points to the necessity of making the existing economic instruments more effective and introducing new ones for stimulating environmental improvement. Furthermore, the NEAP states that environmental taxes must have several functions: provide a financial incentive to polluters to reduce pollution and use natural resources sustainability, as well as form a fund for environmental activities by the State. The NEAP also notes that economic instruments are not always effective and that sometimes it is better to use traditional "administrative-controlling" methods to reduce pollution. At the same time, supervision and management of the taxation system must not be too complex and expensive. Therefore, the current system of environmental taxation in Georgia needs to be overhauled.

The Ministry of Environment and Natural Resources Protection is the leading agency for the development and implementation of economic instruments for environmental protection. Other major institutions involved in the design of new taxes are the Ministry of Finance (including its Tax Collection Department) and the Ministry of Economy, Industry and Trade. The Tax Collection Department collects all revenues from environmental and natural resource taxes. The full amount goes to regional budgets, and the regional authorities use it for their priorities, mainly social ones, such as salaries and pensions.

Economic instruments in use

Instruments for air pollution management

The two instruments for air pollution control from stationary sources are *air emission taxes* and *product charges on fossil fuels*.

The *air emission taxes* have been in force since January 1993, with the introduction of environmental pollution taxes (Government Resolution No. 1010). The taxes are to be paid by all natural and legal entities that have an environmental permit for their activities. The air emission taxes cover 200 different pollutants. The amount is not related to actual emissions but based on the maximum emissions permitted by the Ministry of Environment and Natural Resources Protection or its regional agencies. Each year enterprises have to file information on the expected amount of emissions based on their business plans and submit it to the Ministry of Environment and Natural Resources Protection or its regional agencies for approval. The Ministry and regional agencies compare the estimated emissions with the planned production (based on former Soviet standards on emissions for different industries) and decide whether the emissions will significantly affect ambient environmental quality. If no unacceptable deterioration is expected, the enterprise receives air or water emission quotas (environmental permit).

The tax on the 200 substances depends on the relative toxicity of each. The toxicity indicator is based on former Soviet standards for daily maximum allowable concentrations (MAC). Furthermore, the tax depends on the location of the activity. This regional factor ranges from 1 in the least affected areas to 1.5 for the highly polluted areas. The tax rates for several key pollutants are summarized in table 2.1.

Table 2.1: Tax rates for selected air pollutants

	lari/ton
Air pollutant	**Tax rate per ton of emission**
Carbon monoxide – CO	1.5
Carbon dioxide – CO_2	0.0
Sulphur dioxide – SO_2	90.0
Nitrogen oxides – NOx	112.5
Hydrocarbons – CHx	3.0
Particles	90.0

Source: Tax Code, 1998.

Precise data on the revenues collected for the specific substances are not available. However, official statistics on emissions from stationary sources indicate that NO_x, solid particles and SO_2 have the biggest revenue raising potential. They account for about 95% of potential revenue. CO and CO_2 contribute very little due to their low tax rates.

Enterprises pay the tax quarterly. They file tax forms, which have to be approved by the Ministry of Environment and Natural Resources Protection or its regional agencies. The tax forms then go to the Tax Collection Department, which collects the taxes. The revenues are allocated to the respective regional budgets of the 11 administrative units and are primarily used for social purposes.

The *product taxes on fossil fuels* have been in force since 1998 and have their legal basis in the Tax Code. The tax applies to fuel, natural gas, liquefied gas and kerosene. The tax on fuel oil is differentiated according to sulphur content. The tax on fossil fuels in effect widens the tax base for the environmental pollution taxes on petrol and diesel introduced in 1993 through Resolution No. 1010.

Natural gas is taxed at a rate of 5 lari/m^3, liquefied petroleum gas at 10 lari/ton and kerosene at 20 lari/ton. In 1999, a tax differentiation was introduced for fuel oil. Fuel oil with a sulphur content above 2% carries a tax of 20 lari/ton, whereas fuel oil with less sulphur carries a tax of 10 lari/ton. The tax differentiation is supposed to promote the use of fuel oil with a low sulphur content, but the only threshold is that of 2%.

Instruments related to transport

Transport fuels are taxed as part of the economic instruments for environmental protection. In addition, there are other non-environmental economic instruments in force that may affect the level of transport. Vehicle fuels are subject to excise duty and value-added tax (VAT), and there are various taxes on vehicles (e.g. import of cars, registration tax on cars).

The *taxes on petrol and diesel* have been in effect since January 1993, and their legal basis was provided by Resolution No. 1010. At present, the taxes are to be paid by both the importer and the producer of the taxable fuel. The purpose of the taxes was to limit air emissions from vehicles and to generate revenues for environmental purposes. However, there were no mechanisms to ensure the

latter. Initially, the tax differentiated between leaded and unleaded petrol. This differentiation was abandoned in 1997, reportedly due to difficulties encountered in monitoring and controlling the fuel content. In June 1999, tax rates on leaded and unleaded petrol were again differentiated. However, one month later, Parliament adopted a law banning the import and production of leaded petrol (with more than 13 mg of lead per litre) from 1 January 2000. Nevertheless, the actual phasing-out of leaded petrol has encountered a number of obstacles. There is no efficient fuel quality control and monitoring system for the entire distribution chain (from imports to filling stations). There is also a high percentage of illegally distributed leaded petrol in the Georgian market, which means that taxes worth about US$ 30 million go uncollected annually. This undermines any effort to improve the legal petrol market. It is therefore unclear whether the tax differentiation is relevant. Under the current system, the tax on unleaded petrol is 40 lari/ton and on leaded petrol 120 lari/ton. The actual tax difference of 80 lari/ton (or 0.08 lari/l) is substantially higher than in most other countries of Eastern Europe, the Caucasus and Central Asia and at levels similar to many OECD countries; yet, most cars run on leaded petrol.

Data on revenue from the environmental tax on fuel became available in 1999, when the Tax Collection Department started to differentiate between revenues from the environmental tax on fossil fuel, on the one hand, and environmental taxes on air emissions and water discharges, on the other.

Instruments for water management

Instruments for water management include *water effluent taxes* and *non-compliance fees*. For municipal services there are *user charges* for water supply, sewerage and waste water.

The *water effluent tax* has been in effect since January 1993, and has its legal basis in the Government Resolution on environmental pollution taxes. Since January 1998, these taxes have been unified in the Tax Code. The water effluent taxes as well as the non-compliance fees follow the same general principles as the air emission taxes. All natural and legal entities that conduct economic activities requiring an environmental permit are subject to the water effluent tax. The tax is imposed on about 140 substances that can be discharged into surface waters. It is collected by the Tax Collection Department, based on information on emissions provided by the taxpayers (self-reporting) and controlled by the Ministry of Environment and Natural Resources Protection or its regional bodies.

The amount of taxes to be paid does not relate to the actual emissions, but is based on the "permissible emissions" included in the environmental permit. The system and the procedures for calculating and collecting the taxes are the same as those for air emission taxes. There are substantial variations in the levels of taxation: the tax on sulphates is 0.5 lari/ton, on phosphates 156 lari/ton, on nitrogen 390 lari/ton, and on biological oxygen demand (BOD) 13 lari/ton. Very hazardous heavy metals such as mercury, beryllium, gallium and molybdenum are subject to a tax of 390,000 lari/ton. Precise data on the revenues collected for the specific substances are not available.

The *municipal user charges* include charges for water supply, sewerage and waste water. The supply of water and the collection and treatment of waste water are the responsibility of the public water companies. The current water tariffs barely meet the water companies' operating and maintenance costs and do not allow them to upgrade the distribution networks which have significant leaks. The unrealistically low tariff (0.05 lari/m³ for domestic consumers) combined with poor collection rates (70% overall, but only 50% from domestic consumers) put the water utilities in an unviable financial situation, jeopardizing their operations.

In most households, water consumption is not metered, which does not encourage users to save water. In 2001, households paid 1.2 lari per month as a fixed charge for water supply and sewerage. Enterprises and public institutions pay per cubic metre of water supplied (including sewerage), which amounted to 1.6 lari per m³ in 2001.

The Environmental Financing Strategy of the Municipal Water and Wastewater Sector in Georgia estimated that, using the existing system in 2000, the total cost of producing one cubic metre of water through basic maintenance and operation of the system was 0.27 lari. According to the Strategy, the only sustainable option to close the gap is to increase user charges step by step, to the maximum level that the average household can afford.

Instruments for waste management

The only economic instrument related to waste management is the *user charge for municipal waste*

services. Inhabitants pay a user charge for the collection and disposal of municipal waste. The rate differs from municipality to municipality, with the average at 0.4 lari per capita per month. Enterprises do not pay for waste disposal, and some of the larger enterprises have their own industrial waste sites. Only about 40% of households pay their waste charges. The low tariffs and collection rates do not create true market conditions, and social considerations still dominate when setting waste charges.

Economic instruments for natural resources management

The abstraction of mineral resources, surface and groundwater, and the use of flora and fauna are all subject to taxation. All natural resource use taxes have been incorporated into the Tax Code since 1998.

The *tax on the extraction of mineral resources* has been in effect since 1994. Its purpose is to ensure the rational use of natural resources and to generate revenue for the State budget. All physical and legal entities undertaking activities that are subject to licensing for the use of mineral resources according to the Law on Mineral Resources are liable to this tax. The tax rate is determined by the Inter-ministerial Council on Licensing of Mineral Resources Use, which also issues the licence for the extraction of mineral resources. In establishing the rate, the Council considers the quality and the availability of the resource in question. The rate is a percentage of the market price of the resource (without VAT). The method to calculate the market price is established by the Ministry of Environment and Natural Resources Protection and the Ministry of Economy, Industry and Trade. For each resource, the Tax Code establishes a minimum and maximum percentage (rate) of the market price that can be imposed as tax. For example, for coal the rate varies between 2% and 5%. The taxes are collected by the Tax Collection Department, and the revenues accrue to the regional budgets. The taxes are useful in terms of revenue generation but have limited environmental impact.

The *tax on groundwater abstraction* has been in force since January 1994 and the *tax on surface water abstraction* since January 1998. Their legal basis can be found in the Tax Code. The taxes apply to all legal and natural entities that conduct an activity that requires a licence for the abstraction of water resources according to the 1997 Law on Water and the 1996 Law on Mineral Resources.

There are three different rates for the *abstraction of surface water*; the highest is 0.01 lari/m³, which applies to the Kura river with its tributaries and connected water bodies. The tax on water for irrigation and thermal energy is only 1% of the basic amount of 0.01 lari/m³, making it merely symbolic. The same applies to water for hydropower enterprises, which are supposed to pay less than 1% of the basic amount. For *groundwater abstraction*, the tax is calculated as a percentage of its "price". The method for calculating this "price" is established by the Ministry of Environment and Natural Resources Protection and the Ministry of Economy, Industry and Trade. The tax varies between 2% and 8%, and is determined by the Inter-ministerial Council on Licensing of Mineral Resources Use, which also issues the licence for the abstraction of water resources.

The tax on the use of natural resources includes a specific *tax on tree cutting*. The charge on the extraction of wood from State forests has been in effect for a long time. In 1998 it was included in the Tax Code. This system, too, suffers from the fact that no mechanisms have been established to promote its objectives. The revenues are collected by the Tax Collection Department and go to the regional budgets. The tax rate depends on three parameters: the type of tree, the quality of the wood, and the diameter of the wood. The tax varies from 34 lari/m³ for tree species that have the highest commercial value to 1 lari/m³ for firewood of the lowest commercial value. The tax serves mainly to collect revenue from the forest operations. The overall levels of cutting are managed through licences. The detailed provisions make the tax administratively heavy and compliance difficult to monitor.

A *charge on hunting and fishing* was introduced in January 1998, through the Tax Code. However, it has not yet been fully implemented and enforced. The charge applies to all physical and legal entities carrying out activities that are subject to licensing according to the 1996 Law on Wildlife. However, regulations and procedures for recreational fishing and hunting have not yet been fully drawn up. For commercial fishing and hunting, the licences are allocated by the Inter-ministerial Council on Licensing of Fauna Resources Use. The rate is a percentage of the market price. The Ministry of Environment and Natural Resources Protection and the Ministry of Economy, Industry and Trade regularly determine these prices. There are 24 different tax rates (percentages) and each rate applies to a specific group of species. For example, the rate for bears is 35% and for wolves 25%.

Enforcement incentives (fines and non-compliance fees)

Non-compliance fees can be imposed if evidence is found of a violation of environmental legislation. The penalties are in accordance with the Administrative, Civil and Criminal Codes.

Chapter 48 of the Criminal Code defines different criminal acts against the environment; the punishments vary from 1 to 360 times the daily salary or imprisonment for a period of up to five years, and the deprivation of the right to hold any official position or conduct specific proscribed activities for a period of up to three years.

According to article 311 of the Criminal Code, for example, significant pollution of water bodies that may endanger human life and health is punishable by up to three years' imprisonment. These sentences are rarely carried out due to the weak legal and judicial system. Only an extremely low number of cases are actually likely to reach the courts (see chapter 1 on policy, legal and institutional framework and sectoral integration).

2.3 Environmental financing and expenditures

National sources of finance

State budget

Strategies, objectives and major directions for Georgia's socio-economic development are defined in the Indicative Plan for Social and Economic Development. An indicative plan can be worked out for the short (one year), medium (five years) and long term (10 to 20 years). It is the basis for drafting the State budget. The indicative plan is based on programmes and project proposals from different ministries, agencies and other executive bodies. The project proposals are submitted to the Ministry of Economy, Industry and Trade, which establishes a special commission for the selection of priority projects. When these are approved by the President, they are included in the draft indicative plan for the upcoming year to be subsequently considered in the draft State budget.

The State budgets that were adopted according to the indicative plans over the past ten years show a decline in the expenditures on environmental protection. Table 2.2 shows that total environmental expenditures in 2001 amounted to only 0.002% (or 2.3 million lari) of the State budget. It could be concluded that environmental protection is not considered a priority. In 2002, of the 12 environmental projects proposed by the Ministry of Environment and Natural Resources Protection, only 5 received any financing from the State budget. However, environment-related investment projects are also indirectly grouped under other sectors. The projections of expenditure by sector show that continuing priority is given to public order and safety. Health and education have received substantial increases in spending in recent years.

Most environment-related programmes and plans were developed with the assistance of various international financial institutions. Plans usually include activities that are solely designed to attract future funding from international organizations. Most ongoing and planned measures receive financial support from donor countries and international financial institutions. This comes as no surprise, considering that Georgia has difficulties not only in funding programmes and projects identified in the budget but also in paying wages and pensions regularly. At present the funds allocated from the State budget are not enough to ensure the normal functioning of State agencies and the carrying-out of various measures.

The total amount of the State budget allocated to the Ministry of Environment and Natural Resources

Protection in 2002 was 0.81 million lari (table 2.3). This was sufficient to cover salaries, social security, administration and maintenance. About 87% is spent on the salaries of the staff of the Ministry of Environment and Natural Resources Protection, regional environmental bodies and related environmental institutions. About 25%, or 0.2 million lari, is available for environmental projects.

At the local level, the municipalities are responsible for various public services, some of which are directly related to environmental protection. The municipalities have authority over the natural resources in their area and have to ensure services for water supply, waste water and municipal waste management. At the moment, the municipalities are financially dependent on State budget allocations, which barely cover salaries and related expenditures. Additional sources of revenue under the control of municipalities are property taxes, communal fees and income from municipal services. The municipalities and the regional environmental bodies have additional sources of financing, which originate from penalties for violations of environmental legislation (i.e. illegal pollution, illegal extraction of mineral resources, damage to forests and parks) and the payments for the State ecological expertise. Of these extrabudgetary funds, 70% goes directly to the State budget, and 30% stays within the regional budgets. No data are available about the total amount of this additional source.

Table 2.2: State budget expenditures

million lari

	1997	1998	1999	2000	2001	2002
Total State budget	776.8	797.2	904.8	833.8	908.3	1259.5
Environmental protection expenditures	3.4	15	2.7	1.7	2.3	3.8
Environmental protection expenditures (as % of total State budget)	0.0044	0.0188	0.003	0.002	0.0025	0.003

Source: Ministry of Finance, 2002.

Table 2.3: Share of State budget allocations to the Ministry of Environment and Natural Resources Protection

million lari

	1997	1998	1999	2000	2001	2002
Total State budget	776.8	797.2	904.8	833.8	908.3	1259.5
Ministry of Environment and Natural Resources Protection	..	..	0.8098	0.4915	0.5458	0.8107

Source: Ministry of Environment and Natural Resources Protection, 2002.

Revenue and revenue collection

The revenue from the environmental pollution taxes and the taxes for the use of natural resources amounted to 19.2 million lari in 2001 (table 2.4). Most was generated by the environmental pollution taxes on fuels. The emission taxes on air and water generated much less. The revenue from environmental taxes has increased considerably in recent years.

The revenue from the environmental taxes nearly doubled between 1997 and 1998 and again doubled between 1998 and 1999. This increase can be explained by two factors. First, the tax base for fuels was extended to the fossil fuels used by stationary sources; only transport fuels had previously been taxed. Second, the collection of the fuel tax improved dramatically between 1997 and 1999. The point of collection was changed from fuel retailers to fuel importers. The smaller number of collection points resulted in more effective control and, consequently, led to higher collection rates and lower administrative costs.

The collection of taxes, whether general taxes or environmental taxes, remains one of the most acute economic problems in Georgia. Revenues to the State budget from all taxes amounted to only 7.6% of GDP in 2000, one of the lowest levels in the region. The low level of tax collection is mainly due to the large informal economy and the weak enforcement of tax laws. Moreover, for environmental taxes it is also due to the lack of proper monitoring of emissions and the complexity of the calculation procedures both for taxpayers and tax collectors, leaving room for corruption and non-payment.

Extrabudgetary funds

Unlike other East European, Caucasian and Central Asian countries that have established similar systems of environmental taxes, Georgia does not have a special national or regional environmental fund. Revenues from the environmental taxes are distributed to the regional budgets of the administrative units and are primarily spent on social and other urgent needs.

Despite the efforts of the Ministry of Environment and Natural Resources Protection to establish an environmental fund, which would distribute revenues from environmental taxes for environmental protection purposes, no consensus has been reached on this issue in the Government and Parliament. The main argument of the opposing parties (Ministry of Finance and the Parliamentary Committee on Financing and Budgeting) is that extrabudgetary funds would undermine the policy of fiscal integrity, which is strongly supported by the International Monetary Fund.

The Ministry of Environment and Natural Resources Protection is now pursuing an approach of debt-for-nature swaps, as a means of reducing foreign debt and increasing expenditure on the environmental sector. Georgia has signed an agreement with the "Paris Club" creditors to restructure its official external debt, and a debt for nature swap clause has been included.

Table 2.4: Revenues from the tax on pollution with harmful substances and the tax on use of natural resources from 1996 to 2001

in thousands of lari

	1996	1997	1998	1999	2000	2001
Revenues from pollution taxes	5,326.8	2,581.1	6,880.9	16,547.7	10,001.7	11,939.5
Revenues from mineral resources taxes	2,914.5	2,719.9	2,142.7	5,214.1	7,476.8	7,354.7
Extraction of minerals	1,079.0	..	1,243.3	1,701.3	4,983.2	5,235.2
Water	1,555.1	..	458.2	426.3	357.7	379.5
Forests/tree cutting	300.4	..	299.6	1,232.6	1,582.6	1,209.2
Others	..	..	141.6	1,853.9	553.3	530.8
Total revenues from environmental taxes	8,241.3	5,301.0	9,023.6	21,761.8	17,478.5	19,294.2

Source: Ministry of Environment and Natural Resources Protection, 2002.

2.4   Enterprise privatization and the impacts on environmental protection

Background and current status of the enterprise privatization process

The privatization of State property is an important part of Georgia's economic reforms. The process began in 1992, following the adoption of the Law on the Privatization of State Property (on 9 August 1991) and the introduction of a privatization programme. Under this programme, privatization takes place in two stages. The first stage is directed primarily at small and medium-sized enterprises, and the second at larger enterprises.

The privatization strategy and mechanisms are stipulated in the Constitution, the Civil Code and the revised Law on the Privatization of State Property (adopted on 30 May 1997). The Ministry of State Property Management is responsible for privatizing State property and for controlling related organizational issues. Privatization takes the form of a tender, an auction, a lease with an option to buy or a direct sale.

Around 80% of small and medium enterprises have been privatized. The privatization of large enterprises is progressing slowly. This is mainly due to problems related to their ownership, previous debts, legal transparency, and lack of internal restructuring. In addition, there is still a lack of interest from foreign investors, both because of the social obligations that are included in the privatization contracts and because the remaining State-owned companies may not be commercially viable even if they were to be restructured.

Since 1998, some progress has been achieved in the privatization of the energy sector. A United States power producer became one of the first foreign investors in Georgia, with the purchase of the power distribution company Telasi in 1998. In addition, several small hydropower stations and thermal production units have been privatized. Work is currently under way to develop the strategies for privatizing energy distribution and energy generation sectors, as well as the communications sector and the industrial sector. Privatization of large industrial assets is also envisaged under the World Bank Structural Adjustment Credit. At the same time, those industries that are of no interest to investors will be liquidated or restructured.

Rural and urban land privatization takes place on the basis of the 1998 Law on the Declaration of Private Ownership of Non-Agricultural Land, the 1998 Law on the Administration and Disposal of State-owned Land and the 1996 Law on Agricultural Landownership, and is dealt with in chapter 12 on spatial planning and land use.

Environmental implications of enterprise privatization

The environmental issues to be resolved during the privatization of enterprises can be broken down into compliance issues and remediation problems. Compliance issues, such as emissions and waste management, are related to the environmental performance of ongoing activities. The responsibility for complying with environmental requirements for ongoing activities belongs to the new owners. In many cases, however, the privatized enterprises have been persistent violators of environmental requirements, and it is unreasonable to expect full compliance without process changes and new investments. The introduction of a compliance plan to be agreed by the investor and the Government at the time of the sale could solve environmental compliance issues in the privatization process. The remediation issues refer to the responsibilities for financing the clean-up of past contamination.

The 1997 Law on the Privatization of State Property does not contain any provisions on environmental protection. The Law does not refer to environmental assessments during the privatization process or to regulations on environmental impact assessment. However, article 21 of the Law on Environmental Protection refers to the environmental requirements in the course of privatization. According to this article, the new owner of the privatized enterprise is obliged to fulfil all obligations that were imposed on the former owner. Every new owner of a privatized enterprise should pay for the environmental damage from past pollution. It is not clear if this article is fully applied, but it could deter foreign investors because of concerns over the clean-up costs. The lack of clarity about liability for past pollution can be costly for both the Government and investors.

The Law on Environmental Protection states that "on the basis of a decision of the Ministry of Environment and Natural Resources Protection, an environmental audit may be carried out in order to assess the environmental situation of the enterprise undergoing privatization". However, such enterprises are not systematically subject to environmental audits to assess the extent of environmental contamination.

In practice, the Ministry of Environment and Natural Resources Protection is consulted by the Ministry of State Property Management about privatizations. This cooperation is formalized on the basis of an agreement between the two Ministries. When there are plans to privatize an enterprise, the Ministry of Environment and Natural Resources Protection and its regional agencies check if the enterprise has a valid environmental permit and if all environmental requirements are being followed. Only when the new owner has plans to start a new activity is a new environmental permit needed. Otherwise, the Ministry of Environment and Natural Resources Protection approves the privatization proposal and sends its environmental consent to the Ministry of State Property Management, which will continue the privatization process.

To summarize, while the Ministry of Environment and Natural Resources Protection is involved in the privatization process, it has little influence at the moment. The privatization or sales contract does not require the preparation of an environmental plan, nor are there any other environmental requirements. The new owner is responsible for environmental damage from past pollution, and there seems to be no possibility of negotiating the sharing of environmental liabilities between the investor and the State. An environmental audit can play an important role in identifying the costs of cleaning up contamination and in recommending measures to remediate past damage. But environmental audits are not obligatory, and the Ministry of Environment and Natural Resources Protection is not taking full advantage of the possibilities it has within the privatization process. The Ministry of State Property Management has announced the tenders of several chemical plants, a metallurgy plant and a copper and gold-mining company. These industries are potential environmental polluters, and environmental assessments within the privatization process are needed to identify the risks.

2.5   Conclusions and recommendations

The introduction of economic instruments for environmental protection in Georgia coincided with the beginning of the political reforms and transition to a market economy. The 1993 tax on environmental pollution with harmful substances and the 1994 tax on the use of natural resources are meant to encourage polluters to reduce pollution and to promote the rational use of natural resources, as well as to raise funding for environmental activities. Although their goal was clearly stated in the legislation, no tax performance monitoring system has been set up, nor have institutional arrangements been made for ensuring that the tax revenues are spent efficiently as intended. Despite the stated aim of the environmental taxes, they currently serve to raise revenue.

The effectiveness of economic instruments is based on the flexibility that they give polluters to devise a cost-effective compliance strategy. The application of economic instruments should not be an aim in itself, but should be seen as one of several options to promote improvements in environmental performance and to meet environmental policy goals. The introduction of a pollution charge system in Georgia is one step in the right direction. Still, the effectiveness of the present system is hampered by several factors and it does not provide real incentives to reduce pollution.

One factor that affects the entire system of taxes and charges is its complexity. Pollution taxes are levied on a high number of pollutants, each having its own rate, although there is no adequate equipment to measure the emissions. Pollution taxes could be applied more effectively if they were levied on fewer priority pollutants. The cost of monitoring and administering pollution charges is high, and inspection and enterprises are not adequately equipped to measure emissions. Criteria for selecting standard pollutants should be based on the feasibility of systematic monitoring and inspection, and focus on priority pollutants that can be monitored at reasonable cost.

Another factor is the method for calculating the taxes. The taxes are not related to actual emissions but based on the maximum emissions permitted by the Ministry of Environment and Natural Resources Protection or its regional agencies. This means that the taxes do not encourage enterprises to curb discharges. To provide real incentives, the tax should be based on actual emissions. If there is no monitoring equipment, the tax should be calculated on the basis of emission estimates, in order to give enterprises an incentive to install monitoring equipment.

A fundamental problem is the fact that some major polluters and users of natural resources do not pay the environmental taxes. This inability or unwillingness to pay is a particular problem for municipal services, such as water supply and treatment. In addition, the collection of environmental taxes is further hampered by the extremely limited capacity and resources of the environmental inspectorate of the Ministry of Environment and Natural Resources Protection, the low wages of staff of the controlling authorities, and the low fines and sanctions imposed on defaulters. These conditions make it difficult to improve the collection of revenue and ensure proper enforcement in the short term.

Consequently, Georgia needs to improve its system of economic instruments. An effective system of pollution taxes is based on identifying specific sources and levels of pollution, designing and implementing a reasonable system of pollution taxes, and establishing a monitoring and enforcement network.

The involvement of other ministries and institutions, such as the Ministry of Finance, including its Tax Collection Department, and the Ministry of Economy, Industry and Trade, is essential to improve the effectiveness of the current environmental tax system. Consultation and cooperation among these institutions are needed to make proposals for tax reforms through the Tax Code. The establishment of an inter-ministerial working group could be helpful to investigate ways and means of either deepening and strengthening current tax reforms or implementing new ones.

Recommendation 2.1:
The Ministry of Environment and Natural Resources Protection, in cooperation with the Ministry of Finance, including its Tax Collection Department, the Ministry of Economy, Industry and Trade and other stakeholders, should improve the system of environmental pollution taxes to make it more effective and to provide incentives for polluters to invest in pollution abatement. This could be done by:
(a) Simplifying the tax system by limiting the number of polluting substances and concentrating on major pollutants;
(b) Improving monitoring to identify and make an inventory of the main polluters;
(c) Basing taxes on actual emissions;
(d) Improving enforcement (inspection and control) and collection (through lower administration costs, awareness raising and a stable tax system).

The proposals for improving the environmental pollution tax system should serve as a basis for amendments to the Tax Code.

Financial resources for environmental policies are extremely limited in Georgia. Owing to the difficult economic situation and the small State budget, the pollution and natural resource taxes have, to a large extent, been regarded as an additional source of revenue for the general budget. One possible way to mobilize financial resources for environmental investments is an "earmarked" environmental fund, which would collect revenue generated by economic instruments as well as contributions from foreign donors. Georgia does not have such a fund either at national or at regional levels. Revenues from the environmental taxes are not earmarked; they are distributed to the 12 regional budgets and are primarily spent on social and other urgent needs. Earmarking environmental taxes for environmental spending could secure potentially sizeable revenue sources. Despite the efforts of the Ministry of Environment and Natural Resources Protection to establish an environmental fund, no consensus has been reached on this issue in the Government and Parliament.

The National Environmental Action Plan has identified several environmental priorities. Among these, improving the quality of drinking water supply and providing waste-water treatment have highest priority. The sources for the budget line could be established by earmarking a part of the environmental tax revenue or, alternatively, by increasing the share of government budget spending on water supply and sanitation.

Although preference should be given to establishment of an environmental fund, another solution to allocate more financial resources to environmental investments is the creation of a credit (budget) line for a specific purpose under the supervision of the Ministry of Finance. To make the environmental investments more effective, clear priorities need to be set by the Ministry of Environment and Natural Resources Protection.

Recommendation 2.2:
(a) The Government should take the necessary steps to establish an environmental fund to channel financing for the most urgent environmental projects;
(b) The sources for this fund could either be established by earmarking a part of the environmental tax revenue or by increasing the

share of government budget spending on environmental priority projects;

(c) The Government, under the leadership of the Ministry of Environment and Natural Resources Protection, should establish an independent mechanism to review the allocation of resources for the fund to projects that are consistent with the country's priorities. In addition, all procedures for the use of the funds should be transparent;

(d) The Ministry of Environment and Natural Resources Protection should establish a project preparation unit (see recommendation 4.4).

The Ministry of Environment and Natural Resources Protection is now pursuing a debt-for-nature swap as a means of reducing foreign debt through negotiations with creditor countries, on the condition that a corresponding amount of money will be spent on environmental protection. In a recent agreement with the "Paris Club" to restructure its official external debt, Georgia successfully included a debt-swap clause.

Several institutional options exist to develop the debt-for-nature-swap concept, such as bilateral swaps of official debt, trilateral swaps of private debt, swaps on a project-by-project basis and swaps through an "ecofund", the legal status of the expenditure management institution, and priorities for spending revenues. Active cooperation between the Ministry of Finance and the Ministry of Environment and Natural Resources Protection is needed to analyse and decide about these different options.

Recommendation 2.3:
The Government should further develop and reach consensus on debt-for-nature swaps as a means of reducing foreign debt and increasing expenditure on the environmental sector. Active cooperation between the Ministry of Finance and the Ministry of Environment and Natural Resources Protection is needed to design the swap transactions and expenditure mechanisms.

The privatization or sales contract does not require the preparation of an environmental plan, nor are environmental requirements included. However, the Law on Environmental Protection states that "on

the basis of a decision of the Ministry of Environment and Natural Resources Protection, an environmental audit may be carried out to assess the environmental situation of the enterprise undergoing privatization". In practice, such enterprises are not systematically subject to environmental audits before privatization, and the Ministry of Environment and Natural Resources Protection is not taking full advantage of the possibilities it has within the privatization process.

In addition, according to the Law on Environmental Protection, the new owner should pay for the environmental damage from past pollution. It is not clear if this article is fully applied, but it could deter foreign investors because of concern over clean-up costs. The lack of clarity about liability for past pollution can be costly for both the Government and investors.

The responsibility for complying with environmental requirements for ongoing operations lies with the new owners. In most cases, however, the privatized enterprises have persistently failed to meet such requirements, and it is unreasonable to expect full compliance without process changes and new investments. The introduction of a compliance plan to be agreed by the investor and the Government at the time of the sale could solve environmental compliance issues in the privatization process. The compliance plan should consist of a list of measures to bring the enterprise's operations into compliance with relevant environmental standards and regulations, giving a reasonable time frame.

Recommendation 2.4:
(a) The Ministry of Environment and Natural Resources Protection should fully exploit its role in the privatization process and should require environmental audits to be carried out by enterprises and industries undergoing privatization;

(b) The Ministry of State Property Management should include compliance plans, prepared by the new owner as part of the privatization agreement. These plans should specify the measures that enterprises and industries have to take to comply with environmental standards and regulations.

Chapter 3

ENVIRONMENTAL INFORMATION AND PUBLIC PARTICIPATION IN DECISION-MAKING

3.1 Monitoring and information system

Introduction

Since 1992, there has been no routine environmental monitoring in Georgia, largely due to the economic situation. Over the past decade, monitoring stations and equipment have deteriorated and become unusable; only a few are currently working. Furthermore, the monitoring institutions receive only salaries more or less regularly (see chapter 2, on economic instruments, financing and privatization); the budget for maintenance and for essential analytical equipment has dried up. Nevertheless, some institutions keep an eye on the environmental situation and have early-warning mechanisms to alert the authorities in the event of an emergency. Some institutions also manage to maintain their work, research, competence and knowledge through projects financed by private companies or international organizations. For example, the State Institute of Geology was requested by the Borjomi mineral water company to monitor groundwater, and it also carried out a study on the sediment composition of the Black Sea (21 profiles, 1 to 19 m deep).

Policies and programmes

The Ministry of Environment and Natural Resources Protection participates in the Ad Hoc Working Group on Environmental Monitoring of the United Nations Economic Commission for Europe (UNECE). On the basis of discussions in that Working Group and its recommendations, the Ministry of Environment and Natural Resources Protection with relevant institutions (Ministry of Labour, Health and Social Affairs, Ministry of Food and Agriculture, Ministry of the Interior, State Department of Hydrometeorology and State Department of Geology) developed an environmental monitoring programme (see box 3.1) and sent it to the President for approval. Its aim is to set up a new monitoring system. According to the programme, norms and standards will be harmonized with international norms. It also

foresees the creation of an environmental monitoring agency within the Ministry of Environment and Natural Resources Protection. This agency will coordinate all environmental monitoring activities throughout the country (including self-monitoring of enterprises). Its main functions will be to improve, enforce and implement environmental monitoring legislation; assure the quality of the monitoring, collection and processing of all environmental data collected by the different institutions; assess the state of the environment, provide information to government bodies and decision makers and make environmental information available to the public.

Legislation

Although there is little monitoring at present, there is a strong legislative basis for monitoring the environment. The 1996 framework Law on Environmental Protection calls for State registers and an environmental monitoring system. The State registers should include environmental pollution and natural resources inventories and statistics and their mapping. The responsibilities are divided among the Ministry of Environment and Natural Resources Protection, the Ministry of Labour, Health and Social Affairs and the Ministry of Food and Agriculture, as well as other institutions defined by other environmental laws and regulations. The environmental monitoring system is defined as a system of environmental data collection, storage and analysis, coordinated by the Ministry of Environment and Natural Resources Protection. To comply with Georgia's Constitution, which provides for free access to the information, it should be user-friendly and publicly accessible.

The 1996 Law on Protected Areas System provides for the establishment of State registers of protected areas, with information on their territories, natural resources and environmental status. The 1997 Law on Wildlife provides for a State register of animal species and their use (see chapter 8, on biodiversity and forest management).

Box 3.1: **Monitoring programme**

The main goals of the proposed monitoring programme for Georgia include:

- Restore and modernize the existing systems.
- Establish systems for monitoring background and transboundary environmental pollution, including greenhouse gases.
- Set up environmental systems for monitoring bio-indicators and bio-accumulators.
- Introduce modern methods consistent with international standards for monitoring; compile and evaluate the actual and anticipated status of the environment. (use of models to forecast effects on environmental media under typical weather conditions)
- Establish an effective quality control system for monitoring and meteorological support of measurement tools.
- Establish a system for immediate detection and study of dangerous ecological and toxicological situations resulting from pollution (including accidental pollution).
- Establish an automated system for the collection, processing, electronic dissemination and storage of monitoring data; and create and manage the databases.
- Actively promote the development of national environmental quality standards consistent with international standards.
- Set up a coordinated system of staff training and skills upgrading, and make effective use of international training centres.

To facilitate adoption, the Ministry of Finance has been involved from the beginning and participated in all meetings to help organize the finances. The Ministry of Environment and Natural Resources Protection, as the coordinating body under the Law on Environmental Protection, sent the programme to the President for approval.

Source: Ministry of Environment and Natural Resources Protection.

The 1996 Law on Mineral Resources supports a State register with information on existing mines, mineral resources, the geological survey and other related data. (See chapter 9, on mining, industry and environment.)

The 1997 Law on Water calls for the monitoring of effluent discharges, water quality and quantity (see chapter 7, on water management, including the Black Sea). The 1999 Law on Ambient Air Protection divides the air monitoring system into ambient air monitoring and an air emissions inventory. It covers all air pollutants for which limits have been set. The air emissions inventory includes emissions self-monitored by enterprises and their annual reports. The air monitoring system is part of the environmental monitoring system maintained by the Ministry of Environment and Natural Resources Protection (see chapter 5, on air management).

The 1998 Law on Hazardous Chemical Substances provides for a State register of hazardous substances, with data and information on their life cycle, production, transport and consumption. It also forces industrial facilities to keep records. Facilities working with hazardous substances have to keep records of their use and transport. All operations must be reported to the Ministry of Health, which sets rules on record-keeping,

procedures and format (see chapter 6, on waste, chemicals and contaminated sites). The 1998 Law on Nuclear and Radiation Safety establishes State registers of radioactive substances with information on their use, transport, export-import, radioactive waste, radioactive sources and nuclear facilities and an environmental monitoring system.

Article 17 of the 1998 Law on Pesticides and Agrochemicals requires a State register of agrochemicals and growth stimulators, with information on their export-import, production, transport, storage, consumption, health and environmental effects. All importers, producers and consumers are to report operations on pesticides and other agrochemicals. However, information on banned or restricted pesticides and agrochemicals is kept separately in the register (see chapter 12, on environmental concerns in agriculture).

The 1999 Forest Code calls for a monitoring system based on continuous observations, data analysis and forecasting. There is also a State forestry register with all qualitative and quantitative parameters of State forests and forestry resource balances that are calculated every 10 years.

Although the Law on Environment Protection and other environmental laws require several registers, cadastres or lists, owing to the lack of funding, only two cadastres are available, the State Cadastre of Wildlife managed by the Ministry of Environment and Natural Resources Protection and the State Cadastre of Mineral Resources managed by the State Department of Geology, and one list, the List of Species of Wild Animals. The State Statistical Department does not publish all environmental data, only aggregate data.

Institutions

The monitoring system is widely dispersed, but there does not appear to be any overlap of responsibilities among the institutions.

The Ministry of Environment and Natural Resources Protection is mainly responsible for carrying out and coordinating the monitoring of different environmental media and for maintaining State registers. Owing to the economic situation, and the consequent lack of staff and finances, data stay in paper form. A database should be set up for storage, consulting and publishing. The 12 regional environmental departments should ensure that the self-monitoring by enterprises complies with the requirements. The Ministry of Environment and Natural Resources Protection's Department of Public Relations and Environmental Education is responsible for its external relations with other ministries, the media and the public. It is part of the Department of Management and Supervision of Environmental Activities and is administratively dependent on it. It has to provide environmental information. It cooperates with the Ministry of Education on education programmes. Despite limited funding, the Department has proved its ability and its willingness to manage environmental and EIA information. Six staff members share an office with two desks. This office also is used to receive people requesting information and to store material such as EIA videocassettes and environmental publications. There is no money to set up and maintain a web site; and phone lines could be cut at any time for lack of payment by the Ministry.

The Ministry of Health's State Sanitary and Epidemiology Surveillance monitors drinking-water quality and controls compliance with health standards and requirements. It checks the drinking-water network and ensures safe drinking-water quality. In 2000, the Ministry of Health established new norms in line with WHO norms. If the water is found to be unsafe, it suspends the supply and orders repairs.

The State Department of Hydrometeorology (Hydromet) is responsible for the collection, storage and analysis of environmental data on surface-water quality, air pollution and soil. In the past, a dense network was set up. The current budget is US$ 300,000, which covers only salaries and minimum services. As part of its duties, Hydromet continues to measure air pollution in four towns: Tbilisi, Kutaisi, Batumi and Rustavi. Only dust, sulphur dioxide, nitrogen oxide and dioxide and carbon oxide can be still measured owing to the quality of the equipment (see chapter 5, on air management). For water monitoring, before 1990, 56 physical and chemical parameters were analysed based on Soviet requirements and specifications. Only the most important parameters that the laboratory is able to analyse are measured. Nowadays, only 31 stations are in operation, 16 in the Rioni basin, 5 on different lakes and 9 on the river Kura and its tributaries. Hydromet tries to take samples once a month, but this regularity depends on the budget and allocated resources. An important issue for Hydromet is the clarification on the norms to be followed. The Ministry of Environment and Natural Resources Protection still uses norms and standards established under the Soviet Union, although the Ministry of Health has updated its drinking-water quality norms to be more consistent with those of WHO. For example, for drinking water, the maximum allowable concentrations (MAC) for nickel (Ni) are 0.02 µg/l for the Ministry of Health against 0.1 µg/l for the Ministry of Environment and Natural Resources Protection. There is a similar problem with the classification of rivers. To classify rivers, the Ministry of Environment and Natural Resources Protection uses two categories: fishery; and drinking and irrigation. The Ministry of Health uses three categories: drinking; irrigation; and fishing. Hydromet carries out analyses for both ministries, but the results can vary depending on the norms used. So, for some parameters, water samples may comply with one norm, but fail to comply with the other one. Hydromet currently receives support from several donor organizations, including the United States Agency for International Development (USAID), the European Union (EU) and the North Atlantic Treaty Organization (NATO). USAID has already provided three new gauge stations. Through the European Union TACIS programme for the Kura basin management, Hydromet will receive new equipment. This programme will also involve Turkey and Azerbaijan given the transboundary character of the river Kura. The European Union and USAID will provide groundwater monitoring equipment to determine the water flow. Hydromet will maintain this equipment. Under a NATO project, 90 measuring stations will be set up in the Caucasus (Georgia, Azerbaijan and Turkey), 30 stations will be available for each country. Hydromet will manage Georgia's.

The Ministry of Food and Agriculture maintains the system of State registers of agrochemicals, pesticides and agricultural and eroded land.

The Ministry of the Interior conducts mandatory vehicle emission checks within the State inspection and maintenance programmes. The Ministry's Ecological Police also carries out some environmental inspections.

The State Department of Geology conducts geological surveys, calculates mineral resource balances and maintains a database on mineral resources. The Institute of Geology monitors groundwater. Of the 500 stations, only 30 are operating. Some staff have left the Institute and created their own company, which works with the Institute. The private company performs groundwater measurements for other companies and international organizations. This cooperation enables the Institute to maintain or upgrade some stations.

The State Department of Forestry monitors and keeps the State register of forestry resources. The State Department for the Management of Reserves, Protected Areas and Hunting monitors and keeps records on the environment in protected areas. The State Department of Land Resources and Land Cadastre draws up land-use inventories and the cadastre. Finally, the State Statistical Department develops, and keeps in a database, the country's statistics and publishes environmental data.

In line with the Law on Ambient Air Protection (art. 38), enterprises report on their activities and their environmental impact. Self-monitoring is based on energy and mass balance calculations and not on actual emission measurements, as the equipment for this is either obsolete or non-existent. The forms are regularly sent to the Ministry of Environment and Natural Resources Protection or its regional agencies, which check the validity of the data within 15 days after reception. Self-monitoring concerns only air emissions and not water discharges.

3.2   Access to environmental information, public participation and public awareness

Access to environmental information

Article 37 of the Georgian Constitution grants individuals access to information. Based on that article, all institutions have the obligation to provide any information requested by any citizen, except information classified as a State, professional, commercial or personal secret. However, the 1996 Law on State Secrets (art. 8) stipulates that environmental information and information concerning emergencies cannot be classified as State secret. According to the General Administrative Code, all public information kept by a public agency has to be stored in a public register two days after its acquisition with the date, title and administrative reference. Unfortunately, few agencies (Ministry of Justice, Ministry of Finance and some local authorities) have such public registers.

In addition, article 6 of the Law on Environmental Protection stipulates that a citizen is entitled to obtain full, objective and timely information on the state of the environment where s/he lives, to take part in decision-making and, through the courts, demand changes to decisions on projects deemed dangerous from an ecological point of view.

The Ministry of Environment and Natural Resources Protection's Department of Public Relations and Environmental Education provides information to the public. Furthermore, each year, the Ministry is requested to report to Parliament and the President on the information that it has provided, and explain why in some cases it was not able to provide the requested information. The Department records the debates of the intersectoral expert meetings for environmental impact assessment (EIA) on video. The public can make copies of this video. This is not an official procedure, but an initiative of the Ministry. The Ministry is also drawing up a programme to involve the mass media more in environmental protection. The aim is to provide environmental knowledge to the mass media so as to complement the sometimes insufficient information provided by companies.

The Scientific Research Institute of Environmental Protection within the Ministry of Environment and Natural Resources Protection collects environmental data from the different institutions involved in monitoring. It issues a yearly report on the state of the environment. However, for various reasons, the report has not yet been issued.

Public participation

Since the 1990s, interested people have had a participatory role in EIA. However, few citizens are interested. NGOs and the Ministry of Environment and Natural Resources Protection have established channels of communication with the local population to make people aware of environmental problems that can have an impact on them. The trend is slow, but local residents are -beginning to participate in some EIA processes. However, with the current economic situation, the environment is not a priority for Georgia's citizens, who are more concerned by economic and social issues.

The 1996 Law on State Ecological Expertise, in its article 3, makes provision for publicity of the expertise and public participation and consideration of public opinion. The State ecological expertise helps ensure that environmental concerns are taken into account when decisions are made on the issuance of an environmental permit.

The 1996 Law on Environmental Permits makes provision for wide public participation. Environmental permit applications proceed in four stages:

(a) Within 10 days following the application, the Ministry of Environment and Natural Resources Protection publishes the project proposal in the Official Gazette at the applicant's expense;
(b) The public has 45 days to comment in writing;
(c) Within two months at the most after receipt of the application, the Ministry of Environment and Natural Resources Protection has to hold a public hearing with the participation of the proponent, the Ministry of Environment and Natural Resources Protection, local administration bodies and representatives of the public; and
(d) Finally, after three months, the Ministry of Environment and Natural Resources Protection issues the permit or rejects the application. The Ministry keeps records of the information. Except for confidential information, such as technological processes, the information is made available to the public.

Article 7 of the Law on Environmental Permits stipulates that proponents should enable the public to participate during EIA and provide public access

to the EIA research material. Furthermore, the Ministry of Environment and Natural Resources Protection ensures public participation in the decision-making process for the issuing of environmental permits.

However, NGOs claim that the time frame is too short. Sometimes 45 days is enough only to get all the information and it is too late to put it across to the local population. In Western countries, the consultation period varies from two to three months, depending on the size of the project. NGOs far from the capital are particularly affected.

Although information is available to the public, it could be spread over different ministries or institutions. This can also slow down information collection. TACIS-Georgia will provide bulletins on how and where to find relevant information.

Access to Justice

Article 42 of the Constitution makes provision for the right to appeal to the courts to protect an individual's rights, e.g. access to environmental information. Furthermore, the General Administrative Code's article 5 sets a time limit of 10 days for a public administration or agency to respond to an applicant's request, compared to one month under the Aarhus Convention. Access to information is free, except for copying costs. If access to information is denied, the public administration should inform the applicant within three days after the decision is taken about the decision and about the applicant's rights and the procedure for filing a complaint. An applicant may go to court if:

(a) Access to information was partly or completely denied;
(b) Incorrect information was provided;
(c) Personal data were disseminated; or
(d) Other requirements of the Administrative Code regarding freedom of information were breached by a public agency or civil servant.

There has never a court case on access to environmental information in Georgia. However, it must be pointed out that there are obstacles to going to court: court procedures are long and there are no special legal regulations to speed up environmental court cases. Environmental NGOs cannot represent citizens unless they hire a lawyer and prove sufficient interest in the case. A lawyer is also needed for regional and supreme courts and it is expensive to go in court (State duty). There is no special fund for liability as in Germany. Furthermore, few lawyers or judges have any specific environmental knowledge.

The public has access to an administrative procedure. This concerns an individual's rights, such as the right to access to environmental information. According to the General Administrative Code's article 12, a person may apply to an administrative agency, such as public agency or public service, to resolve matters that are the agency's responsibility and directly affect the applicant's rights and legal interest, e.g. the right to information. Unless otherwise prescribed by law or regulation, the administrative agency should review the administrative complaint and take an appropriate decision. This administrative procedure should start once the complaint is filed, but the complaint should be filed within one month of the official notification. A complaint against an administrative decree issued by the chief official of an administrative agency should be filed in a higher administrative agency. This agency should review the complaint and take a decision within a month: (1) accept the complaint, (2) partly accept the complaint, or (3) reject the complaint. No State duty or supplementary costs should be imposed for the review of an administrative complaint. Moreover, the administrative agency should report the case to the State Chancellery.

Public awareness

Since 1992, Georgians have shown little interest in environmental matters and what little interest there is is dwindling mainly owing to the economic situation and the energy crisis. Nevertheless, there is a will on the part of the Ministry of Environment and Natural Resources Protection and NGOs to raise public awareness. They are working together on seminars and workshops on different environmental topics. Depending on the financing situation, the Ministry meets local people and provides information on environmental topics to them or involves local NGOs in informing the local population about environmental protection. NGOs also provide basic support to the Ministry.

The Ministry has launched several campaigns on urgent topics and financed by special funds from international organizations or donor countries. To carry out its activities, the Department of Public Relations and Environmental Education also tries to raise funds, e.g. USAID provided funds for a campaign in Tkibuli (see below).

For example, the Department launched a campaign to sensitize the local population to the problem of illegal logging and the risk of erosion in Kakheti. The Ministry of Environment and Natural Resources Protection was also asked by a local NGO, Youth Scientific Information Association, to provide to the local population in Tkibuli information on the risks of a coal-fired thermal power plant (e.g. use of poor-quality, high-sulphur coal and location of the power plant on unstable hills). With USAID funds, the Ministry of Environment and Natural Resources Protection published leaflets and organized local seminars to make people aware of the possible hazards related to the construction. According to the Ministry of Environment and Natural Resources Protection and the NGOs involved in the process, local people reacted positively and the project has since been suspended. Another campaign was to provide information on hunting enterprises. Hunting enterprises rent tracts of State land and forest. They are expected to manage rented areas by breeding wild animals and regulating hunting. In certain parts of Georgia, local poachers were against the establishment of hunting enterprises and spread inaccurate information to the population. The Ministry of Environment and Natural Resources Protection stepped in to provide correct information on the status of hunting enterprises.

Education

High education institutions, such as Tbilisi State University, the Technical University and the Agricultural University, train specialists in a limited number of environmental subjects. Environmental law is not part of the regular curricula. NGOs like the Green Movement reach agreements with schools and teach schoolchildren about environmental protection. An ecological primary school was created in Tbilisi five years ago. This private primary school follows the Ministry of Education's requirements, but adds environmental and ecological aspects to its curriculum.

Two years ago, an interdepartmental commission was set up to develop an educational programme. The commission, including the Ministry of Environment and Natural Resources Protection, the World Wide Fund for Nature (WWF) and the Ministry of Education, drafted the "State Programme and Action Plan on Environmental Education". Its aim is to achieve consensus among the State bodies, NGOs and the public on the concept, principles and objective of environmental education. The Ministries of Environment and of

Education have projects to add environmental education to the school curricula. Both wish to introduce environmental subjects at all levels of education.

The World Bank approved a loan for a project to realign and strengthen the education system: phase I, from 2001 to 2005, will cost US$ 25.9 million; phase II, from 2005 to 2009, US$ 20 million; and phase III, from 2009 to 2012, US$ 15 million. The Ministry of Education prepared an environmental educational programme. Its goal is twofold: first, to introduce environment in civics; second, and more ambitiously, to add environment to all fields of education, e.g. maths. The Ministry of Education has started reviewing and updating the books and teaching techniques for children in the first four years of primary school and will gradually extend these efforts throughout primary and secondary school.

Aarhus Convention

Georgia ratified the Aarhus Convention on Access to Information, Public Participation in Decision-making and Access to Justice in Environmental Matters in April 2000. The 1997 Law on International Treaties obliges the Ministry of Foreign Affairs to publish the original text and official translation of all international agreements ratified by Georgia in the "Parliamentary Herald". This has not yet happened for the Aarhus Convention. Only NGOs have published it in the local language.

The Ministry of Environment and Natural Resources Protection has already drafted a law to cover the gaps in the law to comply with the Aarhus Convention. This law is before Parliament for adoption. It contains an exact definition of environmental information, which is missing in the current legislation. A second draft law with amendments to the General Administrative and Civil Codes will help public representatives to overcome obstacles to access to justice. Georgia's Constitution (art. 6) specifies that international agreements or treaties concluded by Georgia take precedence over national normative acts, provided that they do not contradict the Constitution. The 1996 Law on Normative Acts (art. 4) also stipulates that international treaties concluded by Georgia apply in the country. This implies that the Aarhus Convention could be applied without specific local regulations being issued. However, implementation and enforcement require finance and the Ministry

of Environment and Natural Resources Protection has not received enough funding for the implementation not only of the Aarhus Convention but also some of its other legal acts.

Non-governmental organizations

There are approximately 200 environmental non-governmental organizations (NGOs). Some NGOs operate throughout the Caucasus. NGOs are involved in public awareness raising, public information, legal aspects of environment matters, agricultural practices, fighting against illegal logging and poaching, and biodiversity preservation. In cooperation with social NGOs, they explain to local people affected by a project with environmental and social impacts the rights that they have. The largest and most active are financed by international organizations or donor countries. Their cooperation with the Ministry and the Minister is strong and well established. The Ministry of Environment and Natural Resources Protection holds regular meetings with NGOs. These meetings are especially well attended when they deal with a big issue such as the thermal power plant mentioned above, erosion, or poaching. The Ministry of Environment and Natural Resources Protection and NGOs often agree to work together. For instance, the Oil Product Terminal in Kulevi was built without EIA in Poti. Local NGOs contacted the Ministry of Environment and Natural Resources Protection, which subsequently requested an EIA but also forced the enterprise to comply with environmental laws and requirements. Two of the most active environmental NGOs are Green Alternative and Green Movement.

Green Movement is also involved in education. In collaboration with schools, it teaches youngsters to protect and respect the environment through courses, field trips and participation in different campaigns. It launches public campaigns and is active in the whole country. It trains local people in areas where there are no NGOs to create focal points or independent units able to react to environmental issues.

Green Alternative deals with social and environmental impacts on Georgian society. It is involved in the protection of biodiversity, monitoring international financial institutions' programmes and projects in Georgia, especially in the energy sector, and supporting Georgian NGO capacity to deal with such projects in various sectors.

Box 3.2:   Pipelines

The Baku-Tbilisi-Ceyhan Export Oil Pipeline (BTC) and Baku-Tbilisi-Erzrum Gas Pipeline are intended to create an energy corridor to connect the Caspian Sea coast to the Turkish Mediterranean so as to provide oil and gas to European and United States markets. The project depends on the political and financial support from Western Governments and international financial institutions. Three alternative routes were considered, but they present environmental and social hazards. A fourth, the Karakia route, was studied and its environmental impact assessed. This route avoids sensible areas but presents construction constraints. The project is controversial in Georgia.

CEEN together with other national and international NGOs demanded that financing for the project should be stopped until the real development benefits for the population in the Caspian region could be demonstrated. Apart from asking for a realistic assessment of its social, economic and environmental impacts, they have also provided all kinds of information on the pipeline to the local population.

EIA has revealed some important information on the selection of the route, which crosses the Ktsia Tabatskuri Reserve and the Borjomi Mineral Water Field. A spill in the Borjomi Mineral Water Field would be an ecological and potential social disaster. Groundwater will be polluted by infiltration and the economic activity based on the mineral water will have to be stopped.

Environmental risk assessment with EIA is inadequate to address construction risks, public safety, mitigation measures and risks to drinking-water sources.

Non-governmental organization networks

NGO networks are useful to prepare a common view on environmental matters and to share information through different means (press releases, newspapers, web sites). Three networks operate in Georgia.

The Caucasus Environmental NGO Network (CENN) was established to bring environmental information to the public in the three Caucasian countries (Azerbaijan, Armenia and Georgia), but also to people all over the world interested in the environment in the region. Its headquarters are located in Tbilisi. Its aims are NGO capacity building and joint environmental activities in the region, improvement of solutions in a transboundary context, coordination in the development of environmental strategies and policies in the Caucasus, and networking and information exchange. Its web site (http://www.cenn.org) is updated regularly and environmental information is available in five languages (Armenian, Azeri, English, Georgian and Russian). Furthermore, CENN has a mailing list server and disseminates information. It organizes regional thematic seminars and workshops with the NGO community, local people and government representatives. CENN has produced the text of the Aarhus Convention in local languages and posted it on its web site. These translations are also available on the Aarhus Convention's web site.

The Regional Environmental Centre for the Caucasus (REC Caucasus), created in spring 2000 by Armenia, Azerbaijan, Georgia and the European Union, works for environmental and sustainable development in the Caucasus. Its mission is to assist Caucasian States, to bring civil society in the decision-making process, to promote cooperation between NGOs at national and regional level, local communities and businesses, and to provide environmental information. Its web site can be found at http://www.rec-caucasus.org.

The Central and Eastern European Network (CEEN) is a network of NGOs in Central and Eastern Europe. Its mission is to prevent environmentally and socially harmful impacts of international development finance, and to promote alternative solutions and public participation. CEEN is a member of the Central and East European Bankwatch Network (http://www.bankwatch.org).

3.3   Conclusions and recommendations

In Georgia, there is currently no regular, systematic monitoring and data analysis; what little exists could be better characterized as surveillance. Without accurate data, there is no reliable information either for decision-making or for reporting. It is also impossible to comply fully with the laws that call for maintaining registers and cadastres. These tools are reliable only if a reliable monitoring system is in place. They will serve as a tool for public information. The Ministry of Environment and Natural Resources Protection is fully aware of this difficult situation, and it has, in cooperation with other institutions, drafted a programme to restart efficient monitoring based on the conclusions of the Ad Hoc Working Group on Environmental Monitoring of the United Nations Economic Commission for Europe.

Recommendation 3.1:
(a) *The Government should adopt the programme on monitoring drawn up by the Ministry of Environment and Natural Resources Protection and other institutions and should provide funding to carry it out. Monitoring of industrial hot spots and high-polluting facilities should be included in this programme as a matter of priority;*
(b) *After adoption, the Ministry of Environment and Natural Resources Protection and relevant institutions should harmonize the environmental norms and standards with international norms and standards, and should set up an appropriate system for environmental monitoring.*

The Law on Environmental Permits stipulates that the public has 45 days following publication of information on an activity to provide its comments. However, NGOs, which generally have few human and financial resources, sometimes find it impossible to access all the necessary information, analyse it and respond within this time period. This is particularly a problem for NGOs based outside of the capital.

Recommendation 3.2:
The Ministry of Environment and Natural Resources Protection should:

(a) *Prepare an amendment to the Law on Environmental Permits to extend the 45-day time frame for public participation;*
(b) *Improve the exchange and dissemination of all information relevant to the permit procedure, including the environmental impact assessment and the results of the State ecological expertise, for example by creating a depository within the Ministry accessible to the public. (See Recommendations 1.3 and 1.4.)*

The Ministry of Environment and Natural Resources Protection has drafted a law on public access to environmental information and decision-making. The draft laws fills gaps in Georgia's legislation for full implementation of the UNECE Aarhus Convention.

Recommendation 3.3:
The Ministry of Environment and Natural Resources Protection should:
(a) *Actively promote adoption by Parliament of the (draft) law on public access to environmental information and decision-making as soon as it is finalized;*
(b) *Following its adoption, widely publicize and distribute the law and support staff training and public awareness campaigns on the content of the law in order to facilitate its application.*

Chapter 4

INTERNATIONAL COOPERATION

4.1 Framework for international environmental cooperation

International cooperation is a dominant feature and a driving force for environmental reforms in Georgia. Donor assistance has provided significant support for policy formulation and other capacity-building projects, in particular technical capacity.

Water pollution, the management of ecosystems and biodiversity, chemicals and hazardous waste are among the most significant environmental problems in Georgia. Their scale and complexity require an integrated and comprehensive approach and significant financial resources, which are at present limited since the economy is in transition. In this context international cooperation plays an important role in providing access to international funding and investments, expertise and technology transfer.

The main international actors involved in environmental cooperation in Georgia are United Nations system organizations, in particular the United Nations Economic Commission for Europe (UNECE), the United Nations Environment Programme (UNEP) and the United Nations Development Programme (UNDP), the World Bank, other international financing institutions, such as the European Bank for Reconstruction and Development (EBRD) and the European Investment Bank (EIB), the International Monetary Fund (IMF), the Black Sea Trade and Development Bank and the Global Environment Facility (GEF). Another major player is the European Union, primarily through its TACIS programme.

Georgia has been a member of GEF since 1994. It is currently a member of the GEF Council. The Department of Environmental Policy of the Ministry of Environment and Natural Resources Protection is the operational focal point. As one of the main international financing institutes and the financial mechanism for several global conventions, GEF has provided financial support to a number of projects in Georgia to address biodiversity loss, climate change, degradation of international waters, ozone depletion, land degradation and persistent organic pollutants (POPs) (see below).

Georgia became a member of the World Bank in 1992. Priorities for World Bank financing in Georgia include promoting regional environmental initiatives, strengthening institutional capacities and rehabilitating the infrastructure. A number of projects are currently being implemented with regard to, inter alia, integrated coastal zone management, protected areas development and forestry development.

UNDP activities are governed by Georgia's second Country Cooperation Framework (2001 – 2003). UNDP is actively supporting initiatives to improve the management and conservation of natural resources. This includes energy conservation, seeking renewable energy resources and making use of transboundary waters.

Forming part of Georgia's implementation of Agenda 21, the development of the National Environmental Action Plan for Georgia was initiated in 1996 with financial support from the World Bank. The Plan was adopted in 2000. It outlines a number of short- to medium-term objectives for environmental management and the sustainable use of natural resources with chapters on water supply and surface water pollution, air pollution, resource use, chemicals and waste management, land use, protection of the Black Sea, forests and international cooperation.

Georgia actively participated in the development of partnerships and initiatives on health and environment, biodiversity and ecosystem management, agriculture, water and sanitation, energy, and cross-sectoral issues developed specifically in the context of the World Summit on Sustainable Development (Johannesburg, August 2002).

4.2 Institutional arrangements for international environmental cooperation

Several executive agencies in the country are responsible for international environmental cooperation, with the Ministry of Environment and Natural Resources Protection playing the leading role. The Ministry is the focal point for the following conventions:

- The United Nations Framework Convention on Climate Change and the Kyoto Protocol;
- The Vienna Convention for the Protection of the Ozone Layer and the Montreal Protocol on Substances that Deplete the Ozone Layer;
- The Basel Convention on the Control of Transboundary Movements of Hazardous Wastes and their Disposal;
- The Convention on Biological Diversity;
- The Convention on International Trade in Endangered Species of Wild Fauna and Flora;
- The Convention on the Conservation of Migratory Species of Wild Animals;
- The Convention to Combat Desertification;
- The Convention on Wetlands of International Importance Especially as Waterfowl Habitat;
- The Convention on the Protection of the Black Sea Against Pollution;
- The International Convention for the Prevention of Pollution from Ships (MARPOL);
- The Convention on Long-range Transboundary Air Pollution; and
- The Aarhus Convention on Access to Information, Public Participation in Decision-making and Access to Justice in Environmental Matters.

The Ministry of Culture is the focal point for the Convention for the Protection of the World Cultural and Natural Heritage.

The Ministry of Food and Agriculture and the Ministry of Labour, Health and Social Affairs are responsible for the management of chemicals jointly with the Ministry of Environment and Natural Resources Protection.

The Ministry of Foreign Affairs acts as a supervisory body for the implementation of provisions set out in different international agreements.

The national procedures for the ratification, acceptance, approval and accession to international agreements are regulated by the Law on International Agreements of 16 October 1997.

4.3 Cooperation in multilateral environmental agreements (global)

Georgia is a Party to a number of global environmental agreements. The accession and ratification rate has been particularly high within the past few years. Georgia is also becoming increasingly active in the development of these agreements.

Conventions on the protection of air and atmosphere

Georgia acceded to the *United Nations Framework Convention on Climate Change* in 1994 and to its Kyoto Protocol in 1999. To meet Georgia's commitments under the Convention, a national programme and an action plan on climate change were developed by the National Research Centre set up within the Ministry of Environment and Natural Resources Protection. The plan includes a number of prioritized investment projects.

Georgia submitted its Initial National Communication under the Convention in 1999. It contains detailed information on the actions taken to implement the Convention, including:

- A national inventory of greenhouse gas emissions for the period 1980–1997 for five of the six main modules of the Intergovernmental Panel on Climate Change (IPCC) guidelines (energy, industrial processes, transport, agriculture and forests);
- A national strategy for the limitation of greenhouse gas emissions;
- An analysis of the possible consequences of climate change, vulnerability assessments and adaptation measures for agriculture, water resources, the Black Sea coastal zone, and ecosystems;
- The National Action Plan for Climate Change;
- Climate change research, systematic observations and information exchange; and
- Promoting education, training and public awareness relating to climate change.

The Initial National Communication was prepared with financial assistance from GEF and in cooperation with UNDP. It formed part of one of several projects enabling Georgia to implement the Convention on Climate Change. As a non-Annex 1 country, Georgia has no specific obligation to reduce its greenhouse gas emissions. Nevertheless, a number of projects have been developed to achieve a more effective use of energy and thereby reducing emissions of greenhouse gases.

Other internationally supported projects include:
- Promoting the use of renewable energy resources for local energy supply (GEF-funded and co-financed by Germany);
- Additional financing for capacity building in priority areas, focusing on technology needs assessments in the energy and industry sectors. The project included the preparation of 10 project proposals for the abatement of greenhouse gas emissions (GEF enabling activities – part II).

Georgia has been a Party to the *Vienna Convention and the Montreal Protocol* since 1996 as an Article 5 (1) country (developing country for the purpose of the Montreal Protocol). In 2000 Georgia acceded to the 1990 London Amendment, the 1992 Copenhagen Amendment and the 1997 Montreal Amendment. It is in the process of ratifying the 1999 Beijing Amendment.

The Air Protection Department (National Ozone Unit) within the Ministry of Environment and Natural Resources Protection is responsible for domestic and international policy and control of chlorofluorocarbons (CFCs) and other ozone-depleting substances (ODS) controlled by the Protocol. The Customs Department is responsible for monitoring imports, ensuring that they are covered by the appropriate import licence.

Implementing legislation includes the 1999 Law on Ambient Air Protection, which covers the licensing of ODS import and the Presidential Decree on the Control of Ozone-depleting Substances in Georgia, which regulates the import, export and handling of ODS as well as certification of technicians dealing with equipment and storage containers with ODS.

The National Programme and Action Plan for Phasing out Ozone-depleting Substances was developed in 1997. It includes an evaluation of the current and anticipated imports, exports and consumption of ODS, an action plan for the further elimination of ODS and identifies potential projects that need international support to facilitate the phase-out. The following goals for phasing out ODS have been set:

- Phase-out of the consumption of CFCs by 2005, allowing very minor amounts of CFC coolants for maintenance purposes beyond 2005 – up to 2010;
- Follow the phase-out schedules set for non-Article 5 (1) countries regarding HCFCs and methyl bromide;
- Develop and establish an appropriate legal and regulatory framework to ensure the phase-out;
- Develop and establish the necessary monitoring and licensing systems to control imports of ODS and ensure their phase-out;
- Develop a permanent public awareness campaign to support the control measures to be taken; and
- Support local industries to adopt ODS-free technologies.

To meet the set goals for phasing out ODS, a number of projects have been or are currently being implemented with the support of GEF, UNDP, UNEP and the Multilateral Fund for the Implementation of the Montreal Protocol:
- Capacity-building, focusing on institutional strengthening of the Ministry of Environment and Natural Resources Protection. The project included the establishment of a national programme implementation office within the Department of Air Protection;
- Training the trainers for refrigeration technicians;
- Training in the monitoring and control of ODS;
- Disposal and recycling of CFC-12 from existing cooling devices;
- Implementation: monitoring the activities in the refrigeration management programme;
- Incentive programme for end-users in the commercial/industrial refrigeration and refrigerated transport subsectors;
- Phase-out of methyl bromide for soil fumigation; and
- Training of customs officers.

Total ozone-depletion potential (ODP) consumption (CFC-12, HCFC-22, MBr) was 25.96 ODP tons in 1996, of which 24.55 ODP tons were used in the refrigeration sector. The 1999 consumption of CFC-12 was reduced by 4.4% compared to the baseline figures. Georgia is by and large meeting the goals for phasing out ODS.

There are no precise estimates on illegal import of ODS, although there is some concern that such imports are taking place.

Chemicals and hazardous waste conventions

Georgia has taken an active part in several international initiatives in chemical safety and waste. It acceded to the Convention on the Control of Transboundary Movements of Hazardous Wastes and their Disposal (Basel Convention) in May 1999. Georgia has not acceded to the 1995 Ban Amendment to the Convention or the 1999 Protocol on Liability and Compensation for Damage resulting from Transboundary Movements of Hazardous Wastes and their Disposal.

The Department of Land Resources Protection, Waste and Chemical Substances Management within the Ministry of Environment and Natural Resources Protection is responsible for developing policies and legislation on all waste, including hazardous waste and its transboundary movements.

Georgia has no specific legislation on the management of waste. However, the Ministry of Environment and Natural Resources Protection is preparing a framework law on waste to facilitate transposition of general Basel Convention requirements, in particular the definition of waste and hazardous waste, and the EU waste directives. The current draft contains references to the listing and classification criteria for waste and hazardous waste set out in the Basel Convention as well as the EU Framework Directive on Waste, the European Waste Catalogue, the EU Hazardous Waste Directive, the EU Waste Shipment Regulation and the OECD Decision Concerning the Control of Transfrontier Movements of Wastes Destined for Recovery Operations from 1992. This is likely to lead to confusion and often-conflicting definitions and classification of waste and hazardous waste and subsequent difficulties for implementation and enforcement. When finalizing the draft, the Ministry may therefore wish to clarify the definition of waste and hazardous waste, and follow the system in the waste shipment regulation, since that already integrates the EU and Basel systems and therefore provides a ready-made system that can be used as a basis for further waste legislation development. (See also recommendation 6.3.)

Some Basel Convention requirements and the Ban Amendment have been implemented through the Law on Transit and Import of Waste into and out of the Territory of Georgia, as amended by Law No. 957 of 16 October 1997. The Law prohibits the import and transit of hazardous waste, and controls the import, export and transit of non-hazardous waste. For the purpose of transboundary movements, the definition of hazardous waste is broader than that of the Basel Convention. It includes all amber-list waste and some types of green-list waste of the EU Waste Shipment Regulation (259/93). Only the import and transit of non-hazardous ferrous and non-ferrous metal scrap, solid plastic waste, paper waste, textile waste, wood waste, and glass waste for recovery will be permitted. Specific control procedures are set out in the Rules and Procedures for the Regulation of Transit and Import of Waste into and out of the territory of Georgia. Permitting of waste shipments is carried out at national level, by the Department of Land Resources Protection, Waste and Chemical Substances Management (competent authority and focal point for the Convention). Border controls are carried out by customs authorities and border guards.

Despite the legislation being put into place, the control systems for imports are fragmented and insufficient: training and manpower shortages are widespread. Neither the Basel Convention notification, nor its movement document is required. Controls of transboundary movements are often based on the shipment documents using customs codes (and not waste definitions) as a basis. Parts of the border are not controlled, and imports of hazardous waste are often not differentiated from those of hazardous substances.

Georgia is not a Party to the *Convention on the Prior Informed Consent Procedure for certain Hazardous Chemicals and Pesticides in International Trade* (Rotterdam Convention). Georgia has, however, participated in the voluntary Prior Informed Consent (PIC) procedure under the London Guidelines for the Exchange of Information on Chemicals in International Trade. The Ministry of Environment and Natural Resources Protection sees it as a high priority to accede to the Convention in the near future.

Georgia signed the *Convention on Persistent Organic Pollutants* (Stockholm Convention) in May 2002. Upon signing the Convention, Georgia became eligible for GEF funding for the development of a national implementation plan for the management of persistent organic pollutants (POPs) that will describe how Georgia will meet its obligations under the Convention. To this effect the following activities will be undertaken: assessment of the chemical management infrastructures relevant to POPs, establishment of POPs inventories and identification of suitable management options for POPs. A prioritized action plan, including costs, for both management and remediation will also be prepared.

Chemicals are regulated by the 1998 Law on Hazardous Chemical Substances. The Law includes provisions on registration and storage of chemicals, establishment of a database on use of chemicals, and procedures for the licensing and permitting of new chemicals, and the handling, storage and transport of chemicals by producers and users. In addition, the Law contains rules for permitting exports and imports of chemicals as well as the regulatory framework for banning and restricting chemicals. The Ministry of Environment and Natural Resources Protection, jointly with the Ministry of Labour, Health and Social Affairs and the Ministry of Food and Agriculture, is responsible for implementing the Law. Although the Law provides an appropriate framework for regulating chemicals, little has been done so far to implement the legislation.

Chemicals and hazardous waste, in particular illegal imports, are pressing environmental issues in Georgia. It is estimated that as much as 60 to 70% of chemicals, including pesticides, are illegally imported. Storage of obsolete pesticides is also a widespread problem.

Biodiversity-related conventions

Georgia acceded to the *Convention on Biological Diversity* in 1994, and is taking steps to accede to the *Cartagena Protocol on Biological Safety*, including through the preparation of implementing legislation.

Several steps have been taken to implement the Convention on Biological Diversity:
- A biodiversity study programme was completed in 1996 with the support of UNEP.
- A draft biodiversity strategy and action plan was developed with the financial support of GEF and the World Bank. It sets out specific actions to be undertaken to ensure the preservation of biological diversity in Georgia through conservation measures and the sustainable use of natural resources. The draft strategy and action plan is based on the Pan-European Biological and Landscape Diversity Strategy. It has not yet been adopted.
- Protected areas development with support of GEF. The aims are to establish ecologically effective protected areas and wildlife corridors; integrate biodiversity conservation into forestry and range management inside and outside

protected areas; strengthen institutions responsible for biodiversity conservation programmes; support monitoring and applied research on threatened flora and fauna as indicators of ecosystem health; improve public awareness of the values of Georgian biodiversity; support public, private and civil society partnerships for conservation planning and management; and promote regional cooperation in Trans-Caucasus biodiversity conservation.
- Arid and semi-arid ecosystem conservation with the support of GEF. The project aims to protect biodiversity in the arid and semi-arid zones in eastern Georgia. The project is designed to ensure local land users' participation in the design of alternative land uses, and their integration in its implementation. The project complements and enhances proposed protection activities in the target area and coordinates these with neighbouring countries sharing sections of the ecosystem.

Georgia has also been a Party to the *Convention on International Trade in Endangered Species of Wild Fauna and Flora (CITES)* since 1996. The Ministry of Environment and Natural Resources Protection (Convention Unit within the Department of Biodiversity) has been designated as the management authority. The Unit, together with the Customs Department, coordinates the control of exports and imports of animals and plants. A control handbook has been prepared. There are currently 24 Appendix II CITES-listed flora species in Georgia. Draft legislation implementing CITES has been prepared based on World Conservation Union (IUCN) guidelines. It includes export quotas on certain wild flora and fauna species.

In June 2000 Georgia acceded to the Convention on the Conservation of Migratory Species of Wild Animals (Bonn Convention) and is a Party to the Agreement on the Conservation of African-Eurasian Migratory Waterbirds, the Agreement on the Conservation of Cetaceans of the Black Sea, Mediterranean Sea and Contiguous Atlantic Area, and has signed the Memorandum of Understanding concerning Conservation Measures for the Slender-billed Curlew.

Georgia has been a Party to the Convention on Wetlands of International Importance Especially as Waterfowl Habitat (Ramsar Convention, 1971) since 1996. Two wetlands with international importance have been designated: Ispani II marshes and wetlands of central Kolkheti nature reserves, both designated in 1997. The Dzakaxeti nature reserve is currently under consideration as a Ramsar site. A management plan for the wetlands of central Kolkheti has been prepared. Implementing legislation includes the Law on Protected Areas System and the Law on Kolkheti National Park. So far no national action plan for wetlands of international importance has been developed.

In 1992 Georgia acceded to the Convention for the Protection of the World Cultural and Natural Heritage (Paris Convention). Action taken under this Convention is mainly to protect historic monuments. Through its Man and the Biosphere Programme (MAB), the United Nations Educational, Scientific and Cultural Organization (UNESCO) also takes part in certain projects to protect the world natural heritage in Georgia. The Ministry of Culture is the focal point for this Convention.

Desertification

In 1999 Georgia ratified the Convention to Combat Desertification, but little has been done so far to implement it. The preparation of a national action programme to combat desertification was initiated in 2001 with support from UNEP. The programme has not yet been adopted. National reports on the implementation of the Convention were submitted to its secretariat in 2000 and 2002. A GEF project to protect arid and semi-arid ecosystems from degradation through the sustainable management of natural resources is looking at: agricultural practices that protect ecosystems and key species, the management of transboundary ecosystems with the active participation of land users, increasing public awareness and information.

Regional seas – The Black Sea

In September 1993 Georgia ratified the Convention on the Protection of the Black Sea Against Pollution (Bucharest Convention) and its three protocols: the Protocol on Protection of the Black Sea Marine Environment Against Pollution from Land-based Sources; the Protocol on Cooperation in Combating Pollution of the Black Sea Marine Environment by Oil and other Harmful Substances in Emergency Situations and the Protocol on the Protection of the Black Sea Marine Environment Against Pollution by Dumping.

There are a number of internationally supported projects to assist Georgia in implementing the Convention and its regional strategic action plan, including:

- A GEF-supported project to develop the implementation of the Black Sea strategic action plan. Its long-term objective is to foster sustainable institutional and financial arrangements for the effective environmental management and protection of the Black Sea, in accordance with the plan. The project will provide for the development of a national Black Sea strategic action plan, and it will support national and regional institution-building for the development and implementation of such plans;

- The integrated coastal zone management (ICZM) programme. Its activities include the establishment of a legal and institutional framework for planning at the national and local levels; support for an environmental quality monitoring system and information network of ICZM, the identification of cost-effective solutions for coastal erosion, and national oil spill contingency planning.

Other projects include: a GEF/World Bank project for establishing a Danube/Black Sea basin strategic partnership on nutrient reduction and a GEF project for the control of eutrophication, hazardous substances and related measures for rehabilitating the Black Sea ecosystem.

Other environment related conventions

Georgia is a Party to the International Convention for the Prevention of Pollution from Ships (MARPOL), the International Convention on Civil Liability for Oil Pollution Damage, and the International Convention on the Establishment of an International Fund for Compensation for Oil Pollution Damage.

4.4   Regional cooperation in the framework of UNECE

Conventions

Georgia recognizes the importance of the UNECE conventions for the sustainable development of Eastern Europe, the Caucasus and Central Asia, especially with respect to tackling the transboundary effects of water and air pollution and industrial accidents. However, accession to the

UNECE conventions has been slow owing to the lack of financial and technical resources and infrastructure for their implementation.

Georgia acceded to the UNECE Convention on Long-range Transboundary Air Pollution in 1999. However, it has not signed or acceded to any of its eight Protocols. It has no immediate plans to accede to the Protocols due to the anticipated costs of implementation. Whereas international cooperation is high, there is practically no regional cooperation to address transboundary air pollution. At present, there is virtually no information on transboundary movements of the different types of air pollutants and the problems to which they give rise.

Georgia signed the London Protocol on Water and Health to the Convention on the Protection and Use of Transboundary Watercourses and International Lakes in June 1999 and is in the process of ratifying it. A drinking water quality strategy and supply management strategy are being prepared with support from the Government of Denmark (DANCEE). They will build on a pilot project in one region (municipality or district) in Georgia. The strategies will provide recommendations for changes to the institutional set-up of the water sector as well as the legal and the management procedures. Accession to the Convention itself is currently under consideration.

Georgia ratified the Aarhus Convention on Access to Information, Public Participation in Decision-making and Access to Justice in Environmental Matters in April 2000. Activities directed at implementing its provisions and principles were initiated shortly after its adoption, including under various international programmes and projects. Implementing legislation has been prepared and is expected to be considered by Parliament in early 2003. Some new practices to implement the Convention have developed. These efforts have focused primarily on the first pillar of the Convention (access to information), where progress has been made with regard to, for instance, electronic means of information dissemination, including web sites and regular meetings between the Minister of Environment and NGOs. Some progress has also been made with regard to public participation, although more needs to be done. Less progress has been made with regard to access to justice.

A project to support implementation of the Aarhus Convention in a number of East European, Caucasian and Central Asian countries, including

Georgia, is currently being implemented under the TACIS Regional Action Programme, 2000. It includes development of training packages on provision of information and developing public participation as well as a user's guide on how rights under the Convention may be exercised.

Other related projects include the establishment of the new Regional Environmental Centre for the Caucasus in Georgia supported by TACIS and USAID (see below).

Georgia has no advanced plans to accede to the Convention on Environmental Impact Assessment in a Transboundary Context (Espoo) or to the Convention on the Transboundary Effects of Industrial Accidents.

"Environment for Europe" process

In preparation for the fifth Ministerial Conference "Environment for Europe," (Kiev, Ukraine, May 2003), Georgia, together with Ukraine, is playing a key role in developing an environmental strategy for Eastern Europe, the Caucasus and Central Asia. This strategy is intended to provide clear directions for environmentally sustainable policies within and between these countries and to serve as a basis for developing partnerships between East and West.

Georgia is actively involved in a number of other initiatives within the "Environment for Europe" process, including an initiative to develop an agreement for the protection and sustainable management of the Caucasus mountains and their ecosystems, and a proposed water partnership between East European, Caucasian and Central Asian countries and EU countries. Georgia also plays an important role in work undertaken by the Task Force for Implementation of the Environmental Action Programme for Central and Eastern Europe in promoting environmental policy reform and capacity-building. The Minister of Environment of Georgia is currently one of the co-chairs of the EAP Task Force, together with the European Commission.

Cooperation through REC Caucasus

The Regional Environmental Centre (REC) for the Caucasus, located in Tbilisi, plays a significant role in furthering regional cooperation among the Caucasian countries. The Centre was established in 2000 with support from the EU TACIS Programme, which provides the core funding. Other financial and technical assistance has been provided by

Denmark, Germany, Switzerland and the United States.

The Centre has developed a number of programmes for sustainable development, information and public participation, NGO support, and institutional development. Among its activities are several that address transboundary water issues in the Caucasus, including through the development of collaborative partnerships, discussion and determination of policy options and project preparation.

4.5 Other regional cooperation

Cooperation in CIS

Georgia has been a member of the Commonwealth of Independent States (CIS) since 1993. Georgia cooperates in regional integration matters with some members of CIS on the basis of bilateral agreements (see section 4.6 below) as well as with the Interstate Ecological Council, which is a subsidiary body of the CIS Executive Committee. The Action Programme for the Development of CIS until 2025, which was developed and signed by the Heads of State in 2000, includes several measures regarding environmental protection (e.g. environmental monitoring, environmental safety, a uniform classification and labelling system for industrial waste).

Cooperation with the European Union

Georgia entered into a Partnership and Cooperation Agreement with the EU in July 1999. Article 57 of this Agreement sets out the objectives and areas of cooperation with regard to the environment. These include: combating local, regional and transboundary air and water pollution; classification and safe handling of chemicals; water quality; waste reduction, recycling and safe disposal, and implementation of the Basel Convention; the environmental impact of agriculture, soil erosion, and chemical pollution; protection of forests; conservation of biodiversity, protected areas and sustainable use and management of biological resources. The Agreement further calls for the effective monitoring of pollution and assessment of the environment; an information system on the state of the environment; ecological restoration; sustainable, efficient and environmentally effective production and use of energy, and safety of industrial plants.

Under the Agreement Georgia has committed itself to harmonizing its national legislation with the relevant EU environmental legislation. TACIS is the main financial instrument supporting the Agreement's implementation and providing grant assistance for projects in priority areas that are defined on a biannual basis. A number of projects have and are currently being implemented under the respective TACIS programmes (the TACIS Inter-State Programme, the TACIS National Programme for Georgia, the TACIS Cross-border Cooperation Programmes and the TACIS Small Projects Programme).

One of the key areas for TACIS support for environment is water resource management and the control of water quality. This includes improving monitoring capacity, introducing guidelines and regulations for water quality control and establishing the necessary infrastructure. The TACIS programme on joint river management for the Kura basin includes several projects being carried out by national technical working groups in Georgia, Armenia and Azerbaijan.

Environmental policy development and implementation; enhancing the role of civil society; and promotion of sustainable development and management of natural resources in the Black Sea are also seen as high priorities, and €3 million are allocated in 2003 for the Black Sea projects.

Cooperation with NATO

Georgia cooperates with the North Atlantic Treaty Organisation (NATO) in the "Partnership for peace" process, particularly regarding environmental protection through the prevention of, preparedness for and response to natural disasters and industrial accidents, as well as in strengthening the rescue services.

4.6 Bilateral and Trilateral Cooperation

Georgia has concluded a number of bilateral agreements with its neighbouring and nearby countries on environmental cooperation, focusing on the management of transboundary natural resources and pollution prevention, including the management of water, waste, biodiversity and forests. These agreements typically contain provisions on monitoring, joint research and information exchange as well as development and harmonization of legislation.

Georgia has concluded bilateral agreements with Armenia, Azerbaijan, Greece, Kazakhstan, Turkey,

Ukraine and Uzbekistan. A bilateral agreement with Bulgaria is being finalized.

Bilateral and trilateral cooperation is of particular importance in regard to the management and use of transboundary natural resources and ecosystems, such as the transboundary rivers Kura and Arak. Several trilateral water management projects for the Kura-Arak river basin have been initiated with support from TACIS and USAID (see chapter 7 on water management for details of the projects). Another UNDP-supported Kura-Arak river basin management project is in the pipeline.

Georgia has a number of bilateral technical cooperation arrangements with Denmark, Germany, Japan, Switzerland and the United States and with the European Commission providing technical and financial assistance for environmental protection.

4.7   Conclusions and recommendations

International cooperation has and continues to play a critical role in supporting environmental protection efforts in Georgia, e.g. external environmental assistance and financing have been practically the only source for environmental protection. In particular cooperation through multilateral environmental agreements (MEAs) has been an important element of environmental cooperation in Georgia. Georgia has become Party to many global and regional MEAs, several of which have been developed under the aegis of UNECE. Georgia has also entered into subregional and bilateral agreements, in particular to protect enclosed seas and other common resources. This, in turn, has influenced their environmental policies and actions.

While Georgia has a strong record in terms of formal steps of accession or ratification to MEAs and the development of corresponding national laws, implementation has been slow, especially with regard to the MEAs that do not have financial mechanisms to support their implementation. A great deal remains to be done with regard to practical implementation and enforcement.

Effective implementation and enforcement of a number of MEAs, including those on the hazardous waste and chemicals (Basel, Stockholm and Rotterdam Conventions), CITES and the Montreal Protocol, largely rest on the joint efforts of the Ministry of Environment and Natural Resources Protection, as the competent authority, and customs and border controls. So far little has been done with

regard to training of customs officers and setting up communication and coordination mechanisms between the Ministry and the customs officers. Some initiatives, such as training of trainers, are under way to improve the control of the import and export of ozone-depleting substances (ODS). These training projects could easily be expanded to other areas.

Recommendation 4.1:
As soon as appropriate capacities for implementation are available, and pursuant to the Partnership and Cooperation Agreement with the EU, the Government should accede to the following conventions:

- *The UNECE Convention on the Protection and Use of Transboundary Watercourses and International Lakes;*
- *The UNECE Convention on Environmental Impact Assessment in a Transboundary Context (Espoo Convention);*
- *The UNECE Convention on the Transboundary Effects of Industrial Accidents;*
- *The Stockholm Convention on Persistent Organic Pollutants.*

The Government should also accede to the following Protocols:

- *Four of the Protocols to the Convention on Long-range Transboundary Air Pollution (see recommendation 5.3);*
- *The Energy Charter Protocol on Energy Efficiency and Related Environmental Aspects; and*
- *The 1995 Ban Amendment to the Basel Convention.*

Recommendation 4.2:
To ensure effective implementation and compliance, the Ministry of Environment and Natural Resources Protection should take more concrete measures to comply with those conventions to which Georgia is already a Party, including measures to combat and prevent the illegal traffic in hazardous waste and chemicals, ozone-depleting substances and wildlife species. To support implementation and compliance, training of customs officers should be organized regularly.

Within the Ministry of Environment and Natural Resources Protection, the tasks of international cooperation, including development, participation and implementation of MEAs, policy development, harmonization of national environmental legislation with EU law and international project management, are fragmented. Communication and coordination among the units and departments have often been poor, causing an overlap of competences. Lack of coordination also makes it difficult to decide on international environmental priorities.

Administrative and project management needs to be reinforced within the Ministry and in particular within its Department of Environmental Policy.

Recommendation 4.3:
To achieve effective implementation of MEAs and harmonization of national environmental legislation with EU law, including through internationally supported projects, the Ministry of Environment and Natural Resources Protection should identify and rank priorities and draw up preliminary planning for the effective implementation of its international commitments.

A number of initiatives have been taken to make international environmental assistance and financing more effective. These include the establishment of the Department of Environmental Policy and the establishment of the TACIS Coordination Unit within the Ministry of the Economy. However, communication with donors has been insufficient. As a result donors' and international financial institutions' efforts have overlapped in some areas, e.g. water and public participation, while other key issues, e.g. hazardous waste and chemicals, have not received adequate attention. Concerns have also been raised that their activities in Georgia have influenced or driven Georgia's national priorities rather than supported them.

One consequence of this is a lack of ownership by the relevant ministries and therefore a lack of follow-through and implementation. For example, a number of national policy strategies and action plans have been developed with international support, often by foreign experts. While these may be of high quality, they have often failed to generate national commitment. Many have never adopted.

Recommendation 4.4:
The Ministry of Environment and Natural Resources Protection should take the lead in identifying environmental programmes and projects that may need external support. In order to accomplish this, it should take the following steps:

- *Establish a project preparation unit to act as a focus for coordination with donors and international financial institutions;*
- *Set priorities for external funding on the basis of domestic problems and needs, and communicate these priorities clearly to the donor community and international financial institutions; and*
- *Work in close cooperation with the Ministry of Foreign Affairs and other relevant ministries in project identification and dissemination.*

PART II: MANAGEMENT OF POLLUTION AND OF NATURAL RESOURCES

Chapter 5

AIR MANAGEMENT

5.1 State and determinants of air pollution

Air emissions

Road traffic is the major source of air pollution in Georgia, followed by the energy sector and industry. Traffic intensity is high in larger cities and, in extreme cases, it amounts to 60,000 vehicles per day (e.g. in Tbilisi). Georgia has about 3000 stationary sources of air pollution in its main industrial sectors such as energy, iron and steel, chemical and petrochemical, timber and paper, and food. At present, however, few are working at full capacity.

The total emission of selected air pollutants is presented in table 5.1. These data are obtained with the use of the CORINAIR methodology, on the basis of emission indicators and activity indicators (mainly in the form of energy consumption or production rate) for different sectors. They include the following stationary sources: power stations, fuel combustion in both industrial and non-industrial enterprises, and industrial processes. Mobile sources include road transport, railway transport, air transport, marine transport and "other" mobile sources.

The data indicate that there is a high share of mobile source emissions. However, it should be noted that the data in table 5.1 are incomplete. They omit non-methane volatile organic compound (NMVOC) emissions from fuel storage, transport and distribution systems, ammonia emissions from agriculture and all emissions from the municipal sector (households, restaurants, hotels, hospitals and other facilities). If these data were taken into consideration, the relative share of emissions from mobile sources would likely be less.

The share of different activities in the emissions from the industrial sector

Table 5.2 gives a breakdown of emissions by industry for 2001. The data are indicative but may be underestimated. Not all smelting processes have been taken into account, and the production of construction materials does not include asphalt production. In addition, comparisons would have benefited from SNAP (selected nomenclature for air pollutants) classification, which defines data by type of combusted fuel (e.g. gas, heating oil), and from including fuel distribution facilities and terminals.

The industrial flue-gas purification rate is an important factor affecting air pollution. Introducing air pollution purification in industry could considerably decrease air emissions and improve air quality. Data for the industrial sector for 1999 and 2000, which were published in the report of the State Statistical Department of 2002 show that the average rate of purification of all air pollutants amounted to 41% in 1999 and 38% in 2000.

There are wide differences between pollutants. For example, the State Statistical Department states that the rate of dust purification in industry is only 66%. This is quite low and indicates that industry is using very simple dust purification devices with low efficiency. The 24% rate of purification of acidifying substances (SO_2 – 0%; NO_x) is even lower. The situation improves (to a rate of over 90%) only in closed cycles with fully contained process installations (e.g. NH_3 during nitrate fertilizer production or particulate matter during the production of caprolactam).

Georgia needs to modernize its de-dusting treatment systems (or install de-dusting devices where they do not exist) and to take action to reduce NO_x emissions in industry and energy sectors. This could be done at relatively low cost (e.g. by changing traditional burners in energy boilers for low-emission burners, as well as by improving combustion efficiency by installing oxygen content measuring devices in boilers).

Table 5.1: Emissions of selected pollutants

1000 tons

Pollutants	1999	2000	2001	Share of mobile source emissions (average of 1999-2001)
Particulate matter				
Total	**4.96**	**4.58**	**4.72**	
Stationary sources	3.47	3.11	3.24	
Mobile sources	1.49	1.47	1.48	31%
SO$_2$				
Total	**6.52**	**6.14**	**6.35**	
Stationary sources	4.16	3.81	4.01	
Mobile sources	2.36	2.33	2.34	37%
NO$_x$				
Total	**26.79**	**26.04**	**27.7**	
Stationary sources	4.74	4.24	5.03	
Mobile sources	22.05	21.8	22.67	83%
NMVOC				
Total	**28.74**	**27.74**	**28.85**	
Stationary sources	3.26	2.93	3.05	
Mobile sources	25.48	24.81	25.8	89%
NH$_3$				
Total	**0.04**	**0.03**	*	
Stationary sources	0.04	0.03	*	
Mobile sources	*	*	*	*
CO				
Total	**163.84**	**162.26**	**163.22**	
Stationary sources	4.06	3.76	3.91	
Mobile sources	159.78	158.5	159.31	98%
N$_2$O				
Total	**0.96**	**0.84**	**0.86**	
Stationary sources	0.93	0.81	0.83	
Mobile sources	0.03	0.03	0.03	3%
CH$_4$				
Total	**0.73**	**0.62**	**0.64**	
Stationary sources	0.42	0.31	0.32	
Mobile sources	0.31	0.31	0.32	47%
CO$_2$				
Total	**3235**	**3127**	**3253**	
Stationary sources	1472.0	1371.0	1427.0	
Mobile sources	1763.0	1756.0	1826.0	56%

Source: Ministry of Environment and Natural Resources Protection and State Statistical Department, 2002.

Note: * no data available.

Table 5.2: Emissions from stationary sources in 2001

tons/year

Type of activity	Particulate matter	SO$_2$	NO$_x$	NMVOC	CO	N$_2$O	CH$_4$	CO$_2$ (1000 tons)
1 Electric power production and fuel	58.8	1,361.0	782.0	35.8	1,122.0	1.2	101.6	826.0
2 Iron and steel metallurgy	1,069.0	56.5	1,805.0	599.0	228.0	354.0	109.8	153.0
3 Chemical and petrochemical industry	123.0	12.3	46.5	340.0	662.0	331.0	..	144.0
4 Timber and pulp & paper industry	434.0	..	..	..	..	..	..	..
5 Production of construction materials	959.0	223.0	732.0	11.5	173.0	..	..	30.3
6 Food industry	20.5	..	..	1,309.0	..	..	..	274*
Industry (total)	2,665.0	1,653.0	5,366.0	2,296.0	2,186.0	686.0	211.0	1,427.0

Source: Ministry of Environment and Natural Resources Protection, 2002.

Note: * calculated for the whole food industry on the basis of energy consumption.

5.2 Air quality

Before the breakdown of the Soviet Union, the State Hydrometeorological Services were responsible for regularly measuring the concentrations (3 times daily) of the basic air pollutants: particulate matter, SO_2, NO_2 and CO, as well as some specific pollutants from local stationary sources. These measurements were carried out in Georgia until 1991 in 11 large cities at 33 measuring sites. Over time, however, their scope has slowly been reduced. Measurements are now taken only in seven cities for major air pollutants (particulate matter, SO_2, NO_x, CO), and, in certain cities, such specific pollutants as H_2S, NH_3, phenol, formaldehyde and MnO_2. In most cities the maximum allowable concentrations (MAC) are exceeded. Table 5.3 gives the ratio of the measured concentrations at the municipal

measurement stations to the maximum allowable values for four cities: Tbilisi, Kutaisi, Batumi and Rustavi. The situation is similar in the cities of Akhaltsikhe, Zestaphoni and Kaspij, where measurements are also taken (see also chapter 3 on environmental information and public participation in decision-making).

The data given in table 5.3 indicate that almost all measured air pollution parameters in large cities exceed the maximum allowable concentration and are often twice as high as the legal limit. In extreme cases, the concentrations are five or more times greater than the legal limit. The exception is CO concentrations, which appear generally to be lower than the permissible values. This is surprising, because CO emissions from mobile sources are very high.

Table 5.3: Exceedances of maximum allowable concentrations (MAC) of selected air pollutants in selected cities

City / pollutant	Exceeded level coefficient		
	1997	1998	1999
Tbilisi			
Particulate matter	2.0	2.0	2.0
SO_2	3.4	3.8	3.5
NO_x	≤1.0	≤1.0	≤1.0
CO	1.3	≤1.0	≤1.0
Phenol	1.6	1.3	1.6
Formaldehyde	5.0	4.0	4.0
Kutaisi			
Particulate matter	4.0	4.0	4.0
SO_2	1.6	1.2	1.2
NO_x	1.7	1.5	1.2
CO	≤1.0	≤1.0	≤1.0
H_2S	≤1.0	≤1.0	≤1.0
Batumi			
Particulate matter	1.3	1.3	1.3
SO_2	3.2	2.8	3.0
NO_x	1.5	1.5	1.2
CO	≤1.0	≤1.0	≤1.0
H_2S	≤1.0	≤1.0	≤1.0
Rustavi			
Particulate matter	≤1.0	2.0	2.0
SO_2	6.0	8.0	8.5
NO_x	2.3	1.7	1.7
CO	≤1.0	≤1.0	≤1.0
Phenol	2.2	2.0	2.0
NH_3	4.9	4.2	4.4
H_2S	≤1.0	≤1.0	≤1.0

Source: Ministry of Environment and Natural Resources Protection, 2001.

The most detailed data on air quality are collected in Tbilisi, where there are seven measuring sites providing data covering a relatively long measurement period. Table 5.4 presents average values for five-year periods from 1984 to 1998. Data are compared to three sets of standards: World Health Organization (WHO) air quality guidelines, European Commission limit values and the permissible levels of concentration according to Georgian regulations.

The picture presented in these two tables indicates an extremely serious threat to public health in large cities, and this needs to be considered as a priority in local action plans. Particularly serious are the exceedances of permissible concentrations of such air pollutants as: phenol, formaldehyde and particulate matter. Higher SO_2 concentrations may also lead to an increase in upper respiratory system diseases.

All large cities, and particularly Tbilisi, would benefit from a programme of radical action to bring down the concentration of air pollutants to acceptable levels.

Air pollution is not measured in rural areas. There are also no monitoring stations that would comply with the requirements of the Cooperative Programme for Monitoring and Evaluation of the Long-range Transmission of Air Pollutants in Europe (EMEP).

Hot spots

All large cities may be considered as hot spots. In all of these cities the maximum allowable concentrations of air pollutants are exceeded, in many cases by a factor of two to five. Of particular concern are the areas close to the major transport routes, where the situation is worsened by the excess emission of air pollutants from vehicles.

Eight industrial and power plants may also be counted among the hot spots for air pollution. These include:

- Three industrial enterprises in Rustavi: a nitrogen fertilizer production plant, a pulp and paper production plant and a metallurgical corporation;
- An oil refinery in Batumi;
- A smelter producing iron alloys in Zastaphoni;
- A pulp and paper production plant in Kaspij; and
- Two heat and power plants (one combined heat and power plant and one power plant. The first is out of operation now and the second operates at only 20% capacity).

Special protection zones have been established around all of these plants, which means that allowable concentrations of air pollutants are or may be exceeded not only on the premises but also in their vicinity. These protection zones should be eliminated.

Air pollution emission limit values for these eight industrial and power plants are established centrally, by the Ministry of Environment and Natural Resources Protection. Air pollution emission values for all other plants are established by the regional structures of the Ministry.

Table 5.4: Air quality in Tbilisi

Pollutant	WHO air quality guidelines	EC limit value	Georgian MAC	Averages measured over five-year periods		
				1984-1988	1989-1993	1994-1998
Particulate matter, $\mu g/m^3$	50.0	150.0	150.0	400.0	350.0	300.0
SO_2, $\mu g/m^3$	60.0	50.0	50.0	120.0	90.0	140.0
NO_x, $\mu g/m^3$	40.0	..	40.0	45.0	50.0	40.0
CO, mg/m^3	1.0	..	3.0	4.2	4.0	3.2
Phenol, $\mu g/m^3$	..	..	3.0	4.4	7.0	4.4
Formaldehyde, $\mu g/m^3$	..	..	3.0	12.0	12.5	12.0

Source: UNEP-GRID. Tbilisi Environmental Atlas. Tbilisi, 1999.

5.3 Policy objectives and management

The policy framework

According to the 2000 National Environmental Action Plan (NEAP), which was prepared by the Ministry of Environment and Natural Resources Protection, the sources of high air pollution are: the large number of cars that are old and do not comply with emission standards; the poor condition of roads; the high level of transit transport across Georgia; the lack of control on air pollutants emitted by vehicles; the lack of air pollution treatment in power and heating plants and local household combustion systems; and the common use of asbestos in construction materials.

To address these problems, NEAP proposes three priority measures:

- Increase the share of the electric public transport network;
- Introduce a system for monitoring the quality of imported fuels and the quality of fuels at petrol stations, as well as for monitoring exhaust gases from cars;
- Extend the reconstruction of municipal power and heating systems so as to generate both energy for home-heating and electricity.

The NEAP also sets certain targets to amend existing legislation (mainly for transport), to analyse the risks connected with the use of asbestos in the building sector and to introduce appropriate legislation.

While the NEAP is important in addressing a broad range of issues affecting the environment, it would be useful for Georgia to prepare a separate strategy on air protection, inter alia, in an effort to: reduce emissions from cars and vehicles; reduce emissions from the municipal sector (including home-heating systems, and reducing emissions in industry (including crude oil extraction).

The 2001 National Environmental Health Action Plan (NEHAP) is also important for air protection. It sets the following priorities:

- Preparation of short-term, medium-term and long-term air emission reduction programmes in five major cities (Tbilisi, Batumi, Kutaisi, Rustavi, Zastaphoni);
- Implementation of complete systems and databases on air quality for industrial centres and large cities;

- Introduction of highly efficient flue-gas purification systems in the energy sector and industry;
- Decreasing the import and use of heavy metals, sulphur and oil containing hazardous substances;
- Development of stationary and mobile vehicle inspection units; and
- Encouraging the use of primary energy sources (sun, wind) and decreasing technological energy consumption.

It is worth noting that certain elements of what could become an air protection strategy are included in Georgia's National Assessment Report for Sustainable Development, chapter 2 on energy security.

The legislative framework

The major legal act regulating air protection issues is the Law on Ambient Air Protection of 22 July 1999. This Law requires a series of implementing laws, some of which are being developed, including the draft law on non-ionizing electromagnetic radiation, noise and vibrations. Laws that have not yet been drafted concern the environmental monitoring system; climate change; and integrated environmental pollution control system (expected for 2005).

The Law on Ambient Air Protection is a modern and sophisticated legal act, similar to many framework acts adopted in Western and Central Europe. In many places the Law makes use (partially) of standards and procedures included in the European Union's environmental legislation (the following directives are quoted in the text: 70/220/EEC; 72/306/EEC; 88/77/EEC; 93/12/EC; 96/62/EC; 96/96/EC).

The requirements of certain international legal acts have also been incorporated into the Law, including those of the Vienna Convention and the Montreal Protocol, the United Nations Framework Convention on Climate Change and the Convention on Long-range Transboundary Air Pollution.

The Law on Ambient Air Protection is a framework law (although it also regulates several issues in detail). It foresees issuing 29 executive regulations (presidential decrees and regulations of the Minister of Environment), which, in line with article 61 of the Law should be published between 2000 and 2006. The following have already been issued and published in the Official Gazette:

- Approval of the provision on controlling ozone-depleting substances throughout Georgia (2002);
- Ambient air pollution indices for extremely polluted, highly polluted, polluted and unpolluted areas (2001);
- Approval of ambient air pollution index calculation guidelines (2001);
- Approval of guidance on ambient air protection guidelines during landfill operations (2001);
- Approval of the provisions on the calculation method of annual limitation and temporarily agreed values of emissions and guidelines for completing applications for permission (2002);
- Approval of the provisions on guidelines for identifying and inventorying the stationary sources of pollution (2001);
- Registration and reporting of pollutant emissions from stationary pollution sources (2001);
- Approval of the provisions on the operation of air pollution abatement devices at stationary pollution sources (2001);
- Approval of the provisions on guidelines for calculating environmental damage resulting from the impact of harmful human activity on ambient air (2001).

Some of these regulations introduce detailed procedures for air protection. For example, the 2001 Regulation of the Minister of Environment divides the country into four: very heavily polluted, heavily polluted, polluted and unpolluted areas. A differential index has been established for fees for air emissions for each category, with the highest rate for very heavily polluted areas (1.5).

These few examples indicate that Georgia is attempting to follow European environmental standards and procedures, although, in practice, some elements of the old Soviet Union legislation remain. The issuing of all executive acts to the Law on Ambient Air Protection with its derivative laws, which is due to be accomplished by 2005, will complete the modernization of air protection legislation in Georgia.

Regulatory instruments

Enterprises that exceed emission limits require environmental emission permits. The limits are: for dust and soot, 10 tons/year; for SO_2, 10 tons/year; for NO_x, 1.5 tons/year; for CO, 100 tons/year; and, for hydrocarbons, 30 tons/year.

Prior to obtaining a permit it is necessary to carry out an environmental impact assessment that covers only air emissions (see chapter 1 on Policy, legal and institutional framework and sectoral integration). The EIA technical reports on air pollution are verified and approved by the regional environmental body of the Ministry of Environment and Natural Resources Protection. In exceptional cases the Ministry carries out this procedure itself; at present this is done for eight major industrial plants. The Ministry supervises the regional issuing of permits. All technical reports are submitted to the Department of Air Protection in the Ministry for further review.

The plant that, according to the technical report, exceeds the permissible emissions, receives a "provisional decision" for five years, prepares a remedial programme and each year submits a progress report. The responsibility for follow-up lies with three persons in the Ministry and between one and three persons each in the regional bodies of the Ministry. These services, due to their lack of financial resources, are unable to carry out regular inspections to see whether the approved emission limits are met.

Regarding emission fees and fines, the Law on Ambient Air Protection incorporates the "polluter pays" principle. The fee structure and levels, as well as the payment procedure, are regulated by Georgia's tax legislation. Fees for emissions go to the State budget.

The Ministry is involved only in the procedure of calculating the fees. Each enterprise fills in a quarterly questionnaire entitled: "Declaration for air pollution taxes", using the earlier set emission limits and the level of actual production. These declarations are verified (approved) by the regional bodies of the Ministry of Environment and Natural Resources Protection, and then submitted to the regional tax inspectorates. After filing the declaration, the manager of the enterprise is obliged to pay the tax into the tax inspectorate's account.

The current mandatory fines for emissions exceeding the permitted limits are five times higher than the tax on emissions within the limits. They have been set for 26 groups of pollutants. Some examples of fees for excess emissions of major air pollutants are presented in table 5.5 (see also chapter 2 on economic instruments, financing and privatization).

Table 5.5: Fines for excess air pollution

No.	Pollutant	Fees (lari/ton)
1	NO_2; NH_3	562.5
2	SO_2, Particulate matter	450
3	Benzo(a)pyrene	22,500,000
4	Hydrocarbons (total)	15
5	Benzene	225
6	CO_2	0.05
7	Phenol; formaldehyde	750
8	Mercury, Lead	75,000
9	CO	7.5

Source: Ministry of Environment and Natural Resources Protection, 2001.

It seems worth mentioning here that the system of setting emission limits for different stationary sources is based entirely on legally binding air pollution indicators (MAC). In 2001, after the new legislation on air protection was adopted, a decision was made to apply more stringent emission limits than those of 1988.

Georgia intends to transpose European environmental law into its own legislation, including, from 2006, to implement the Integrated Pollution Prevention and Control (IPPC) Directive. This will have several advantages: in several cases the procedure for setting "emission limits", according to the existing legislation, will be significantly facilitated by reducing the cost of technical reports on air emissions.

The institutional framework

The Ministry of Environment and Natural Resources Protection is the major governmental body responsible for initiating and preparing environmental legal acts, including those concerning protection against air pollution, as well as supervising the implementation of strategies, policies and action plans. In carrying out its mission, the Ministry cooperates closely with several other ministries and central bodies. Among them are: the Ministry of Health, the Ministry of Industry, the Ministry of Justice, the State Department of Geology, the State Inspection, the State Department of Standardization, Metrology and Certification. These bodies participate together with the Ministry of Environment and Natural Resources Protection in the development of air protection legislation, in particular the executive acts to the Law on Ambient Air Protection. Furthermore, the Ministry of Environment and Natural Resources Protection is involved in the work of several other national bodies in implementing the Law. Among them are the State

Statistical Department and the Department of Hydrometeorology.

Within the Ministry of Environment and Natural Resources Protection, both the Department of Air Protection and the Department of State Ecological Expertise are involved in air protection. Furthermore, the Agency for Climate Change is subordinate to the Ministry.

The Department of Air Protection employs ten people, of whom three are involved in national matters (emission inventories, emission permit verification, cooperation with regional bodies) and seven primarily with the implementation of international conventions and the preparation of new legislation.

There are 15 regional environmental bodies, which are the main units for implementing air protection policy and legal acts. They are directly subordinated to the Minister of Environment. These regional bodies have two functions. They implement legal acts (e.g. issue emission permits, set emission limits for stationary sources, approve and verify quarterly declarations on air emission fees and annual reports on air emissions from enterprises). The regional bodies also carry out control and inspection duties connected with the implementation of legal requirements by enterprises.

The institutional arrangements for air management are adapted to the requirements of Georgia's legislation on air protection, and they operate properly. However, due to the insufficient numbers of trained personnel in air protection at the regional level, the lack of modern laboratory installations and measurement systems, and the lack of financial resources for carrying out regular inspections at company premises, the work is less than efficient.

5.4   International obligations

Georgia is a Party to, has signed or intends to accede to several international agreements (conventions and protocols) regarding air protection. These agreements are listed below with a brief description of their implementation.

- The United Nations Framework Convention on Climate Change. Georgia is a Party to this Convention. The Agency for Climate Change is subordinate to the Ministry of Environment and Natural Resources Protection. A very detailed report has been prepared on the implementation of the Convention in Georgia, within the framework of a UNDP/GEF assistance project. A special law on climate change is being drafted.

- The Vienna Convention and the Montreal Protocol. Georgia is a Party to both agreements. The President has issued a decree on the control of ozone-depleting substances throughout Georgia; it includes obligations concerning 20 substances controlled by the Montreal Protocol.

- The Stockholm Convention on Persistent Organic Pollutants. Georgia has signed this Convention and is preparing its implementation. A draft proposal for a UNDP/GEF project on "Enabling activity funding for ratification and implementation of the Stockholm Convention on Persistent Organic Pollutants" has been prepared. For details concerning the implementation of the Convention, see chapter 4 on international cooperation.

- The Convention on Long-range Transboundary Air Pollution. Georgia acceded to this Convention on 11 February 1999, but it has not acceded to any of its eight protocols. The Ministry of Environment and Natural Resources Protection considers it impossible at present to accede to certain protocols due to the ensuing financial obligations. However, it should be noted that article 2 of the Convention requires Parties to "reduce emissions".

These legal instruments are implemented to different degrees. The highest priority has been given to the implementation of the global conventions. The Convention on Long-range Transboundary Air Pollution has, so far, been implemented to a limited extent. Georgia has prepared the national emission balances with the use of EMEP procedures, although it is not a Party to this Protocol.

5.5   Conclusions and recommendations

The annual inventory of national emissions of air pollutants is limited to only three sectors: energy, industry and transport. Emissions from agriculture are not taken into consideration (except for greenhouse gases), nor are emissions from the municipal sector. In addition, NH_3, heavy metals (HMs) and persistent organic pollutant (POP) emissions are not inventoried. This means that the CORINAIR methodology, along with the classification of emission sources according to

SNAP, is used only partially in Georgia. Full application of this methodology to emission sources and emitted substances is not costly and will be required at a later stage should Georgia decide to comply with EU directives or accede to the 1984 Protocol on Long-term Financing of the Cooperative Programme for Monitoring and Evaluation of the Long-range Transmission of Air Pollutants in Europe (EMEP) to the Convention on Long-range Transboundary Air Pollution.

Recommendation 5.1:
The Ministry of Environment and Natural Resources Protection should broaden the scope of the national emission inventory to include additional substances and emission sources, to enable the use of the CORINAIR system, the SNAP classification and EMEP provisions to their full extent.

In Georgia the emission limits for enterprises are set as a MAC derivative. Direct emission standards in the form of permissible concentrations in flue gases (mg/m³), permissible losses of resources (mg/ton of resources) or waste generation of the technology process (mg/ton of product) are not used for certain types of production. Such technology standards are widely used in the European Union member countries and applicant countries. As Georgia is planning to adopt a law on integrated pollution control system by 1 January 2006, regulations concerning direct emission standards in the energy sector, metallurgy, waste incineration and some other types of production should be adopted before that date.

Recommendation 5.2:
The Ministry of Environment and Natural Resources Protection should modify the procedure for setting emission limits for industrial plants, by progressively introducing, where possible, direct emission standards, similar to those included in the protocols to the Convention on Long-range Transboundary Air Pollution. This would significantly facilitate the present procedure for setting emission limits and reduce the cost.

Three countries of the South Caucasus (Armenia, Azerbaijan and Georgia) have acceded to the Convention on Long-range Transboundary Air Pollution. This creates a good basis for subregional cooperation among the three countries to reduce air pollution. Only Armenia has signed both 1998 Aarhus Protocols on Heavy Metals and on Persistent Organic Pollutants, and the 1999 Gothenburg Protocol to Abate Acidification,

Eutrophication and Ground-level Ozone. Georgia has not signed any of the protocols.

As these protocols contain less strict obligations than the European Union directives, the implementation of the Convention (through the protocols) would be an important step toward implementing EU directives, which the 1999 Law on Ambient Air Protection sets as a goal.

Recommendation 5.3:
The Government should consider acceding to the following four protocols to the Convention on Long-range Transboundary Air Pollution:

- *The 1999 Protocol to Abate Acidification, Eutrophication and Ground-level Ozone;*
- *The 1998 Protocol on Heavy Metals*
- *The 1998 Protocol on Persistent Organic Pollutants (POPs); and*
- *The 1984 Protocol on Long-term Financing of the Cooperative Programme for Monitoring and Evaluation of the Long-range Transmission of Air Pollutants in Europe (EMEP).*

The Ministry of Environment and Natural Resources Protection should assess and advise on the activities related to these protocols.

Chapter 6

WASTE, CHEMICALS AND CONTAMINATED SITES

6.1 Introduction

The management of municipal and industrial waste, hazardous chemicals and contaminated sites has not been a priority for the Ministry of Environment and Natural Resources Protection and other ministries and institutions involved. The political and economic conditions during the transition have not been favourable for investment into waste management or the decontamination of sites, especially former Soviet military sites. This area requires financial resources, strong and well coordinated institutions, further research and an inventory of waste sites, including quantities of waste, hazardous chemicals and their composition.

Here are some of the major issues confronting this sector:

- There is no overall government strategy for waste and hazardous chemicals management and radioactive sites, nor is there yet a comprehensive law on waste management, although a draft law has been prepared;
- The Ministry of Environment and Natural Resources Protection lacks capacity to manage municipal and industrial waste disposal and hazardous chemicals and contaminated sites;
- There are no economic incentives for good management, and little funding;
- There is no inventory of the sources of industrial waste or its composition, or of stored hazardous chemicals, including obsolete pesticides;
- There is no monitoring of soil, air or groundwater quality in the vicinity of municipal and industrial waste disposal sites;
- Abandoned radioactively contaminated sites pose a serious potential adverse effect on the population and the environment;
- There are no sanitary landfills for municipal waste disposal;
- In many cases industrial waste, including hazardous waste, is dumped together with municipal waste;
- There is no service for municipal waste collection and disposal in rural areas;

- Research and development in waste collection, treatment, reuse and recycling have ceased, and there is essentially no system for the separate collection of medical waste;
- There are no facilities for the reuse of scraps from old cars.

Among the main reasons for this situation are: poor governance; low economic development; lack of sufficient information and information technologies for decision-making; and little public information and participation in decision-making.

6.2 Industrial waste

The quantities of industrial waste and hazardous chemicals have decreased considerably during the past five years. In 1990 industry contributed about 30% of GDP; this share fell to about 9% in 1998 (NEAP). At present, industrial facilities work at 5 to 50% of their capacity. The exception is copper production in Bolnisi, with the "Madneuli" ore mine, including a copper and barite ore-processing plant, working at full capacity. However, at the oil refinery plant in Batumi 40,000 tons of acid tar and 1,500 tons of aluminium silicate are stored; and at a glass packaging plant in Khashuri about 370,000 tons of plastic waste has accumulated (see chapter 9 on mining, industry and environment).

Information on the amount of waste generated is based on accumulated waste, presented in table 6.1.

At present there are no treatment facilities for industrial waste; all industrial effluents and industrial solid waste are discharged into the environment without any treatment. There is also no classification system for industrial waste and no identification of the toxicity of accumulated waste. The statistical data on waste generation and accumulated waste are not classified and therefore cannot represent the real situation regarding their physical state and chemical composition. Further research is necessary to carry out a detailed inventory of waste in order to propose a solution for recycling or safe disposal.

Table 6.1: Main sources of accumulated industrial waste

Location	Name / type of plant	Type of waste	Quantity (tons)
Batumi	Oil refinery	Acid tar	40,000
		Aluminium silicate	1,500
Batumi	Wood-processing	Sawdust	450 m³
Khashuri	Glass packing	Plastic bottles	370,000
Kvarciti	Gold-quartzite processing	Abandoned mines	88.8 mill. m³
Kazreti	Ore reprocessing	Solid, dark colour mining waste	22.5 mill.
Rustavi	Metallurgy	Overburden and slag from mining reprocessing	11.5 mill.
Kutaisi	Lithopone	Slag containing Barium and Zinc	200,000
Zestaphoni	Ferro-alloy	Slag and dust from thermal treatment and slag from electrolysis process	368,000
Chiatura	Manganese reprocessing	Slag with manganese (mn)	9,318,200
Racha	Mining Chemical Substances	Ash containing arsenic	1,000

Source: Ministry of Environment and Natural Resources Protection. Survey of industrial waste, 1999.

In addition, industry needs to invest in technology to reduce waste generation and to recycle or reuse accumulated waste.

6.3   Hazardous waste and chemicals

During the 1980s, up to 35,000 tons of pesticides per year were used in Georgia. Now about 1,700 tons of pesticides (80% of copper sulphate) are imported. In the past, in addition to pesticides transported from Russia, Georgia produced blue vitriol at a metallurgical plant in Rustavi and a lithopone plant in Kutaisi. Pesticides and fertilizers were stored at the Saksophqimia facilities. After the dissolution of the Soviet Union, these chemicals remained in place. Originally about 2000 tons of pesticides were at the main storage facilities, and another 400 to 500 tons in 81 small storage facilities. DDT, which was banned for use in the 1970s, may be among these obsolete pesticides. There are also 3,000 tons of obsolete fertilizers. Sixty-four facilities were completely destroyed and all chemicals are exposed to the elements. The quality of soil, groundwater and air has never been monitored.

The biggest and the most dangerous threat to the environment is the storage of hazardous chemicals, including pesticides, in the Iagluji mountains (Marneuli region). Here, from 1976 to 1985, 2,572 tons of pesticides and toxic chemicals were buried in an area of two hectares at a depth of 15-20 metres.

There are no precise data on the composition of the hazardous chemicals that are stored. Some data

exist, but they have not been collected, compiled and aggregated. The site is now abandoned and covered by a layer of soil. The soil, air and groundwater nearby have never been monitored, and no risk assessment has been undertaken. There is no fence around the area and no warning signs posted. People and domestic animals have full access to the area, and the population has not been informed of the health risks. The site is situated in a populated area and poses a real threat to the population and the environment.

All other storage sites for obsolete pesticides and hazardous chemicals have similar problems. It is estimated that more than 100 tons of polychlorinated biphenyls (PCBs) have accumulated at industrial sites. One of the storage areas for PCB waste from transformers and condensers is in Gardabany, near Tbilisi. There is also mercury waste, derived primarily from old thermometers and mercury lamps. There are two natural deposits of ore containing mercury: one in Akhey and another in Avadkhara.

For none of this hazardous waste is there an inventory either of the exact location where it is stored or of the amounts. None of the known storage sites or disposal sites is under environmental control. Nor has their risk ever been assessed.

The environmental information management centre of GRID-Tbilisi is drawing up an inventory of waste and products containing PCBs through the geographic information system (GIS), and Georgia has begun working with the Global Mercury

Assessment Working Group to address the mercury problem.

It is general practice for pesticides and hazardous chemicals to be incinerated. There are several installations for this in the world, but it is very expensive (some US$ 4,000 per ton of pesticides) and Georgia cannot afford it.

6.4 Municipal waste

Urbanization and recent economic development have increased municipal waste generation. In the cities municipal waste is collected and transported to landfills for disposal.

However, there are no reliable statistics on the generation of municipal waste. Only in the municipality of Tbilisi are statistics kept on the amount of waste transported to the municipal dumps. There is no information on the composition of waste, although it is clear that the share of paper and plastics has increased.

There is no monitoring of air, soil and groundwater quality at the disposal sites, and geological and physical characteristics and conditions were not investigated before the landfills were constructed. Legal landfills were not planned and are not managed in an environmentally sound manner. For example, there are no warning signs or fences around these dumps.

Unfortunately, the effects of landfills on air, surface and groundwater are not known. According to unofficial data from the Ministry of Environment and Natural Resources Protection, approximately 27 ha of land are occupied by illegal municipal dumps, but there is no inventory, so the exact number of legal and illegal dump sites is unknown.

A special project to draw up an inventory of existing landfills was developed by the Ministry of Environment and Natural Resources Protection, but ran out of money. The data on the composition of municipal waste in the main cities date from Soviet times and do not reflect to the current situation.

At present there are no facilities for separating, processing or recycling plastics, paper and glass from municipal waste. A detailed study is necessary to assess the situation and propose a solution.

The main landfills are listed in table 6.2.

Table 6.2: Main municipal landfills

Location	Surface of landfill (ha)	Started in
Batumi	12.0	1965
Kobuleti	12.0	1960
Kutaisi	42.0	1962
Poti	8.0	1968
Senaki v.Teklati	10.0	..
Ozurgeti	5.0	..
Lanchkhuti	5.5	1987
c.Gori	4.0	1985
c.Kareli	4.0	1984
Lilo	10.0	1989
Gldani	8.0	1992
Iagluji	5.0	1985
Total above	125.5	..
Other landfills	114.2	..
Grand Total	**239.7**	..

Source: Ministry of Environment and Natural Resources Protection. Survey of industrial waste, 1999.

There are three landfills for Tbilisi: Gldani, Lilo and Iagluji. Gldani became operational in 1972, and the quantity of waste disposed there is 572,400 tons a year. Lilo came on stream in 1989 and receives 658,800 tons a year. Iagluji started operating in 1985, with an annual quantity of waste of 93,600 tons. It is estimated that these three landfills will run out of space in two or three years' time. Sanitary landfills are needed, but the main problem is finding suitable locations for them. In the vicinity of Tbilisi the groundwater table is very high, preventing any landfills from being built there.

Groundwater in the vicinity of these landfills and other landfills is contaminated by heavy metals and toxic organic chemicals resulting from the decomposition of municipal waste. In addition, surface water and rain water leach soluble hazardous chemicals and penetrate into groundwater that is used by the local population as drinking water. Unfortunately, there are no data on groundwater contamination available since it is not monitored.

The municipality of Tbilisi is obliged by court order to plan a new municipal landfill in Gldani. This decision was taken following a complaint filed by the citizens of Tbilisi based on the Aarhus Convention.

In Rustavi, 2,700,000 m^3 of municipal waste, including household rubbish and street sweepings, has accumulated over 10 years. Daily about 115 m^3 of municipal waste is generated and transported to landfills. There are two landfills near Rustavi. Like the landfills in other cities, the Rustavi landfills are filled to capacity and do not meet any sanitary requirements. A project for reprocessing municipal waste in Rustavi is under development, with the support of the European Bank for Reconstruction and Development (EBRD).

All household and street rubbish is disposed together. There is no system for waste separation, for instance of plastics and glass bottles. There is shortage of containers and lorries for collecting municipal waste in Tbilisi. At present the municipal services have only 250 lorries instead of the 350 that are needed to collect and transport all municipal waste generated in Tbilisi. The situation in the other cities is worse.

All dumps are almost full. They need to be extended or new sanitary landfills need to be built urgently. In many cases municipal waste is dumped together with industrial waste and even together with medical waste without any analysis of the adverse effects on the environment. Many illegal dumps are situated either in the cities or in their vicinity.

There are a few projects to ease the situation. One is a project under the Integrated Coastal Zone Management Centre on integrated municipal water management in Georgia (MUB 97016P1), which also includes a part on solid waste management in the city of Poti. The aim is to develop a waste policy plan so as to:
- Reduce the risks to public health from municipal waste and improve living conditions;
- Make the city more attractive for tourism;
- Improve institutional, organizational and operational activities for the collection, transport and disposal of solid waste; and
- Keep commitments to the Black Sea Convention regarding municipal waste disposal in the coastal area.

The project will concentrate on reducing municipal waste discharges into rivers and illegal waste dumps and overall control over waste disposal.

At present municipal waste is dumped at a landfill on the banks of the river Rioni. The landfill does not meet any sanitary standards. It is estimated that the city of Poti, including the port, generates about 130,000 m^3 or about 40,000 tons of municipal waste a year. Of this waste 40,000 m^3 or 12,000 tons are collected, but 90,000 m^3 or 27,000 tons are dumped illegally along the banks of the Rioni, which is directly connected to the Black Sea. During periods of heavy rain, when the river breaks its banks, this waste is carried directly to the Black Sea and pollutes the Black Sea coast and its tourist resorts. No study on the effects of such events on the population and marine life has ever been conducted.

In addition, when there is not enough transport, municipal waste is stored at illegal sites, which are not fenced off and to which people and domestic animals have access. The Poti city landfill should be closed, but at present there are no plans to construct a new one. For the municipality, the main obstacles to organizing the environmentally sound management of municipal waste are the poor waste management system in general and the lack of financial resources.

6.5 Medical waste

The State Health Inspectorate is responsible for medical waste management. In Tbilisi alone, about 40,000 tons of medical waste are generated. There is no statistical information on medical waste generated elsewhere in the country. In the past medical waste was treated and deposited separately.

At present medical waste is disinfected at the source. The most dangerous anatomical medical waste is collected separately, transported to special centres and, after investigation, buried in cemeteries. The other (non-anatomical) medical waste is transported and deposited with municipal waste. There are also four incinerators for pathological medical waste, but they are not always in operation. Only anatomical waste is incinerated at one new hospital in Tbilisi. There are plans to construct a new crematorium in Tbilisi for anatomical waste in 2003.

At present the main problems concerning medical waste management are:
- The absence of separate collection for different kinds of waste;
- The lack of technical means for separate collection and treatment;
- The lack of nationwide statistics;
- The lack of trained personnel for the environmentally sound management of medical waste.

There have been no special studies on the health effects of medical waste and there is no register of diseases caused by it.

6.6 Radioactive waste and contaminated sites

There is no precise statistical information on quantities of radioactive waste, nor are there special sites or facilities for radioactive waste treatment and disposal. It is usually stored at the place of generation. Its environmental effects have not been investigated or defined. Some radioactive waste is stored at the Institute of Physics and the institute of Radiology, but these storage facilities do not meet safety requirements and they are potential sources of radiation. It is therefore necessary and urgent to construct one central storage site for radioactive waste.

There are no concrete studies on the effects of radionuclides on health. The adverse effects of former USSR military sites on population and the environment have been documented. According to the Ministry of Environment and Natural Resources Protection, there are about 300 former Soviet military sites in Georgia. Most are under the Ministries of Defence and the Interior and the State Border Control; some are under the Russian military representation in the South Caucasus. All military sites are contaminated by chemicals and radiation; wind and soil erosion are dispersing radioactive soil. The exact kinds of contamination are difficult to define because there is no technical documentation on these sites. (For health effects of these sites, see chapter 14 on human health and environment.) About 223 radioactive sources of mainly Caesium Cs-137 and Strontium Sr-90 have been identified. The contaminated sites are listed in table 6.3.

Table 6.3: Main radioactive sources discovered on former Soviet military bases

	Discovered substances	Amount	Radiation dose rate, R/h activity, Ku	Location	Date of discovery
1	Caesium Cs-137	43 containers 61 sources		Zestaponi Military chemical defence unit	Jan-95
2	Caesium Cs-137	6 containers 11 sources	160-600 R/h	Georgia State Department of Frontier Protection Village of Lilo	Sep-97
3	Caesium Cs-137	2 containers 11 sources	30 R/h 17R/h	Tbilisi Anti-aircraft Brigade (Makhata)	Oct-97
4	Caesium Cs-137	4 containers 6 sources	600R/h 30R/h 17R/h	Akhaltsikhe Tank Battalion	Oct-97
5	Caesium Cs-137	2 sources	75 mR/h 20 mR/h	Kutaisi The 35th military area	Jan-98
6	Strontium Sr-90 Radium Ra-226	40 sources	Total-6 R/h	Kutaisi Village of Godogani	Jul-98
7	Caesium Cs-137	2 containers 2 sources	600 R/h 17 R/h	Khoni, village of Matkhoji - store of former civil defence base	Jul-98
8	Caesium Cs-137	11 sources	1-600R/h 10 mR/h-each	Vaziani vicinity of N555 Military Unit Rocket Base	Aug-98
9	Caesium Cs-137	2 containers 3 sources	600 R/h 30 R/h 17 R/h	Poti Naval Infantry Battalion	Sep-98
10	Caesium Cs-137	2 containers 2 sources	600 R/h 30 R/h	Senaki "Kolkhi" Airport	Sep-98
11	Caesium Cs-137	2 containers 3 sources	600 R/h 30 R/h 17 R/h	Tbilisi Black Sea St.	Feb-99
12	Caesium Cs-137	1 container 1 source	600 R/h	Gori	Apr-99
13	Caesium Cs-137	2 containers 3 sources	600 R/h 30 R/h 17 R/h	Tbilisi Tsitsamuri St. 22	Apr-99
14	Americium Am-241	1 source	60 mR/h	Anaklia	May-99
15	Strontium Sr-90	4 sources	each 2400 R/h 35000 Ci	Svaneti Khaishi	May-99
16	Cobalt Co-60	1 source	0.8 R/h	Tbilisi Asatiani str.	Jun-99
17	Caesium Cs-137	2 containers 3 sources	600 R/h 30 R/h 17 R/h	Rustavi Metal works	Jul-99

Table 6.3 (Continued)

18	Caesium	Cs-137	3 pots in ground	Total activity 5-6 Ci	Poti Ship building plant	Aug-99
19	Caesium	Cs-137	2 containers 3 sources	600 R/h 30 R/h 17 R/h	Dedoplistskaro Village of Zemo Keda, Military Base	Apr-00
20	Caesium	Cs-137	1 container 2 sources	30 R/h 30 R/h	Ozurgeti district Meria Air Base	Jun-00
21	Americium	Am-241	1 source	60 mR/h	Tbilisi airport	Sep-00
22	Strontium	Sr-90	1 container 1 source	90 mCi	Tbilisi Didi Digomi	Oct-00
23	Caesium	Cs-137	5 containers 7 sources	3 – 600R/h 2-30 R/h 2-17 R/h	Vaziani Former Russian Military Base	Jul-01
24	Strontium	Sr-90	4 containers 14 sources	Total activity 90 mCi	Vaziani Former Russian Military Base	Aug-01
25	Caesium	Cs-137	4 containers 6 sources	2-600R/h 2-30 R/h 2-17 R/h	Vaziani Former Russian Military Base	Aug-01
26	Caesium	Cs-137	1 source	30 R/h	Daba Surami	Sep-01
27	Strontium	Sr-90	2 sources	35 000 Ci	Tsalenjikha region	Dec-01
28	Strontium	Sr-90	1 source		Zestaponi Former Russian Military Unit	Feb-02

Total: 223 sources

Source: Ministry of Environment and Natural Resources Protection, 2002.

Radioactive waste is a serious hazard in many respects. There is always the risk of an accident. For example, in 1996, three people were injured when they opened a container with radioactive medical waste. An attempt had been made to send these containers to the Russian Federation for disposal, but transport problems prevented this. They are now stored on the premises of the Institute of Physics of the Academy of Sciences between Tbilisi and Mchketa.

Another accident occurred in 1997, when 11 soldiers were seriously contaminated by radiation at the Vasiani training base. And, in the winter of 2002, three people received high doses of radiation in western Georgia when they dismantled two radioactive sources.

Radioactive contamination of the air is another significant risk. Tests are taking place in western Georgia, and a map of contaminated areas is being drawn up. All highly populated areas have been investigated and the main sources of radioactive contamination identified, but further research is needed.

In addition to radiation contamination, former military sites are contaminated by liquid rocket fuels, which consist of acid and hazardous organic substances, and are explosive. There is no precise information on all the substances in the

contaminated soil. The Government should urgently draw up an inventory of all sites with detailed information on its contamination.

A project to recover rocket fuels at a former military air base in Meria in the Guria region of western Georgia has already been completed. It was supported by the Organization for Security and Co-operation in Europe (OSCE). There is also a joint programme of the Ministry of Environment and Natural Resources Protection of Georgia and the Federal Ministry of Environment, Nature and Nuclear Safety of Germany to train Georgian experts in the environmental assessment of contaminated military sites.

A commission has been established to draw up an inventory of highly toxic waste and contaminated sites, but it has not begun to work because of a lack of funds. A project to assess the conditions at former Soviet army sites and industrial landfills was developed, but also discontinued for lack of money. National and international contributions are needed to draw up an inventory of contaminated sites and to clean them up.

In 2001 a project was initiated with support from the International Atomic Energy Agency (IAEA) to rid former Soviet military bases in Georgia from chemical and radioactive waste. The main purpose was to carry out further investigation in order to identify the sources and concentration of chemicals and the level of radiation at the contaminated sites, to start their rehabilitation and to raise public awareness about the health risks (publication and dissemination of special brochures). The aerial photography project will be carried out in accordance with IAEA norms and regulations.

6.7 Policy objectives and management

The policy framework

There is currently no comprehensive governmental strategy or policy on municipal and industrial waste management, or on hazardous substances and contaminated industrial and radioactive sites.

The National Environmental Action Plan (NEAP) is the main recent policy document on environmental protection. It outlines action, including investment projects, that covers, inter alia, the following:

For municipal and industrial waste management:
* Providing equipment for the collection and transport of municipal waste;
* Building sanitary landfills for municipal waste;
* Building special environmentally sound storage facilities for the disposal of radioactive, toxic and other hazardous waste;

For the management of chemicals:
* Environmentally sound treatment of obsolete hazardous chemicals;
* Development of regulations for the environmentally sound management of hazardous chemicals;
* Improvement of the system for testing and control of hazardous chemicals;
* Development of a system for monitoring pollution from hazardous chemicals;
* Development of a programme for the treatment of hazardous chemicals as an integral part of State policy on environmental protection.

The strategy and action plans for the management of waste and hazardous chemicals and the rehabilitation of contaminated sites have to be part of a strategy for sustainable development, as recommended in Georgia's submission to the World Summit on Sustainable Development.

According to the Law on Environmental Protection, the priority for waste management is the development of new technology to minimize industrial waste generation.

Georgia does not have a governmental programme on waste management. A solid waste management master plan for the city of Tbilisi was prepared in 1997, but it was never implemented because waste management is not priority for the Government and because of the lack of good governance and financial resources during the past 10 years.

The legislative framework

A new law on waste management has been prepared and is now being considered by the Government. The law covers the classification, collection, transport, recycling and reuse as well as disposal of municipal and hazardous waste. It also contains provisions on health and hygiene norms and standards for different kinds of waste management, the movement of hazardous waste, and a reporting system for waste generation. It is expected to be submitted to Parliament by the end of 2002.

Three major laws concern waste management and hazardous chemicals:
* The Law on the Transit and Import of Wastes Into and Out of the Territory of Georgia (1995, amended in 1997);
* The Law on Hazardous Chemical Substances (1998); and
* The Law on Pesticides and Agrochemicals (1998).

This legislation bans the import and transit of hazardous and radioactive waste into Georgia. Non-hazardous waste, such as ferrous and non-ferrous metal scrap, waste paper, wood and textile waste and glass, can be imported or allowed to transit. Two other laws in theory contain provisions for the registration of hazardous chemicals and a permitting system for new chemicals, and the setting-up of a database for hazardous chemicals. These laws have never been applied. The main reason is that the national regulations and sub-legal acts for the application of existing laws on municipal and industrial waste management, including hazardous substances and contaminated industrial and radioactive sites, are not being developed and passed. In addition, the country's economic situation hampers implementation.

It is necessary to speed up the adoption of draft laws and the drafting of new regulations, technical standards and norms for their application taking into account already existing laws mentioned above in order to solve the problem of waste and hazardous chemicals management.

Georgia has acceded to the Basel Convention on the Control of Transboundary Movements of Hazardous Wastes and their Disposal and signed the Stockholm Convention on Persistent Organic Pollutants (POPs). The enabling activities project proposal for Georgia to develop a national implementation plan to meet its obligations under the Stockholm Convention is in the review process. The proposal is to be submitted to GEF for funding. For details, see Chapter 4 on International Cooperation.

Economic incentives

There is a charge of 4.8 lari per person per year for municipal waste collection, transport and disposal. The rate of collection stands at about 40%. The Government contributes more than 50% of the cost of municipal waste collection and disposal. There are, consequently, no funds available to improve the collection and transport of municipal waste or to manage the waste at the landfills, for example by covering it with a layer of soil to prevent fire and the release of hazardous substances.

There are taxes on environment pollution with harmful substances (Tax Code, chapter XI) (see chapter 2 on economic instruments, financing and privatization). Unfortunately, the Code does not provide for taxes on hazardous substances and waste; it covers only air and water management. According to the Ministry of Economy, Industry and Trade, industrial facilities are not charged for solid waste generation and disposal.

The institutional framework

There are many institutions involved in waste and hazardous chemical management, but their responsibilities are not clear and coordination is poor.

The Ministry of Environment and Natural Resources Protection is responsible for developing and implementing national waste legislation, controlling the norms and standards for environmentally sound disposal or treatment of industrial, including hazardous, waste as well as municipal waste. The Ministry carries out governmental control over hazardous waste

movements (export, import and transit) under the provisions of the Basel Convention.

Developing and implementing health, hygiene and epidemiological standards and norms are the responsibilities of the Ministry of Labour, Health and Social Affairs.

The Ministry of Economy, Industry and Trade issues licences for the export and import of ferrous and non-ferrous scrap and other industrial waste. Industry itself is responsible for the recycling and disposal of industrial waste.

The Ministry of Environment and Natural Resources Protection (Nuclear and Radiation Safety Service) also coordinates and carries out investigations at former Soviet military sites and their rehabilitation. This work covers radiation sources and radioactive waste. The Service has a staff of 10, which is insufficient to provide a complete radiological service.

Only two staff at the Department of Land Resources Protection, Waste and Chemical Substances Management deal with waste and hazardous chemicals. In practice this is not enough to manage such a broad and important area of environmental protection. Georgia's entire waste and hazardous chemicals management system needs to be overhauled.

Municipalities and regional departments of the Ministry of Environment and Natural Resources Protection are responsible for municipal waste collection and disposal. This covers the collection, transport and disposal of municipal waste, providing information on household waste, sweeping public areas and maintaining local landfills.

6.8 Conclusions and recommendations

A new law on waste management has been prepared and is now being considered by the Government. The draft law covers the classification, collection, transport, recycling and reuse as well as disposal of municipal and hazardous waste. It also contains provisions for health hygiene norms and standards for different kinds of waste management, the movement of hazardous waste, and a reporting system for waste generation. There are already three major laws on waste management and hazardous chemicals; they have not been applied because the necessary regulations were not developed.

In addition, there is no comprehensive governmental strategy or policy on municipal and industrial waste management, hazardous substances and contaminated sites. There is also no action plan or programme on waste management.

Recommendation 6.1:
(a) *The Ministry of Environment and Natural Resources Protection should promote the adoption of the draft law on waste management and its enforcement through the development of regulations, technical standards and norms for this law and other existing legislation on waste management;*
(b) *The Ministry of Environment and Natural Resources Protection, in coordination with other relevant ministries, should prepare action plans for the management of waste, including the rehabilitation of contaminated sites. This action plan should be integrated into the strategy for sustainable development.*

There is no monitoring for air, soil or groundwater quality around landfills. Geological and physical characteristics and conditions are not investigated before landfills are constructed, and the landfills are not managed in an environmentally sound manner. There is no precise inventory of existing landfills and no information on illegal dumps. The majority of dumps are now almost full, and their extension or the construction of new sanitary landfills, processing plants or incineration facilities is needed. In many cases municipal waste is dumped together with industrial waste and even with medical waste, without any analysis of the adverse effects on the population and the environment.

Recommendation 6.2:
The Ministry of Environment and Natural Resources Protection, in cooperation with the municipalities, should:
(a) *Develop an information management system for municipal waste generation, handling and recycling;*
(b) *Draw up an inventory of legal and illegal landfills;*
(c) *Monitor air, groundwater and soil in the vicinity of landfills, with priority given to those that are situated near big cities;*
(d) *Support the construction of sanitary landfills, processing or incineration facilities, on the basis of positive environmental expertise and environmental impact assessment; and*
(e) *Raise public awareness about the environmentally sound management of municipal waste.*

There is no classification system for industrial waste, and it is therefore difficult to gather and process information on waste generation, accumulation, treatment, recycling or disposal. In addition, the chemical composition of accumulated waste is not known, making it impossible to apply proper methods of treatment. Further research is necessary to draw up a detailed inventory of waste in order to propose a solution for its sound management.

Recommendation 6.3:
The Ministry of Environment and Natural Resources Protection, in cooperation with the Ministry of Economy, Industry and Trade, should:
(a) *Introduce and implement a classification system for industrial waste and hazardous chemicals, including pesticides, on the basis of the Globally Harmonized System of Classification and Labelling of Chemicals (GHS);*
(b) *Develop a permitting system for hazardous waste and draw up an inventory of major sources of hazardous and industrial waste in order to introduce the technologies for its recycling or environmentally sound treatment;*
(c) *On the basis of the above, start the rehabilitation of abandoned industrial waste sites and, where technically and economically possible, recycle industrial waste as a secondary raw material.*

The biggest environmental threat is the storage site of hazardous chemicals, including pesticides, in the Iagluji Mountains (Marneuli region), which is situated in a populated area. Unfortunately, there are no precise data on the quantities and composition of the hazardous chemicals stored at the site. There has been no analysis of the groundwater, soil and air nearby; and there are no fence or warning signs around the storage area. No risk assessment has ever been carried out.

Recommendation 6.4:
The Ministry of Environment and Natural Resources Protection, in cooperation with the Ministry of Economy, Industry and Trade, Ministry of Food and Agriculture and municipalities, should:
(a) *As a first and most urgent step, take appropriate measures to protect the population and to limit access to the Iagluji site;*
(b) *Develop a plan for the environmentally sound management of the site that also identifies the institutions that will be responsible for carrying it out;*

(c) Carry out a risk assessment of the site in cooperation with the Ministry of Labour, Health and Social Affairs and other relevant institutions;

(d) Identify the quantities and composition of the hazardous chemicals that are buried at the site; and

(e) Develop a plan for its rehabilitation.

Special attention should be given to the sound management of medical waste, including its separate collection, disposal and storage. At present medical waste is disinfected at the place of generation. The most dangerous anatomical medical waste is collected separately, transported to special centres and buried at cemeteries. Non-anatomical medical waste, however, is dumped with municipal waste without any separate treatment.

Recommendation 6.5:
The Ministry of Labour, Health and Social Affairs, in cooperation with the Ministry of Environment and Natural Resources Protection, should:
(a) Organize the separate collection of medical waste, including non-anatomic medical waste, and provide for its environmentally sound disposal or incineration throughout the country; and

(b) Train personnel in the environmentally sound management of medical waste.

About 223 radioactive sources have been identified in old contaminated military bases. Because there is no technical documentation concerning these sites, it is difficult to know precisely what kinds of contamination exist. It is essential that an inventory and classification of the contamination should be undertaken as soon as possible in order to provide the information required for rehabilitation.

Recommendation 6.6:
The Ministry of Environment and Natural Resources Protection should strengthen its Nuclear and Radiation Safety Service and identify sources of financing to:
(a) Further inventory and investigate all sites to provide detailed information on kinds of contamination and methods of rehabilitation;
(b) Speed up existing projects for the rehabilitation of contaminated sites; and
(c) Build storage facilities for radioactive waste according to the standards of the International Atomic Energy Agency.

Chapter 7

WATER MANAGEMENT

7.1 Water resources

Availability

Georgia is the richest country in the South Caucasus in terms of available water resources. Water balance calculations suggest that, theoretically, Georgians have four times or more water available per capita than their neighbours in Armenia and Azerbaijan. Distribution of water resources in Georgia is uneven, however, in large part due to the range in precipitation from the humid western part of the country to the semi-arid east.

The country lies in two major water basins, with the western portion of Georgia draining to the Black Sea and the eastern part to the Caspian Sea. The Rioni river is the largest tributary to the Black Sea in Georgia, draining approximately 20% of the country. Additional contributions to the Black Sea come from smaller rivers such as (moving southerly) the Kodori, Inguri, Supsa and Chorokhi. Drainage to the Caspian Sea is dominated by the Kura (also known as the Mtkvari) river. While the main stem of the Kura drains 23% of the country, other rivers such as the Iori and Alazani to the north of the main stem join the Kura downstream in Azerbaijan. With the Kura originating in Turkey, and tributaries joining in Georgia from Armenia, the Kura is clearly the most important transboundary water resource to Georgia and its neighbours.

Georgia has 860 lakes and reservoirs, with 74% of total storage in five: Paliastomi, Sagamo, Paravani, Ritsa and Tabatskuri. The 43 reservoirs in the country are used primarily for irrigation and hydropower generation, and less for water supply. Thirty-five of the reservoirs are in east Georgia and eight are in west Georgia. Groundwater resources are plentiful in the country, both in hard-rock aquifers and in alluvial deposits along rivers. This abundance supports 90% of the nation's drinking water supplies, which are groundwater-dependent.

Water quality

Data on quality of the country's surface waters is extremely limited. At best in recent years, the State Department of Hydrometeorology has collected data for up to 10 conventional indicators of pollution at up to 42 monitoring locations. Annual average data are typically cited in reports, but these unfortunately reflect at best a few measurements during any year. The infrequency of monitoring, and questions as to the quality control on sample collection and analysis compared to international norms, complicates any ability to draw conclusions on true ecological health and threats to Georgian water resources. Based on published and unpublished data, and qualitative interpretations by experts, one can draw some tentative observations:

- Ambient surface water quality probably exceeds Georgian (and comparable international) norms many times over throughout the main stems of both the Rioni and Kura rivers;
- The main stem of the Kura is reportedly affected downstream from the cities of Borjomi, Gori, Tbilisi and Rustavi;
- Tributaries to the Kura of concern include the Vere river in the Tbilisi area, the Alazani river downstream from Telavi, the Mashavera river downstream from Madneuli, and the Suramula river downstream from Khashuri;
- Relatively greater impacts on the Rioni river are reported to be downstream from Kutaisi and at Poti near the Black Sea;
- Groundwater quality at the source is believed to be very good but essentially no data are available to support this claim. Data are insufficient to assess whether more vulnerable groundwater (such as in alluvial deposits) is being contaminated by municipal, agricultural or industrial pollution;
- Ambient water quality has improved somewhat since the break-up of the Soviet Union, not from the introduction of pollution control technologies, but from dramatic reductions in industrial production and subsequent waste-water discharges; and

- Relatively high nutrient readings (especially ammonia) in surface waters are likely to result form untreated discharges of municipal waste water. Synthetic organic chemicals, oil products and metal contamination probably originate from industrial sources since only 10% of industrial discharge is treated.

Water use

The Ministry of Environment and Natural Resources Protection receives annual reports of water use. For example, in the year 2000 reports on 90% of total national water use reached the Ministry, with 345 users reporting. Total water use was 2,010 billion m^3 with 39% going to irrigation, 36% to thermal power production, and 25% to municipal water supply. From this total, 398 million m^3 was returned as permitted discharge, predominantly as municipal waste water (71%) and cooling water (27%). The slowdown in industry is apparent since less than 2% of discharge volumes came from industry. One note, however, is that these data are not controlled for accuracy through independent surveys by the Ministry, and users typically estimate rather than measure use, so there may be significant inaccuracies and inconsistencies. The Ministry also receives records from hydropower stations (nearly 100 stations withdrawing almost 15 billion m^3 per year), though such "once-through" use is considered non-polluting.

7.2   Drinking water

System overview

Drinking water is provided through centralized systems in 77 cities and larger towns in Georgia. The top four systems in terms of population served are Tbilisi (1,272,000), Kutaisi (241,000), Rustavi (159,000) and Batumi (137,000). Centralized distribution to some extent is present in approximately 870 smaller towns and villages. The Ministry of Labour, Health and Social Affairs estimated that, in 1999, 75% of Georgians living in urban areas were served by centralized systems delivering water to individual dwellings. Of the remainder, 8% received water from taps in their yards, 3% from public taps, 10% from unprotected springs, and the balance through other means. The situation in rural areas was quite different, with 37% being served by unprotected wells and springs, 20% by water piped in their yards, 13% from public

taps, 10% piped to individual dwellings, 13% from rainwater harvesting, and 4% from protected wells and springs.

Quality and health considerations

The quality of drinking water is of particular concern. The Ministry of Labour, Health and Social Affairs has been able to maintain a minimum level of water system surveillance, though questions of quality control do arise, and this must be taken into account in interpreting official statistics. Test methods, especially for microbiological constituents, are not directly comparable to World Health Organization recommendations. Drinking water standards were set by the Ministry of Labour, Health and Social Affairs in August 2001, and were generally adapted from old Soviet norms. Despite these limitations, concerns over systems' violations are real. In total (and depending on data source), approximately 18% to 24% of samples collected from centralized water systems in the years 2000 and 2001 violated Georgian norms for chemical and microbiological constituents. Samples from 13 towns and cities exceeded microbiological norms by 50% or more. Except for the larger cities, monitoring by water utilities for even such basic parameters as disinfection residual is not carried out.

Perhaps a more direct measure of concern regarding drinking water is the occurrence of water-borne disease outbreaks. Water-related diarrhoeal illnesses affected Rustavi during 1997-1998 with 1902 reported cases and in 2000 with 450 reported cases. Outbreaks between 1997 and 2000 also affected Kobuleti (3582 cases in 1997-1998), Khashuri (244 cases), Borjomi (294 cases in 1997-1998), Poti (267 cases in 2000) and five other cities (361 cases). Outbreaks of amoebiasis have occurred in Tbilisi each year since 1997, with a total of 2423 cases up until 2001. Senior officials in the Ministry of Labour, Health and Social Affairs in charge of epidemiological surveillance believe that there is significant underreporting of illness (i.e. most people affected do not visit their clinics and the illness goes unreported.) Therefore, they believe that the actual number of cases is far greater.

Sector constraints

Many related factors have caused these violations of health norms and water-borne outbreaks. Based on published and unpublished sources, as well as discussions with experts, the key reasons are:

Breakdowns in physical infrastructure and the prevalence of cross-connections with waste-water systems. Many of the drinking-water systems were either installed or last upgraded in the 1980s, when construction quality was particularly poor. Drinking-water distribution pipes are often co-located in the same ditches as waste-water collectors. Frequent power failures and pressure drops in drinking-water distribution systems can then create hydraulic conditions whereby contaminated water can enter the drinking-water network. This hazardous condition is believed to be common in the majority of systems in the country.

Inadequate drinking-water disinfection. Georgia does not produce chlorine, the basic chemical that is used most commonly for disinfection of drinking water. Import costs are high and disinfection equipment at many treatment plants is not functioning. As a result, it is estimated that 70% or more of systems are not disinfected. While groundwater sources are generally considered safe (a fact that could be contested due to lack of data) this absence means that no chlorine residual is present in distributed water. Without this residual there is no barrier to the transmission of microbiological pathogens. The adequacy of chlorine residual in the 30% of systems that do disinfect could also be questioned.

Financial needs of water utilities. Utility companies are burdened by payments for energy -- in some cases 2/3 or more of total budgets. This is exacerbated by the inefficiency of the old pumps and other equipment. Water metering of homes is rare, and some believe that Georgian law must actually be changed to allow metering of domestic water use. With very low tariffs set by local government for residential customers, and collection rates of 20% or less in poorer communities, cash flows cannot support operations, maintenance needs and service improvements. To cite Tbilisi as one example, not only have water tariffs been unrealistically low (US$ 0.013/m³), but even in the relatively richer capital city, collection rates reached only 70% overall, with 40% from residential customers.

Inadequate quality control and surveillance. At least 70% of water utilities do not have even rudimentary laboratories to optimize treatment or check on the quality of water delivered to consumers. Surveillance and testing by local offices of the Ministry of Labour, Health and Social Affairs can only substitute for a very small part of this need.

Inadequate sanitary protection zones. While Georgian law requires that there be three zones of protection around water-supply intakes or wells, official statistics show that even the most rudimentary protection (zone 1) is lacking in at least 14% of urban systems and 46% of rural systems. Unofficial reports suggest the numbers are much higher (i.e. less protective). Additional protection zones are only theoretical and not mapped or enforced to any significant degree.

Lack of incentives for private sector participation in drinking-water services. Other countries facing similar obstacles have been able to take significant strides in breaking down the barriers to public-private partnerships. Such progress has been very slow in Georgia, with only Tbilisi as a current candidate for a lease contract (facilitated by a proposed World Bank loan). The reasons for this condition include the major factors noted above, and an institutional framework not yet conducive to open and transparent public-private partnerships.

Plans for improvement

The working group of Georgia's National Environmental Action Plan (NEAP; November 1997 report) proposed a number of activities to address drinking-water concerns, ranging from furnishing water meters to all industrial users, to reducing operational water losses in Tbilisi and Kutaisi, to ambitious reconstruction of rural water systems (with a goal of 10% of systems improved each year). The final NEAP (adopted May 2000) also recommended improvements in water-supply safety in Kutaisi and Abastumani (the latter for concerns over tuberculosis clinic issues), and included an overarching recommendation for a project preparation unit to develop these and other proposed investments.

Despite such recommendations, progress in attracting investments and loans to address drinking-water concerns has been very slow. While several capacity-building efforts are being supported by donors, only two major investment efforts are now under way on urban drinking-water supply. They do, however, appear to be good examples of integrated and targeted approaches.

- Tbilisi Water Supply and Sanitation Project. Facilitated by a World Bank loan (expected to reach the World Bank Board of Directors in spring 2003), this US$ 25 to 35 million project includes two key components; a repair and rehabilitation fund to improve drinking water and associated sanitation conditions, and a technical assistance component to improve legislative conditions and utility management. The core effort will be a lease contract to bring in private sector operations. Investments will cover water loss reduction, water demand management, repairing and replacing broken or energy-inefficient pumps, reduction in cross-connections with waste-water collection pipes, and rehabilitating treatment technologies.

- Municipal Development and Decentralization Project. Another World Bank project (in its second stage) seeks to increase "the effectiveness of participating local government units in their identification, planning, delivery, and cost recovery of local infrastructure, and utility services." Over US$ 25 million will be allocated for investments; an estimated 20% of this will go to water supply, sanitation and urban flood control. Investments must be targeted given the US$ 600,000 ceiling per activity. Nevertheless, such investments can be crucial; under the first phase of the programme, Rustavi for example, was able to improve disinfection performance of drinking-water treatment with a direct reduction in water-borne illness as a benefit.

7.3   Waste-water management

Infrastructure

Perhaps nowhere in Georgia is the decline in water sector investment and conditions as obvious as in the area of waste-water management. As noted in table 7.1, only 5 of the 29 municipal waste-water treatment plants in the country are currently operational, albeit at the reduced efficiency of mechanical mode. Biological treatment units (which are more effective at reducing organic and nutrient loading to surface water) are not operational at any of the 22 facilities in Georgia initially fitted with them.

Municipal waste-water plants, too, were often constructed poorly and, due to inadequate operation and maintenance, have degraded further. The case of the regional treatment plant in Gardabani (serving Tbilisi, Rustavi and Gardabani) is instructive in this regard. According to unpublished reports (prepared in 1999 for a possible donor grant), while the plant was initially designed to treat 1 million m^3 per day, only an estimated 600,000 m^3 per day pass through the plant. This reflects the fact that only 43 out of 100 connections to the sewer collectors were actually installed. The rest of the waste water (estimates range from 30% to 50% of the total) from Tbilisi discharges directly to the Kura river without even rudimentary treatment. Some components within the treatment plant (such as the sludge digesters) were never completed. Needed improvements to waste-water collection and treatment systems are extensive and encompass all components.

Box 7.1:   Cross-sector relationships; the case of Rustavi
The industrial centre of Rustavi is an excellent example of the crucial linkages between the water and energy sectors, especially in times of economic difficulties. Rustavi has been affected by several water-borne disease outbreaks, the most severe of which (in 1997-1998) saw 500 people hospitalized out of a total of over 1200 cases. According to a senior elected official in Rustavi, 3 million lari (approximately US$ 1.38 million) is needed each year just for the cost of energy to run the drinking-water distribution and treatment system. Energy represents 70% of total drinking-water utility costs. Theoretically, each family of four in Rustavi would need to pay 10 lari per month to cover all costs of service. Given average household income at 60 to 70 lari per month (and pensions at 18 lari per month), this is not considered practical. With the economic crisis, citizens are charged a radically reduced rate of approximately 1.3 lari per month per family. While collection rates are high (65% to 85%) compared to the rest of the country, the total municipal income from water bills of 120,000 lari per year falls far short of the 3 million lari billed for energy alone. As a result, the city of Rustavi is 16 million lari in arrears for energy payments. On the positive side, however, Rustavi has been assisted by the World Bank's Municipal Development and Decentralization Project, and has greatly improved the microbiological safety of its water supply through targeted investments in distribution systems disinfection.

Table 7.1: Status of municipal waste-water treatment plants

Town	Technology	Operational since	Design capacity	Current condition
Black Sea Basin				
Kutaisi	MB	1980	110.0	Mechanical only
Batumi	MB	1983	85.0	Mechanical only
Kobuleti / Ozurgeti	MB	1985	50.0	Out of order
Zugdidi	MB	1975	23.3	Out of order
Poti	M	1981	23.1	Out of order
Samtredia	MB	1978	17.0	Out of order
Tskhaltubo	MB	1976	13.0	Out of order
Zestaphoni	MB	1976	11.5	Out of order
Chiatura	M	1978	8.2	Out of order
Sairme	MB	1978	0.8	Out of order
Kura River Basin				
Tbilisi / Rustavi	MB	1986	1,000.0	Mechanical only
Tskhinvali	MB	1983	25.0	Out of order
Gori	MB	1968	18.0	Mechanical only
Sagarejo	MB	1975	10.2	Out of order
Khashuri	MB	1971	10.0	Mechanical only
Kareli	M	1968	5.3	Out of order
Telavi	MB	1975	4.5	Out of order
Java	MB	1982	3.5	Out of order
Kaspi	M	1978	2.5	Out of order
Bakuriani	MB	1978	2.1	Out of order
Dmanisi	MB	1983	1.4	Out of order
Abastumani	MB	1981	1.4	Out of order
Tetri Tskaro	MB	1981	1.0	Out of order

Source: Ministry of Environment and Natural Resources Protection Background data for report: European Commission Project: SCRE/111232/C/SV/WW.

Support to the Implementation of Environmental Policies and NEAPs in the NIS. Sub-Project Georgia: Increasing the Effectiveness of Economic Instruments.

Working Note: Targeted Analysis of the Georgian Environmental Problems, October 2002.
Notes:
MB = mechanical and biological treatment
M = mechanical treatment only
Design capacity expressed in thousand cubic metres per day

The situation regarding industrial waste water reflects the extensive downturn in industrial production in the country. Water use, one measure of productivity and pollution impact, dropped from a reported 1,542 million m^3 in 1985 to 975 million m^3 in 1992 and to 211 million m^3 in 1998. Only nine major industrial enterprises are listed in most reports as being operational to some extent. In addition, there are more than 130 smaller industrial enterprises that have permits from the Ministry of Environment and Natural Resources Protection (obtained either from headquarters in Tbilisi or from regional agencies) to withdraw water or discharge effluents. One of the principal industrial categories is food processing, which can generate organic contamination. Pretreatment of waste water by the vast majority of industrial users is the exception rather than the rule. The Ministry of Environment and Natural Resources Protection estimates that more than 80% to 90% of industrial waste water is not treated before being discharged to sewers and municipal waste-water treatment plants (where there is a network), or directly to surface waters (where there is no network). If biological treatment units were in operation at municipal waste-water plants (which unfortunately they are not) pretreatment to neutralize metals, acids and other contaminants would be essential for good operation.

Water quality impacts

Published and unpublished data on waste-water discharge to surface water and subsequent impacts are sparse and conflicting. It is believed that most treatment plants do not monitor either the quantity or the quality of their waste water, and reports to the central authorities are rough estimates. As noted earlier, ambient water quality may have improved over the past few years given the slowdown in industry. While municipal waste water is projected to be the major contributor of organic pollution to surface water, there is evidence to suggest that inflow to municipal plants is diluted by storm water, wastage from leaking drinking-water systems, and groundwater infiltration. This means that if waste-water plants were working properly, they would not be able to operate as effectively as possible due to such dilution. Plants in Georgia are typically designed to handle inflows with biological oxygen demand (BOD) in the range of 120 to 200 mg/l. Limited monitoring data show that inflows are at half this concentration or less (i.e. 60 to 80 mg/l). Ammonia concentrations in surface water do appear consistently higher than recommended norms, likely attributed to the cumulative impact of these somewhat dilute but untreated municipal waste-water discharges.

Waste water is not routinely disinfected. This can increase the spread of water-borne diseases. Concern has been expressed that waste water from health centres and hospitals, including those that treat patients with tuberculosis, may not be disinfected at municipal plants. Possible "hot spots" include: (1) the Kvabliani river and its tributary the Otskhe river downstream of Abastumani village; (2) the Mtkvari river and its tributaries the Borjomula river and the Gujaretistskali river in the Borjomi region; (3) the Mtkvari river and its tributary the Ksani river in the Mtskheta region; and (4) the Vere river within Tbilisi city limits. Water quality and health data to assess the validity of these concerns are lacking.

Plans for improvement

Donor assistance has been sought by Georgia for proposed improvements in waste-water collection and treatment, for example: (1) a US$ 21,500,000 extension and rehabilitation of waste-water collection in Tbilisi, Rustavi and Gardabani, as well as overall improvement in the regional waste-water treatment plant serving these communities, and (2) rehabilitation of the waste-water collector systems for the Kobuleti resort at over US$ 10 million. Except for the most crucial components in the World Bank projects noted above (aimed at preventing cross-contamination), no significant investment effort or programme plan for waste-water management is in the pipeline.

Apart from infrastructure investments, there are only a few donor-supported activities aimed at building stronger regulatory institutions, such as for the compliance and enforcement of waste-water regulations. A major limiting factor in making progress in this area is the lack of basic equipment for carrying out independent field inspections.

7.4   Watershed and transboundary water management

Context

Experts recognize that comprehensive and effective water sector improvements are best supported within an overall watershed-based framework. This has also been the conclusion from numerous international development policy meetings, such as the World Summit on Sustainable Development (September 2002). Article 79 of the Law on Water of Georgia ("Multipurpose Water Use and Protection Plans") supports this approach in that: "Master, basin and territorial multipurpose water use and protection plans define the principal water management and other measures to be implemented for satisfaction of population's and natural economy's perspective water requirements, as well as for protecting water and preventing its adverse impact." Many of these same concepts are seen in the European Union's Water Framework Directive, on which so many countries in Eastern Europe, the Caucasus and Central Asia seek to pattern their efforts. The importance of the Kura river basin for Georgia and its neighbours is, furthermore, a critical regional issue.

Despite setting the stage in law, there are no effective regulations or incentives in Georgia to launch either watershed-based plans, or administrative bodies to share information or manage quality or quantity on a watershed basis within the country. Georgia is a party to the Convention on the Protection of the Black Sea Against Pollution but not to the Convention on the Protection and Use of Transboundary Waters and International Lakes. There has been considerable high-level attention on transboundary issues of the Kura river basin, though no formal international commission at the government-to-government level has been formed. Instead, informal and promising discussions and pilot projects are ongoing.

Box 7.2:   Programmatic initiatives with donor support

Beginning at the regional or transboundary scale, the European Union's TACIS programme on Joint River Management for the Kura Basin includes several projects being carried out by national technical working groups in Georgia, Armenia and Azerbaijan. These groups meet in plenary workshops, which allows country-to-country interaction. Steady progress is being made to upgrade technologies and monitoring of water quantity and quality in the Kura basin, all with an eye towards consistency within and across countries, and data sharing. Transboundary reviews and management can be done only when all three countries have a sound understanding of conditions and threats, and this programme is making important progress in this direction. Capacity-building components include reviews of water management practices, raising of public awareness, and early stages of pollution "hot spot" identification. Broader political concerns mean that a formal basin-wide steering group, international commission, or other high-level and politically endorsed entity is not now possible. Nevertheless, all three countries are clearly supporting and will benefit from technical cooperation. This effort clearly helps set the stage for longer-term formal transboundary cooperation.

With a similar goal of fostering cooperation, the United States Agency for International Development (USAID) has been working in Georgia and neighbouring countries under the Water Management in the South Caucasus programme. As with the TACIS programme, the emphasis is on "parallel bilateral" activities among professionals, with workshops to share experiences regionally. In particular, work has focused on subregional watershed-based planning for two pilot sub-basins to the Kura: the Alazani river basin (north-eastern Georgia and north-western Azerbaijan) and the Khrami-Debed river basin (south-central Georgia to north-central Armenia). Project tasks include data sharing, improvement of technologies and capabilities for water monitoring, assessment of problems and solutions, and preparation of lists of dozens of candidate institution-building and investment projects. It should be noted that while the list of projects has benefited from stakeholder input, there are no current funds identified for the vast majority of proposals. While the final reports from the programme are not government-endorsed (or legally binding) watershed plans, they do set a good basis for future adopted plans.

In addition to these programmes, transboundary and watershed planning has been a topic of other discussions and meetings. For example in July 2001, the Regional Environmental Center for the Caucasus (REC) held an international meeting on "Water Resources Management in the Countries of the South Caucasus" which brought together a wide range in specialists and policy makers from inside and outside the region to discuss these questions. A non-binding resolution to continue dialogue and actions was released, and REC has secured funding to help support continued sharing of information on programmes and initiatives.

Regarding additional pilots, the World Bank-supported Agricultural Research, Extension and Training effort includes pilot projects to reduce nutrient loading from small watersheds in western Georgia through better manure containment and management.

7.5   Protection of the Black Sea

Water quality conditions

The Black Sea is an important recreational and fishery resource for Georgia, and Georgia's actions that affect the Black Sea have regional consequences. Taking the regional view first, the Black Sea has been heavily contaminated with nutrients (i.e. nitrogen and phosphorus series), causing severe eutrophication, with a subsequent steady, steep decline in fish production over the past 25 years. The greatest sources of organic pollution are municipal waste-water treatment plants and agriculture. Poorly treated waste water means that many beaches are unsafe for swimming. Additional contaminants from industrial facilities, oil refineries and leaking tankers affect overall conditions in the Black Sea. Lower-quality invasive species, such as the jellyfish-like *Mnemiopsis leidyi*, and the presence of a hypoxia layer (or "dead-zone") at depth are serious ecological concerns. On the positive side, the comparatively small watersheds that traverse Georgia and contribute to the Black Sea mean that Georgia is by far the smallest contributor of organic pollutants among the six countries that ring the Black Sea. In 1996, for example, Georgia's contribution of BOD was about 4% of the regional total, phosphorus about 3% of the regional total and nitrogen less than 1% of the regional total. Given the limited mixing of the Black Sea, however, these comparatively small contributions can have a disproportionally large impact in the eastern part of the Black Sea nearest to Georgia.

As was noted earlier, the main waste-water treatment plants in Georgia that discharge municipal sewerage to the Black Sea basin are in poor condition. Those closest to the Black Sea coastline include: Batumi, where there is only mechanical treatment; Kobuleti and Poti, which are not operating at all; and Sukhumi (in Abkhazia), which is also believed to be not operating. In addition to waste water from residents, these facilities receive ship-generated waste water and bilge water, which are also inadequately treated. The short distance from the waste-water plants (which discharge to tributaries of the Black Sea) to the Sea itself allow for very little natural attenuation. This means that tourists and residents who depend on nearby beaches for summer recreation are threatened with microbiological illness from contact with polluted bathing waters. Health officials close down beaches along the Batumi to Poti coastline each year due to microbiological contamination, a condition that can only be solved unfortunately by the costly and difficult reduction of pollution to coastal waters.

Beach quality is further hampered by poor industrial facility maintenance and inadequate industrial waste-water treatment, particularly from old oil refineries (such as the Batumi refinery) and port facilities. Anecdotal evidence suggests that erosion of solid waste landfills in Batumi also contributes to reduced recreational water quality. Quantitative data on near-coastal water quality are sparse at best, and are of questionable accuracy. Finally, as noted above, insufficient treatment of drinking water in several coastal cities has also led to water-borne outbreaks, notably in Kobuleti and Poti.

Programme initiatives and needs

A number of initiatives supported by donors and international financial institutions are under way to tackle some of the issues noted above, though improving water quality will take considerable time.

Georgia is a party to the Convention on the Protection of the Black Sea Against Pollution adopted in Bucharest in 1992 and ratified by all six countries surrounding the Black Sea by early 1994. The Convention includes specific protocols on the prevention of land-based sources, dumping of waste and coordinated action in response to spills. The Convention itself is a general framework that does not, however, provide sufficient legal or financial impetus for investments and other interventions needed to improve water quality. The Black Sea Environmental Programme (based in Turkey) coordinates implementation actions and is beginning a second year of its second phase of operations.

The Integrated Coastal Zone Management (ICZM) Programme, financed largely by a US$ 4.4 million credit from the World Bank and a US$ 1.3 million grant from the Global Environment Facility, targets

several crucial needs. It will establish an institutional framework for integrated management, help protect and restore critical wetlands to improve water quality, bolster monitoring and coastal erosion-prevention programmes, and develop a national oil spill contingency plan. The programme is a key initial step in meeting Georgia's part of the regional Black Sea Strategic Action Plan.

A number of technical projects implemented through the Black Sea Environmental Programme have both country-specific and regional benefits. The most recent initiative (currently in the bidding process) calls for an international study group to be formed to conduct consistent and accurate field surveys of water quality and ecological conditions of the entire Black Sea. The effort seeks to define "…the main gaps in setting targets for nutrient control in the Black Sea and how these can be closed or reduced by good and cost-effective science".

The Department for Black Sea Protection of the Ministry of Environment and Natural Resources Protection serves as a central point for cooperation and coordination. The Black Sea Inspectorate (based in Batumi) is staffed to a somewhat better extent than the Ministry's other regional arms. Proposed new investments in refineries and port facilities along the Black Sea coast in Georgia will be subjected to full environmental review and are expected to include more up-to-date pollution control facilities.

Despite such positive signs, key deficiencies remain, for example:

- There are no active, funded programmes in place to improve the water and waste-water infrastructure of key port cities, particularly Batumi, Kobuleti and Poti. Some initial facility improvement plans were considered in the past few years for Poti (with possible European Union partnership), and for Kobuleti (with possible Japanese Government partnership) but do not appear to be active at present. Industrial and municipal pollution, with consequent human health impact, will continue without such basic investment.
- The ICZM programme will set a good basis but does not include sufficient capital for the mitigation of coastal erosion, oil spills, ports and ship-based waste. Investments in hardware and equipment for oil spill response and port/ship waste-water treatment are not included.

- There is still a lack of resources to strengthen basic needs for field surveillance by the Ministry of Environment and Natural Resources Protection (to oversee waste-water discharge) and the Ministry of Labour, Health and Social Affairs (to oversee drinking-water quality, bathing-water quality, and track water-borne illness).
- There is still a need to translate knowledge of resources and threats into a specific national action plan for Black Sea protection by Georgia.

7.6 Policy objectives and management

The policy framework

While there is no separate policy document that directly spells out Georgian policy for protecting and managing water availability and quality, the Law on Water does outline a number of key principles that comprise a policy framework. Some of these are:

- Water protection is a major element of environmental protection for Georgian citizens, with consideration of both current and future needs;
- Drinking water for the population is the highest priority of all uses;
- Both groundwater and surface water are under State control;
- Management of water varies depending on the hydrologic importance;
- A system of "user-polluter pays" is key; and
- Pollution is not allowed (though specifics as to what defines pollution are lacking).

The legal framework

There are more than 10 major laws in Georgia that have significant influence over the protection and management of water resources and associated environmental concerns. The most comprehensive is the Law on Water, which has been in force since October 1997 and was last amended in June 2000. The 96 separate articles of this Law cover a very wide and comprehensive set of issues such as pollution control policies, protection of drinking-water sources, licensing of water use and discharge, categorization and protection of resources, particular measures for the Black Sea, flood control, and many others. All surface waters, groundwater and near-coastal waters are deemed to be under the control of the national Government. Many of the provisions of the Law are supplemented by legislative orders and decrees, as well as by regulations of the Ministry of Environment and Natural Resources Protection, which specify necessary actions in greater detail. The Ministry holds overarching responsibility for implementing the Law on Water, though other Ministries are key players on specific topics. Implementation of the Law is carried out by personnel at the regional or municipal level.

The Law on Water does provide for the licensing of water use and the discharge of pollutants, an approach that has been in place since 1999. Licences for waste-water discharge are good for 3 to 5 years, those for municipal water systems and irrigation for 25 years. There are 99 operating licences in Georgia, with 72 of these for abstraction of water, 27 for industrial waste-water discharge, and 10 for recreational or resort use. Decisions on major facility licences and those affecting the highest priority water bodies are taken by the Inter-ministerial Council for Water Use.

It should be noted that none of the municipal waste-water treatment plants is operating under licence, and the 27 industrial facilities under licence represent only about 5% of total waste water generated by industry. Facilities in place before 1999 operate under a system of allowable limits. Under both systems, users pay a fee to withdraw clean water and discharge waste water (i.e. that has been contaminated to some allowable level). If the discharge is above the allowable limits, a proportionally higher fine is paid. The core of the system is self-reporting by users to national authorities. Since a small minority of industrial users carry out accurate monitoring of their discharge and the Ministry's oversight is minimal, the system is not believed to be an effective means for discouraging pollution. Industrial discharge that goes to municipal treatment plants is not subject to licensing by the Ministry or limits; instead the quantity and quality of discharge are set by negotiation and contract between the industry and the waste-water utility.

Water quality standards are issued administratively. The Ministry of Labour, Health and Social Affairs set standards for drinking water and recreational use, as well as waste water used for land irrigation, in August 2001 (order No. 297/n). The Ministry of Environment and Natural Resources Protection set surface water quality standards in September 1996 (order No. 147). Most of these standards are adapted from those in place during the Soviet era, albeit with some regard to international norms.

Even those updated to reflect international norms (such as those of the World Health Organization) are essentially not implemented due to the lack of monitoring, testing and oversight in the field.

The institutional framework

In addition to the Ministry of Environment and Natural Resources Protection, several other Georgian government bodies have key roles in the water sector:

- Ministry of Labour, Health and Social Affairs, which sets drinking water and recreational water standards and oversees the quality of drinking water delivered by water utilities. The Ministry also tracks and responds to major water-borne disease outbreaks. Budget and personnel restrictions mean that the Ministry can now maintain only the most rudimentary oversight role, with significant questions as to quality control.
- State Department of Geology. While having some nominal role in oversight of groundwater development, it is largely the repository of geologic and hydrologic data on aquifers used for water supply.
- State Department of Hydrometeorology. While technically responsible for monitoring surface water quality, its current network is severely constrained. As noted above, improvements in equipment and methodologies have been a major focus of several donors.
- Ministry of Finance, which historically has made funds available from the central Government for water investment (albeit now quite limited with decentralization), now primarily acts as the counterpart for disbursing and managing funds from the limited programmes of the World Bank. This Ministry also sets water use and emission rates incorporated in the licences from the Ministry of Environment and Natural Resources Protection.

Despite the fact that a structure appears to be in place for water quality management and control, concerns over effectiveness remain. Field personnel of the Ministry of Environment and Natural Resources Protection do not have the basic tools for monitoring compliance by industry with either licences or emission limits. These deficiencies include vehicles for transporting inspectors to field sites, sampling equipment, field and central laboratories, and computers for aggregating data, among other things.

Georgian legislation that prohibits on-site inspections without a court order (instituted reportedly as an anti-corruption measure) hampers the ability of field personnel to carry out effective inspections. Municipal authorities in Tbilisi could get such orders in only 4 out of 10 situations that they deemed worthy of unannounced environmental inspections.

A permit programme or compliance effort for municipal waste-water treatment plants appears to be totally lacking. Fines and fee structures do not appear to provide the right incentives to encourage pollution control or investments in better water efficiency. Innovative approaches such as investment tax credits or targeted loan programmes for good compliance are not in place. There is no competitive domestic programme for providing funds for water infrastructure improvement (e.g. a water fund or revolving loan programme).

Citizens' suits and legal actions to force the Government and polluters to improve practices are either not allowed or not effective in forcing change. Public participation in the vast majority of decisions on water is not the norm.

7.7   Conclusions and recommendations

Georgia is rich in available ground and surface water resources, but the infrastructure and management systems currently in place to use these resources effectively and sustainably are severely constrained. Surface water quality may have improved to a small degree over the past decade due to the dramatic reduction in industrial productivity and subsequent pollutant discharge. Unfortunately, the risks of water-borne disease and other negative health impacts have increased due to breakdowns in water infrastructure, and reduced prevalence of drinking-water treatment. More than 80% of urban waste-water systems fail to provide even the most rudimentary treatment. Water utilities are unsuccessful at raising sufficient revenue from water tariffs to meet even basic operating expenses for energy and treatment chemicals. Incentives for mobilizing capital from public and private sources are lacking. Legal and policy instruments available to local and national authorities are insufficient to deter further degradation.

Given the scope of these difficulties and serious budget constraints in the country, recommendations for sector improvement need to be both feasible and focused on areas that can make a real difference in the near to mid term. Some promising donor-supported activities are under way to address drinking-water quantity and quality, watershed and transboundary water management, and protection of the Black Sea.

Given the expense of treatment chemicals and the high cost of energy faced by water utilities, it is reported that 70% of utilities do not disinfect their water supplies. With the prevalence of cross-connections (i.e. mixing) with raw waste-water collection systems, water-borne disease outbreaks are on the rise, and health risks from contaminated water are significant. Public officials and utility representatives should try all legal and policy means to correct this immediate health risk. It is acknowledged, however, that some systems may not be able to maintain an adequate disinfection residual due to elevated natural or human-induced organic constituents. Severe taste and odour concerns, or fears over dramatic increases in disinfection by-products could arise. In these cases, alternative sources of water (including bottled water, fuel subsidies for boiling water, and tanker trucks) should be found to the extent practical.

Recommendation 7.1:
The Ministry of Labour, Health and Social Affairs in cooperation with the Ministry of Environment and Natural Resources Protection and local governments should ensure that:
- *Drinking-water utilities disinfect their water supplies with chlorine or other chemicals so that sufficient disinfection residual is maintained within distribution systems to ensure microbiological safety;*
- *The public is notified of particularly hazardous drinking-water conditions, suggesting, inter alia, alternatives for children and boiling of water; and*
- *Utilities that do not disinfect are justified in this decision; for example those systems tapping protected wells or springs with very short, protected distribution networks.*

Investments are needed to reduce water losses, eliminate cross-connections with waste-water collectors, and improve cost-recovery through water metering and other means. This is the approach that has been taken in Tbilisi, which has brought in a private sector operator (under a leasing contract). While this may be difficult to replicate in other cities, management contracts with central government support could be a viable strategy. Grant money from foreign donors could be used (as in the case of the World Bank's municipal

programme) to finance infrastructure investments with the greatest health benefit, for example disinfection technologies and strengthening of surveillance laboratories. The project preparation unit could also coordinate donor assistance and partnerships for innovative financial mechanisms such as revolving loans and development credits, and help foster institutional change to sustain positive results from the pilots (see recommendation 4.4).

The overall degradation in the municipal waste-water system infrastructure, constraints on raising revenue for improvements and greatly reduced industrial productivity limit practical recommendations for improvement. Some of the largest industrial "hot spots" are not operational, or are working at a fraction of their design capacity. Nevertheless, cooperation with industrial subsectors that are relatively more viable economically can set the stage for broader improvements in the future. To cite one example, Georgia is an agricultural centre for the region and food processing is comparatively strong. Waste-water discharge from food processing can be high in nutrient concentrations, but treatment schemes are comparatively simple.

Voluntary cooperation between the industry (to assess and implement changes in operations and treatment schemes) and regulatory authorities would be a positive sign for overall sector reform. Additional candidate activities include more thorough and accurate self-monitoring and reporting by industry to regulatory authorities, and quicker notification of unintentional releases of industrial waste water.

Recommendation 7.2:
The Ministry of Environment and Natural Resources Protection, in cooperation with other relevant ministries, should begin to tackle the problems of waste-water management through the launching of a waste-water programme for the most urgent hot spots.

Good watershed-based planning can assist in the implementation of more cost- and health-effective water services and water pollution control. Positive outcomes and processes (such as stakeholder involvement, better monitoring and critical needs assessment) that have shown to be promising in EU and United States-financed pilot projects should be seriously considered for wider application. The role of the Ministry of Environment and Natural Resources Protection in partnerships in these pilot schemes could be strengthened to foster dissemination and sustainability. Inter-ministerial working groups could be formed as one way to expand cooperation and engagement on pilot schemes. Regulations to accelerate the adoption of improved approaches, including the formation of watershed- or river-basin-based organizations could then be developed. Finally, opportunities should be sought (to the extent politically feasible) for engagement by senior officials and policy makers in Georgia with their counterparts in Armenia and Azerbaijan on transboundary water issues.

Recommendation 7.3:
The Ministry of Environment and Natural Resources Protection should:

- *Undertake a policy review on the use of watershed-based planning for the implementation of improved water services and water pollution control;*
- *Draft regulations, including incentives, for watershed-based planning; and*
- *Accelerate transboundary cooperation in this area.*

This coming year will see a number of positive initiatives to improve the country's understanding of near-coastal water quality and threats. Oil spill contingency plans will be developed; the institutional framework for integrated coastal zone management will be strengthened; and it is hoped that new port and energy facilities will be designed with greater environmental protection. The next step, attracting investments in critical water and waste-water infrastructure, needs to be taken but will be challenging. Taking the experience of other regional programmes (such as the Danube and Baltic Sea efforts), it is recommended that Georgia should move forward with developing a national action plan. The plan would examine needed improvements in municipal and industrial facilities, and provide a consistent basis for evaluating investment needs and benefits from both human health and ecological perspectives. A draft plan has been developed and received some Parliamentary review, but more serious attention to making this a centrepiece for investment attention should be considered.

Recommendation 7.4
The Ministry of Environment and Natural Resources Protection should accelerate preparation of a Georgian national action plan for the Black Sea.

Water management should also take into consideration good irrigation practices and the introduction of environmental sound technologies (see recommendation 11.2).

Chapter 8

BIODIVERSITY AND FOREST MANAGEMENT

8.1   Current state of nature

Landscapes and ecosystems

Georgia is located in the southern Caucasus. The Caucasus is recognized as one of the world's 25 biodiversity hot spots and Georgia is rich in biodiversity.

The most important physical-geographic features that support this biodiversity are a complex geological history, a very diverse and developed relief, a diversity of climate types (see Introduction), a variety of soils, a developed hydrographic system, as well as a rich cultural history. The country's relief is made up of very high and low mountains, valleys and plains. Its major mountain ranges are the High (north) Caucasus Mountains, the Lesser (south) Caucasus Mountains and the Volcanic Mountains of south Georgia. Georgia's altitude ranges from 0 (Black Sea coast) to 5,069 metres above sea level (Mtsvane Shkhara in the Caucasus Mountains). Valleys along the river flows belong to two different major watersheds – the Black Sea and the Caspian Sea – divided by the Likhi Range (Surami). This range divides the two main flatland areas – the Kolkheti (west Georgia) and the Iberia Plains (east Georgia) – into two distinct orographic (relief) regions with completely different bio-geographic entities. Kolkheti is a very humid, Mediterranean-type refugial zone, and the Iberia Plains is a semi-arid to arid subtropical region.

Beside the horizontal climatic differences, there are marked climatic and vegetation zones along the vertical gradient, with clear distinctions between the west (Kolkheti) and the east of the country. There are five major zones in west Georgia – from forest belt (from coastal plain to 1,900 m) to the nival zone (above 3,600 m). In east Georgia the situation is even more complex with six major zones – from semi-desert, steppe and arid sparse woodland (150-600 m above sea level) to the nival zone (above 3,700 m).

Georgia has a rich variety of landscapes owing to the junction of temperate and subtropical climate zones in the Caucasus mountain range, Quaternary history, cultural development, vegetation zones and other geographic features. In total there are 16 types, 22 subtypes and 72 landscape genera in both plain and foothill and mountainous landscape classes. In all, there are 260 kinds of landscape.

In addition, Georgia has a great diversity of ecosystems. Major ecosystems can be compared to bio-geographical biome division. In Georgia there are at least nine inland biomes: floodplain forest, semi-desert, steppe, arid light woodland and hemixerophyte scrub, forest, subalpine, alpine zone and subnival (see figure 8.1). Wetlands can be added to this list. However, the division and classification of ecosystems differ greatly among the scientists.

Land use

Most land is used for agriculture (43.4% of the country), of which 64.2% are meadows and pastures and only 26.2% is arable land. The main crops are wheat, maize, grapes, tea, citrus fruit, potatoes and vegetables. About 40% of Georgia is forested. The rest is urban land, water bodies and glaciers. At present, 4.1% of the country is protected, mostly forests (see figure 8.2).

Species diversity

Due to its bio-geographical characteristics, Georgia has a rich flora and fauna. More than 28,900 species have been recorded, of which 2,745 are algal species, more than 8,000 fungi and lichens, 4,100 vascular plants and about 14,100 known animal species. Of the animals, 576 are vertebrate species, including freshwater fish species (see table 8.1).

Georgia's flora and fauna are characterized by a high degree of endemic, subendemic and relict species. There are 300 endemic and 600 subendemic (Caucasus region endemic) vascular plant species. There are no complete data on invertebrate animals' endemism, but it is probably very high, since among the vertebrates species 59 are endemic (table 8.1). Three bird species are also endemic: the Caucasian black grouse (*Tetrao mlokosiewiczi*), the Caucasian snowcock (*Tetraogalus caucasiacus*) and the Caucasian warbler (*Phylloscopus lorenzii*). Most of the other birds are migratory species, mostly characteristic of the Kolkheti area. Such a great diversity, and especially endemism, is not common in temperate climate countries like Georgia. However, according to the actual biodiversity index (ABI) and the average biodiversity index (BDI), Georgia ranks first in Europe and 36th in the world.

Not all of the invertebrate groups in Georgia are well studied, although some groups (especially among arthropods) are quite well known. According to some calculations and prognoses 26,355 invertebrate species are to be found in Georgia. Vertebrates, on the other hand, are very well studied. A special characteristic of Georgia is its large mammal diversity. Until the beginning of the 20th century these species were found throughout Georgia. For example, Asian leopard, lynx and wolf ranges covered almost all of Georgia. Since the 1920s there has been a significant decline

on all these mammal populations. Only few leopards remain in very remote and inaccessible areas. Similarly, the striped hyena population has declined to several individuals and the goitered gazelle is now extinct. Caucasus mountain goat populations, some of which are endemic, have severely declined due to poaching. This rich biodiversity also has a very high economic value. Besides wild flora and fauna diversity, Georgia is very rich in agro-biodiversity. It is one of the centres of plant and animal domestication. The country's agro-biodiversity includes original breeds as well as many sorts of grapes, fruits and cereals.

Black Sea

The Black Sea is not only a significant natural resource for the Georgian economy, it is also a very important part of its natural heritage. In addition to the extremely diverse land ecosystems and landscapes, the Black Sea represents a sea ecosystem with its different bioceonoses, and together with its associated coastal habitats, it contributes to Georgia's exceptional biodiversity. The diverse fish and whale species are of great importance for the country's biodiversity, and they also have an economic value.

Table 8.1: Flora and fauna diversity

Species	Number	Endemic for Caucasus Number (%)
Algae (taxa)*	2745	
Fungi	> 7000	
Lichens (taxa)	987	
Vascular plants	4100	900**(21)
Ferns	74	
Gymnosperms	17	
Angiosperms	4009	
Invertebrates	13514	
of which arthropods	11443	
Vertebrates		
Fishes	84	
Amphibians	13	3 (23)
Reptiles	52	15 (29)
Birds	322	3 (1)
Mammals	105	38 (36)

Source : Beroutchachvili, N.: Georgia's Biodiveresity against a global background, from: Biological and landscape diversity of Georgia (Proceedings).

Notes :* Continental waters and soil taxa, ** 600 Caucasian and 300 Georgian species.

Figure 8.1:   Map of major biomes

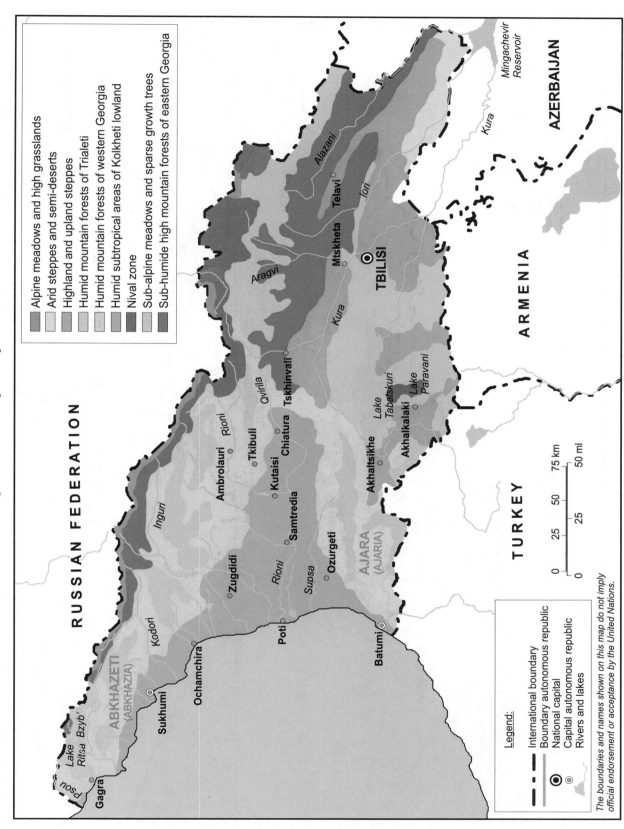

Legend (biomes):
- Alpine meadows and high grasslands
- Arid steppes and semi-deserts
- Highland and upland steppes
- Humid mountain forests of Trialeti
- Humid mountain forests of western Georgia
- Humid subtropical areas of Kolkheti lowland
- Nival zone
- Sub-alpine meadows and sparse growth trees
- Sub-humide high mountain forests of eastern Georgia

Legend:
- International boundary
- Boundary autonomous republic
- National capital
- Capital autonomous republic
- Rivers and lakes

The boundaries and names shown on this map do not imply official endorsement or acceptance by the United Nations.

RUSSIAN FEDERATION

AZERBAIJAN

ARMENIA

TURKEY

ABKHAZETI (ABKHAZIA)

AJARA (AJARIA)

TBILISI

0   25   50   75 km
0   25   50 ml

Figure 8.2:   Map of land use

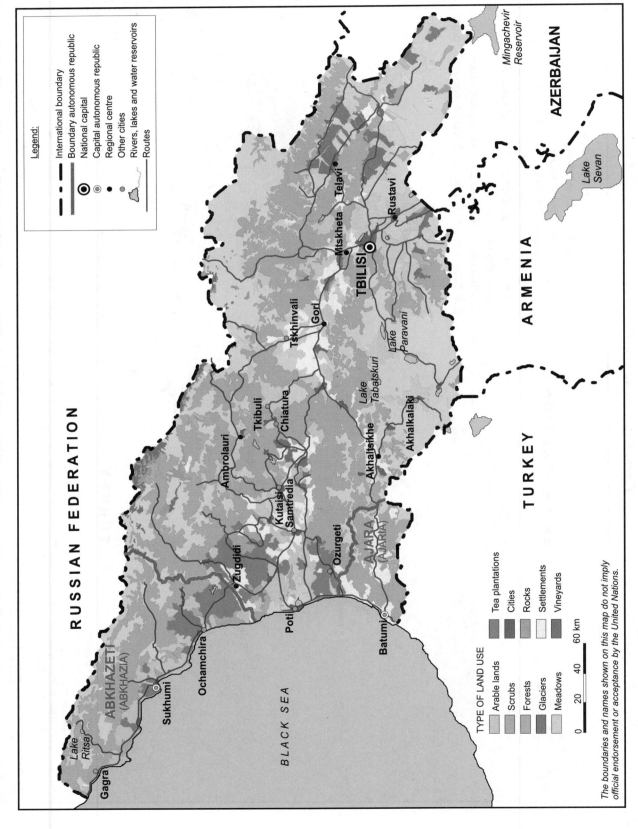

The boundaries and names shown on this map do not imply
official endorsement or acceptance by the United Nations.

The Black Sea was under strong anthropogenic pressure (both overexploitation and pollution). Currently, the situation is slightly improved, but there is still a threat (oil industry and trans-Caucasus pipelines). Georgia has ratified all the regional conventions on the Black Sea (see chapter 4 on international cooperation) and is committed to its protection. More information is available in chapter 7 on water management.

Forests

Almost 2.77 million ha of forests and forestland make up 41% of the country's total territory, with a total wood stock of 452 million m^3 and an annual increase of about 4 million m^3 (table 8.2 and figure 8.3). This percentage is higher than in most European countries. These figures show that Georgia contributes 0.13% to the world's total timber volume. On average there is 0.6 ha of forest and 98 m^3 of timber per person in Georgia.

All forests belong to the State; 84% are controlled by the State Department of Forestry, 2% by the Mountain Forest Institute, 6% by the State Department for the Management of Protected Areas and 8% by the former collective and State farms. The new Forest Code does not foresee their privatization.

The forests in Georgia are unevenly distributed. There are areas with less than 10% forest cover. About 98% of forests are in the mountains and only 2% are plain forests in both east and west Georgia. About 26.8% of the forests are below 1000 m, 66.2% between 1000 and 2000 m, and 7.0% above 2000 m. Commercially valuable tree species, like chestnut, beech and oak, are rare above 1500 metres. Most of the forest cover of Georgia is on steep slopes, which makes exploitation very difficult and dangerous from the erosion point of view. Only 5.5% of the forests are on slopes of less than 10 degrees, 16.5% grow between 11 and 20 degrees, 34.8%, between 21 and 30 degrees, 19.6%, between 31 and 35 degrees, and 23.6%, on slopes above 36 degrees.

The average economic value of the timber harvest turnover in Georgia is not very high, since the average density per hectare is around 158 m^3, well below European peak values.

There are almost 400 different tree and shrub species in Georgia's forests. The most abundant is beech. Beech forests cover 52.9% of all forest land. Other deciduous species make up 22.5%, conifers, 15.7%, and other species, 8.9%.

Georgia has well preserved forest ecosystems. About 98% of the forests are natural or near natural, and 800,000 ha are virgin forests, which are usually natural reserves or restricted areas. This is mainly owing to their inaccessibility. The forest road network is not developed since the forest industry in Soviet times was dependent on cheap wood imports from Russia. At present about 100 km of forest roads are built annually and about 800 km are repaired. The natural character of the forests is clear since more than one third (35.4%) is over age, one third (33.4%) is middle age and the rest is under age. Forest cover has expanded naturally during the past 40 years from 2,555,000 ha to 2,773,000 ha, i.e. almost 5,500 ha per year.

Georgia's forests are classified as follows: valuable forest massifs, green zone forests, resort forests, soil-protecting and water-regulating forests and protective-exploitative valley forests. As can be seen in table 8.3, there are very restricted areas where logging is allowed. The main cut is supposed to be sanitary. At present about 8.5-8.7% of the forests form part of protected areas.

There is no organized State monitoring in Georgia's forests, neither is Georgia part of international monitoring programmes. Even worse, its forests are under serious threat because the responsible institutions do not have enough money to operate normally. During the past five years the budget of the State Department of Forestry has been cut more than fivefold, and the most serious cut affected the funds for forest protection. Thus, without State control and owing to the severe drop in living standards, illegal logging (both by private individuals for home heating and by enterprises) has increased to a threatening rate. It is especially significant that the forests are clear-cut close to the roads, because there are few forest roads. There are no reliable data (or no data at all) to indicate the extent of illegal logging related to the total forest area or to the valuable wood, although it is undoubtedly very high.

Figure 8.3:   Map of forests

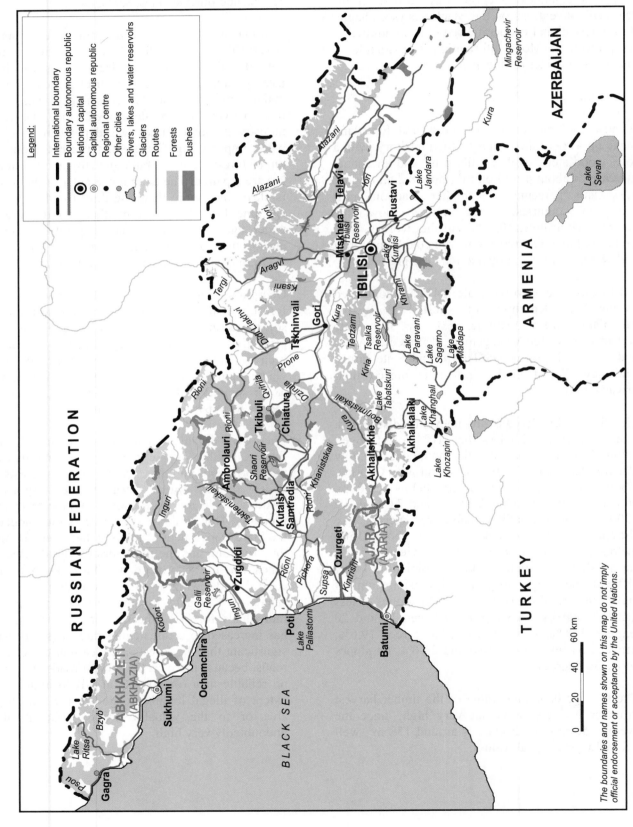

Table 8.2: Forest data

	1995	1999
Total area of forest fund (thousand ha)	2,991.4	3,006.4
Actual forest cover (thousand ha)	2,760.6	2,773.4
% of the total country area	39.7	39.9
Total wood stock (million m^3)	434.8	451.7

Source: State Department of Forestry, 2002.

Figure 8.4: Species composition

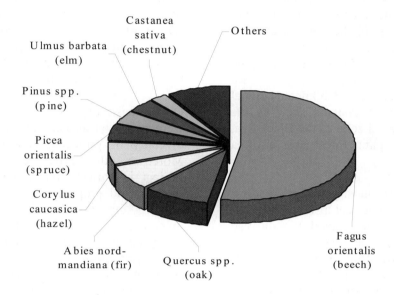

Source: State Department of Forestry, 2002.

Table 8.3: Forest functions (1999)

	1,000 ha	%
Reserve	169.0	5.6
Valuable wood massif	4.7	0.2
Green zone forest	276.5	9.2
Close forest resort	119.4	4.0
Remote forest resort	923.6	30.8
Soil-protecting and water-regulating forest	1,465.7	49.0
Protective-exploitative valley forest	35.1	1.2
Total	2,994.0	100.0

Source: Metreveli, K. Forest and Forest Product Country Profile - Georgia 2002. Final version of the report for Georgian Forest Development project. World Bank.

Protected areas

There are 24 natural protected areas in Georgia under the administration of the State Department for the Management of Protected Areas. This represents 4.1% of the country's territory. According to the 1996 Law on Protected Areas System, other categories are administered by different stakeholders, such as the Ministry of Food and Agriculture, the State Department of Forestry, local governments, and others. It is hard to get a clear picture of the status and protection regimes of areas other than these noted in table 8.4. The State Department for the Management of Protected Areas does not have data about these territories. They are protected areas of IUCN categories III, V and maybe VI and VII, but they do not have management plans or administration bodies, i.e. no one takes care of them. Their protection status may be changed and new protected areas designated under ongoing projects. The Law defines the protected areas according to the IUCN categorization (standards).

The two national parks - Borjomi-Karagauli and Kolkheti - have been established only recently and are administered and functioning according to international IUCN standards. However, their future administration and functioning are in jeopardy since funding from foreign donors will soon stop and current State financing is insufficient. Borjomi-Karagauli was established on the basis of an existing State nature reserve and encompasses pristine conifer and broadleaf forests and subalpine pastures and meadows (790,000 ha together with Borjomi State Nature Reserve). Kolkheti National Park comprises diverse ecosystems such as the continental shelf and coastal zone of the Black Sea, meadows, wetlands and plain forest over an area of 44,313 ha.

State nature reserves were mostly set up on forest land. They were created to protect different types of forests, like beech, oak and mixed broadleaved forests, including rare type of forests like conifers, common yew and Zelkova. But some reserves were created on grassland and sparse juniper and pistachio woodlands (Vashlovani), alpine pastures (Lagodekhi and Kazbegi), or wetland (Kobuleti).

There are two Ramsar sites in Georgia. The wetlands of central Kolkheti (33,710 ha) and the Ispani II marshes (513 ha), both designated in 1997. A third, Javakheti Lake (high mountain wetland) has only recently been nominated.

Although administered by the State Department for the Management of Protected Areas, the policy and designation of the protected areas are the responsibility of the Ministry of Environment and Natural Resources Protection. Its control and monitoring are to a certain extent parallel and independent of the State Department for the Management of Protected Areas. This overlapping of competences could create problems.

Several projects for protected areas are ongoing. They are mainly developing the country's protected area system and creating a protected area network. Examples are the World Bank project for Integrated Coastal Zone Management (ICZM) in the Black Sea Region (ICZM Project Implementation Unit), the UNDP/GEF project for the Conservation of the Arid and Semiarid Ecosystems in the Caucasus (implementation agency NACRES), the World Bank/GEF Georgia's Protected Areas Development Project, and other smaller projects. All these were preceded by projects of the WWF regional Caucasus branch in Tbilisi.

On the basis of these projects several other areas were proposed as national parks. In this way the diversity of protected ecosystems will increase. Moreover, the Protected Areas Development Project is drawing up a strategy for connecting existing and proposed protected areas, which are currently cut-off, into a network of protected areas by creating bio-corridors. The bio-corridors will be protected areas of IUCN category VI, ensuring a loose protection regime and enabling parallel economic activities. This idea seems realistic, since it also has political support. On 3 April 1997, in connection with the Living Planet Campaign - WWF 2000, the President of Georgia announced Georgia's first "gift" to the world: by the year 2010, 20% of the country will be protected under several categories. About 15% of that will be in forests. Furthermore, the EMERALD Network pilot project has selected eight sites for development. The Emerald Network is a network of areas of special conservation interest (ASCIs) to be established in the territory of the Contracting Parties and Observer States to the Bern Convention, including Central and East European countries and EU member States.

Table 8.4: Protected areas according to IUCN category

	IUCN (approx.)	Number	Area (ha)
State nature reserves	I	16	168,705
National parks	II	2	102,293
Restricted areas	IV	6	12,822
Total		24	283,820

Source: State Department for the Management of Protected Areas, 2002.

8.2 Pressures on nature

Forest exploitation

Total standing wood is estimated at 434 million m^3 with an average of 163 m^3 per hectare (1999, see table 8.2). The annual increment is almost 1 million m^3 (0.22% of the stock) and about 25% of this may be cut. According to forest management plans for 2002, this amount was 229,550 m^3 (84,450 conifers), of which 117,100 m^3 (51,800 conifers) for the wood-processing industry and the rest for fuel.

Timber is harvested by private individuals or firms. On the proposal of the regional forestry offices, the State Department of Forestry can change the 10-year forest use plan if protective measures are necessary (additional sanitary cut).

Industrial production (primary processing of wood; paper industry and especially the construction wood industry) is declining owing to the decrease in traditional markets (mainly Russian Federation) and to the obsolete technology that is still used. Some wood-processing sectors have decreased their production 20-fold. There are no strategic plans for improving this situation. After the break-up of the Soviet Union, the loss of cheap wood imports forced timber processors to harvest Georgian forests. There is also a highly visible trade in illegally harvested timber, with trucks hauling unrecorded high-quality beech logs across the border, but this accounts for only 6% of the total estimated harvest. The most immediate threat to Georgia's forests is the harvesting of fuelwood. Declining GDP, rising poverty and the disruptions in the supply of fossil fuels have boosted the use of fuelwood. At present, nearly 60% of the annual forest harvest (or about 720,000 m^3) is unrecorded fuelwood.

The forest sector made up 4-5% of GDP during the period of central planning, but there are no reliable statistical data for this sector at the moment. The same is true for the trade (export) of wood. Turkey is the main importer of Georgian wood, but statistical data from both countries are quite different. A large quantity of wood goes there illegally. Most timber (except for firewood) is used by the Ministries of Construction and Communal Economy for building; furniture production took 20% and packaging 14%.

Forest products other than wood are also an important exploited resource. Picking forest fruits, mushrooms, medicinal plants and other products for personal use is allowed. In some cases this is an important source of income for the local population.

Hunting

Hunting is regulated by the 1996 Law on Wildlife. This Law permits hunting only in specially designated area (hunting reserves) and on the basis of a licence from the Animals Division of the Ministry of Environment and Natural Resources Protection's Department of Biodiversity. The Ministry is responsible for enforcing the hunting regulations. Hunting reserves are established on the basis of a comprehensive ecological, biological and economic study. The study is carried out by the proponent and it is intended to safeguard the sustainable use of game - and all biodiversity - in the hunting reserve, as well as to sustain the balance in the ecosystems. So far six hunting reserves have been established. They are controlled by the State Department for the Management of Reserves, Protected Areas and Hunting Farms.

The potential for hunting in Georgia is considerable, but it is also evident that wildlife populations are currently very small, mainly as a result of intensive poaching. There are no reliable statistics on game and hunting from 1990 onward, but a broad overview of some game species is given in table 8.5.

Fishing

Fishing too is regulated by the 1996 Law on Wildlife. According to this Law, fishing for personal needs (recreation and sport) is permitted in all water bodies, including the Black Sea continental shelf. Restrictions apply only to water systems in natural reserves and other protected areas, which require a special licence. The Department of Biodiversity's Fishing Division issues these licences, as well as commercial fishing licenses. The fishing of all sturgeon and salmonid species and marine mammals is banned.

The fishing industry is not developed in Georgia and there is no appropriate infrastructure for fish processing. Consequently and as a result of the loss of traditional markets for raw fish, the total annual catch collapsed, from more than 100,000 tons in 1990 to almost nothing in 1992. However, the pressure on fish populations has not eased since illegal fishing has increased significantly. Although the fish catch is regulated by existing legislation, enforcement is very weak. For example, the number of commercial fish species in the Black Sea had dwindled to 3-4 species by 1990, down from 24 in 1960.

Another threat to fish and other organisms in the inland waters and the Black Sea is pollution. Although the economic collapse of the 1990s has resulted in a tremendous drop in industrial production, transport via the Black Sea has had a very negative effect on the fauna (see chapter 7 on water management).

Exploitation of wild flora and fauna species

The economic and social importance of wild plants and animals has increased during the past decade owing to the total collapse of the country's economy. The picking of wild medicinal plants and wild fruits and the catching of game and other animals for individual consumption, trade or export are a significant additional economic activity for many people. More than 150 tree and shrub species produce fruits, berries, nuts and bark. Among the 100 species of edible mushrooms, only 12-15 are regularly used. There are more than 60 native trees and bushes used in veterinary medicine and more than 110 woody species are used in medicine. In addition, a great number of indigenous medicinal plants are used for treating people and animals. Georgia's forests are also rich in honey, ethereal and decorative plants.

Table 8.5: Population and density of game animals according to the 1987-88 inventory

Species	Population	Density (per 1,000 ha)
Bear	6,000	3.0
Boar	5,000	3.0
Deer	1,100	0.7
Roe deer	12,000	6.0
Wolf	3,000	1.0
Fox	26,000	9.0
Hare	34,000	12.0
Squirrel	40,000	20.0
Marten	22,000	11.0
Muskrat	65	
Duck	6,000	
Partridge	14,000	35.0
Grey partridge	5,000	5.0
Black grouse	12,000	20.0

Source: State Department of Forestry, 2000.

The use of plant products by people is free of charge and allowed even in protected areas. Some of the medicinal herbs and species that are included in the red book of Georgia are also used, but this does not seem to be the most important threat to biodiversity. There are no enterprises for processing mushrooms and berries. Exploitation of wild animals and fish is more serious (see above).

The regulation of trade (especially export) is governed by the Convention on International Trade in Endangered Species of Wild Fauna and Flora (CITES), to which Georgia is a party. The Ministry of Environment and Natural Resources Protection issues licences (about 80 were issued in 2000) for the species listed in the Convention's annexes. An important trade exists in endemic snowdrop and cyclamen species, for which the quota is 15 million plants and 300,000 tubers respectively, including cultivated plants.

Impact on biodiversity from other sectors

Water quality is threatened not only by industry, but also by mining, municipal waste water and agricultural run-off. Opencast mining of non-ferrous metals, manganese, coal, gravel, sand and quartz has prospects for future development. Consequently, the threat of pollution to rivers and the Black Sea, as well as land degradation and local soil pollution still exists (see chapter 9 on mining, industry and environment). Energy is an important sector with a negative impact on biodiversity. Hydropower is considered the most important energy resource in Georgia. The use of hydropower instead of coal or other fuel reduces air pollution, but it leads to habitat degradation and conversion and watercourse fragmentation (fish migration) (see chapter 10 on energy and environment).

The permanent shortage in energy supply has resulted in widespread illegal logging for firewood close to the settlements. Not even parks were spared.

In Georgia road and railway transport are not very well developed. There are almost no highways, which means that transport is not a significant threat to biodiversity at present (see chapter 13 on transport and environment). However, oil and gas pipelines that pass through Georgia are a possible threat to biodiversity.

8.3 The framework for biodiversity and forestry protection

Policies and strategies

The Ministry of Environment and Natural Resources Protection, and its Department of Biodiversity, are responsible for establishing, promoting and implementing policies and strategies for biodiversity conservation and the sustainable use of natural resources. The main policy goal is to increase the percentage of protected areas and to include different ecosystem types and bio-corridors in the system. The Ministry of Environment and Natural Resources Protection is also determined to protect species outside the protected areas by establishing a system of quotas, which will safeguard the sustainable use of biological resources. It is responsible for issuing licences and permits for the use of these resources. However, the implementation of this policy is very weak (especially monitoring and control) owing to the lack of finance, except for the protected areas' planning and the designation of new ones, which receive foreign donations. The Ministry of Environment and Natural Resources Protection also shares responsibility for forestry policy and strategic plans with the State Department of Forestry. This is stipulated in the Forest Code and mainly concerns the protection of the non-timber forest products and protected forests.

The National Environmental Action Plan (2000) gave adequate priority to both biodiversity and forestry. The following priorities were envisioned:

For forestry:
- Preserving the diversity of forest ecosystems;
- Ensuring the stable regeneration of forest resources;
- Improving the relevant legal base;
- Training persons in sustainable management, ensuring better social and economic conditions for staff;
- Reforming the forestry system by making it independent from entrepreneurial activity;
- Providing conditions which will attract private investments into forestry.

For biodiversity:
- Conservation, e.g. preservation of rare and endangered species in bio-reserves;
- Creation of a genetic fund for wildlife;
- Sustainable use of renewable natural resources;

- Reproduction - breeding of rare and endangered species and their introduction into nature.

The National Biodiversity Strategy and Action Plan has been drawn up, but it has still not been approved. It is being reviewed by the Ministry of Environment and Natural Resources Protection. Its priorities are species conservation, improvement of the legislation, research and monitoring, hunting and fishing, agriculture and agro-biodiversity and enlarging of protected areas.

For forestry, there is no strategic document, although this is the goal of the World Bank project on forest development. The Red Data Book and red lists are very old and outdated. The Ministry of Environment and Natural Resources Protection intends to issues new ones.

Legal framework

The basis of Georgia's environmental legislation is the 1995 Constitution. It states that everyone is entitled to live in a healthy environment and to use natural resources but is obliged to protect them. It stipulates the State's obligation to ensure the rational use of natural resources. All international treaties ratified by Parliament become part of domestic legislation.

The 1996 Law on Environmental Protection calls for the preservation of biodiversity and states that activity should not lead to irreversible degradation of biodiversity. Regarding nature protection, the Law also specifies that environmental impact assessment should be compulsory in the initial phase of projects, programmes or activities.

Georgia has developed extensive nature protection legislation. All laws foresee numerous bylaws and regulations. Few have been adopted, making enforcement complex and difficult. In fact, the enforcement of all laws is very weak, not only because of the unfinished legal framework (vertical regulations), but also because of the overall economic situation.

The following legislation is relevant to biodiversity and forestry management; other laws on water, agriculture and air indirectly affect nature protection and biodiversity:
- The Law on Plant Protection (1994);
- The Law on Protected Area System (1996);
- The Law on State Ecological Expertise (1996);
- The Law on Environmental Permits (1996);

- The Law on Wildlife (1996);
- The Law on Creation and Management of Kolkheti Protected Area (1998);
- The Forest Code (1999);
- Presidential Decree No. 280/2001 on Coordinated Planning and Implementation of Ongoing and Prospective Programmes Related to Bojomi-Kharagauli National Park and its Supporting Zone;
- The Tax Code (1997);
- The Administrative Violation Code (1984).

Georgia has signed almost all worldwide conventions and agreements on biodiversity conservation, as well as regional and bilateral (including Black Sea) conventions and treaties (see chapter 4 on international cooperation). Georgia is in the process of ratifying the Bern Convention and the Cartagena Protocol on Biosafety. An ongoing GEF-UNEP project is considering the drafting of national legislation on genetically modified organisms and biosafety.

The implementation of these conventions is the responsibility of the Division of Conventions of the Ministry of Environment and Natural Resources Protection's Department of Biodiversity. Georgia has been a strong advocate of enlarging the lists of species protected by these conventions. It has proposed more than 120 species to the three different agreements of the Bonn Convention and many species to CITES. However, actual implementation of the conventions is very weak owing to the lack of finance. Georgia has ratified the Agreement on the Conservation of Cetaceans of the Black Sea, Mediterranean Sea and Continuous Atlantic Area and is implementing it.

Institutional arrangements

The Ministry of Environment and Natural Resources Protection is the national body responsible for establishing, promoting and implementing the policies and strategies for nature protection (including forests), biodiversity conservation, and the use of natural resources (flora and fauna). While forest management has been with the State Department of Forestry, the protection of forests, control and policy remains the responsibility of the Ministry of Environment and Natural Resources Protection. Its Department of Biodiversity (20 staff in six Divisions: Forestry, Protected Areas, Fishery, Wild Animals, Plant Protection and Conventions) is responsible for coordinating nature conservation activities, drawing up the policies and strategies, proposing measures and normative acts, participating in the approval of ecological impact studies and assessments, and applying legal measures concerning the sustainable use of biodiversity components. The Ministry of Environment and Natural Resources Protection (Department of State Ecological Expertise and Environmental Permitting) is responsible for issuing licences for natural resources use and setting quotas in cooperation with scientific bodies.

It is difficult to coordinate protection and control measures as the responsibilities of the State Department of Forestry and the State Department for the Management of Protected Areas overlap. The State Department of Forestry has direct responsibility for improving the ecological and economic efficiency of forest production, to support scientific research, to make proposals concerning the implementation of anti-monopoly and privatization policy in the forestry sector, to draw up an inventory of the State forest resource base in collaboration with the Ministry of Environment and Natural Resources Protection, to regulate resource use, to draft legislative and normative acts and initiate projects for the control of forests and, to a certain extent, for protected forest areas. The State Department for the Management of Protected Areas is directly responsible for the administration and control of the protected areas. As already mentioned, however, the lack of money undermines the enforcement of all these responsibilities. Besides the main State policy for transferring forest exploitation into private hands, there is also a debate on transferring ownership of the Caucasus forests from the State to lowest possible local government level, the so-called *sakrebulo* (local communities, lower level than municipality).

Regional offices have direct responsibilities for control in nature protection, periodically monitoring, surveying the enforcement of management plans, issuing authorizations, and identifying affected areas.

Several research institutes and the University of Tbilisi are involved in the work of the Department of Biodiversity. They participate in the drawing-up of strategic documents whenever necessary. They are also part of the decision-making process when the Ministry of Environment and Natural Resources Protection (Department for Biodiversity) has to set quotas or issue licences.

There are many non-governmental organizations (NGOs) in Georgia dealing with biodiversity protection. Some are very effective in carrying out projects and their influence is considerable. There is a constant brain drain of well-trained and experienced experts from the scientific institutions and the Ministry of Environment and Natural Resources Protection to NGOs, which offer more attractive salaries.

Monitoring

There is no biodiversity monitoring. Even the regular visits to different sites and protected areas have almost stopped owing to the lack of funds.

Economic instruments and financing

The main financial instrument is taxes on the use of natural resources, as stipulated in the Law on Wildlife and the Law on Plant Protection. They are payable in accordance with the Tax Code. Non-compliance fees are the second financial instrument. They are payable according to the Administrative Code. The regional offices of the Ministry of Environment and Natural Resources Protection or the State Department of Forestry collect these non-compliance fees. The most important problem for the biodiversity and forest protection institutions is that all taxes and fees go directly to the State budget and are not used for nature protection (see also chapter 2 on economic instruments, financing and privatization).

So far, the only way to raise money for nature conservation is external (international) funding. The severe and constant shortage of finance is the main obstacle to achieving biodiversity objectives.

Research and information

Georgia has sufficient well-trained scientific personnel. But the economic crisis is reflected in the scientific institutions as well. It has limited the research on biodiversity issues during the past ten years. However, the diversity of Georgia's fungi, flora and fauna has been quite well investigated. Now the most important problem is that most data are not updated and correlated to recent worldwide investigations.

The lack of a national information network and information databases is another major problem affecting biodiversity conservation. Monitoring, when performed, is adequate, but irregular or ad hoc, thus the related data are not processed efficiently and therefore cannot be used as a decision-making and management instrument.

Georgia has not developed a clearing-house mechanism, although this is an obligation for the implementation of the Convention on Biological Diversity.

8.4   Conclusions and recommendations

Georgia's share of the world's natural heritage is substantial. This extraordinary richness is worth protecting. Its potential lies in large undisturbed areas containing well-preserved ecosystems and rich natural resources. The minimum use of forest resources during the 1970s and 1980s due to the wood import from Russia has led to the preservation of virgin forests and to the successful recovery of Georgia's forest ecosystems.

However, there are many threats to this extraordinary natural heritage. They result from past activities, especially improper land use, and heavy pollution of the water ecosystems and soils. In the past decade industrial and agricultural pressures on nature have been reduced owing to the collapse in the economy, but other threats have become stronger (e.g. the unsustainable use of biological resources, especially poaching).

Georgia has developed an extensive legislation, covering all main aspects of biodiversity. Some of this legislation is outdated, but, in general, it tends to be harmonized with modern laws. Perhaps the biggest deficiency of the laws is the tendency to distribute responsibilities among several institutions, producing in that way overlapping jurisdictions. The legislative framework for nature protection is also very complex, with multiple laws, sub-laws and regulations.

Environmental departments have been established in some other sectoral ministries, but there is still a lack of coordination and intersectoral approach to biodiversity. The very complex issue of biodiversity conservation and the sustainable use of its resources have not been given adequate treatment and priority. The sector-specific environmental departments should be reinforced with biodiversity experts and staff should be trained in nature protection and more attention should be given to inter-ministerial coordination.

Attention needs to be given especially to clarifying and strengthening the activities of institutions responsible for biodiversity management. The Ministry of Environment and Natural Resources Protection is the national body responsible for establishing, promoting and implementing the policies and strategies for nature protection, including forests, biodiversity conservation, and the use of natural resources (flora and fauna), but forest management is the responsibility of the State Department of Forestry, an agency that reports directly to the President. Among other tasks, the State Department of Forestry is responsible for forestry policies, management plans and rehabilitation, and, to a certain extent, for forest protected areas. A second agency under the President, the State Department for the Management of Protected Areas, is responsible for the administration and control of the protected areas. Other government agencies also have some functions related to bioresource use, including the Ministry of Food and Agriculture, the Ministry of the Interior, the State Customs Department and the State Department for the State Board Protection. Duplication of functions and lack of coordination have created a situation marked by the ineffective use of financial, technical and human resources and poor implementation.

Recommendation 8.1:
The Government should rationalize the institutional responsibilities for biodiversity, nature conservation and protected areas. Among other tasks, the Ministry of Environment and Natural Resources Protection should have full responsibility for managing protected areas, including those located within forests.

Recommendation 8.2:
The Ministry of Environment and Natural Resources Protection should take the initiative to harmonize all existing legislation and regulations related to biodiversity, in an effort to simplify it and to rationalize implementation.

To date, there are no management plans, except for the inventories of most of the protected areas. The Law on Protected Areas stipulates that management plans must be drawn up. The current economic situation, along with the lack of institutional clarity, makes it difficult to enforce the law and implement protection measures. At present protection is

concretely implemented only in those protected areas that have gained international support through particular projects. The other protected areas are neglected. Among these neglected areas are less valuable areas that could serve as bio-corridors. These also need to be included in the overall strategic planning for protected areas.

Recommendation 8.3:
(a) The Ministry of Environment and Natural Resources Protection, together with the State Department for the Management of Protected Areas, should:
- *Develop a strategy for protected areas that, inter alia, implements the requirements of the Pan-European Biodiversity and Landscape Diversity Strategy, climate change action plans, and bio-corridors;*
- *Develop management plans for all protected areas as stipulated in the Law on Protected Areas;*

(b) The State Department of Forestry, in cooperation with the Ministry of Environment and Natural Resources Protection, should develop a general strategy for the sustainable use of forests, ensuring the accomplishment of all forest functions and their stable regeneration.

Monitoring of the different levels of biodiversity is the most complex task in integrated monitoring. It needs the involvement of numerous experts. However, it is essential for biodiversity protection. There is no biodiversity monitoring in Georgia, nor is it foreseen in existing policy documents.

Recommendation 8.4:
The Ministry of Environment and Natural Resources Protection should:
(a) Develop a system for biodiversity monitoring, based on existing scientific information and implemented by the regional environmental offices;
(b) Create an information system and database for biodiversity.

PART III: ECONOMIC AND SECTORAL INTEGRATION

Chapter 9

MINING, INDUSTRY AND ENVIRONMENT

9.1 Current situation in mining and industry

General overview

In the 1980s, Georgia's industrial sector accounted for 65% of gross domestic product (GDP). The situation changed dramatically in 1991, when Georgia started a difficult transition from a centrally planned to a market economy. The decline in industrial production reached its critical level between 1990-1995, when the average GDP growth rate plummeted from 0.5% to –26.9%. In 2000, industrial output accounted for 10% of GDP, whereas agriculture, trade and services accounted for the main share (figure 9.1). The mining sector also experienced a sharp decline. In the early 1990s, this sector accounted for 10% of GDP; currently this figure is reduced to only 2%. The problems faced by Georgia's industrial and mining sectors are attributed to a combination of factors such as inefficient management, lack of investment in the modernization of enterprises, the energy crisis, the disruption of economic ties between the former Soviet republics, and civil war.

Signs of industrial revival have appeared since 1995, when Georgia achieved positive GDP growth, after political stabilization and the introduction of legal and economic reforms. Industrial output in 2000 increased by 10.8% compared to 1999, and by 50.2 % compared to 1995.

Mineral resources and mining

Georgia is relatively well endowed with mineral resources (see figure 9.2), and its mining industry experienced a period of development between 1960 and 1990. Mineral production has significantly decreased since 1990. Some mines ceased operations; others are still operating, but at a low capacity (see table 9.1). The Madneuli complex (JSC Madneuli), a copper-barite polymetallic deposit, where barite, copper and a range of subproducts, including gold and silver, are mined, is an exception. About 1 million tons of ore

are extracted annually, and high-quality copper concentrate is produced for exports. In addition, gold is extracted from accumulated tailings in Madneuli using modern techniques. Georgia was a major producer of manganese from the Chiatura complex during the Soviet period, producing 5.37 million tons of manganese concentrate in 1980. At present, production has fallen to only 63,100 tons per year (see table 9.2). The manganese is used domestically for ferroalloy production at the Zestafoni ferroalloys plant, which has been adversely affected by the lack of raw material supply from the Chiatura mine. Small amounts of iron ore were mined in the Tkibuli-Shaori deposit. Lead and zinc were mined at the Kvaisi lead-zinc deposit, and arsenic was mined from the Lukhumi and the Tsansa deposits. These mines are currently out of operation. Georgia produces a range of industrial minerals, including bentonite, diatomite, talc and zeolites. Decorative stones for use as building materials are mined at more than 100 deposits, and there is also mining of semiprecious stones. Many clay deposits as well as high-quality quartz sand and sand and gravel deposits are developed for the production of bricks and ceramic products. Georgia also has abundant mineral water reserves, which are characterized by unique properties such as those from Borjomi, Ajaria-Trialeti, and Tskhaltubo.

The country also produces coal, oil and natural gas. There are two refineries, one at Batumi and a smaller one in Sartichala (GAOR). Hard and brown coal deposits occur in Tkibuli-Shaori, Tkvarcheli and Akhaltsikhe, with total reserves of 473.3 million tons. The largest coal deposit is Tkibuli-Shaori, which alone contains 378 million tons of hard coal with an ash content of 10-12%. Georgia possesses limited oil and gas reserves, which amount to 11.4 million tons and 82 million m^3 (estimated on 1 January 2001), respectively. Its importance for the world energy market is as a potential oil transit centre between the hydrocarbon-rich Caspian Sea countries and western markets. Nevertheless, Georgia has taken steps to increase domestic oil production and has negotiated several production-sharing agreements and joint ventures, mostly in the Kura basin east of Tbilisi, as well as in the Black Sea region. Gas deposits are small and unexplored, and the country must import a large share of its natural gas. The Georgian authorities have estimated that, between 2001 and 2005, US$ 453 million will be invested in oil and natural gas exploration and production in Georgia by the existing joint-venture companies. Although the current production level of mineral commodities is low, there is a recent growth in the crude oil and gas output, as well as in the manganese, copper and non-metal ores production (see table 9.2).

Figure 9.1: Structure of GDP, 2000

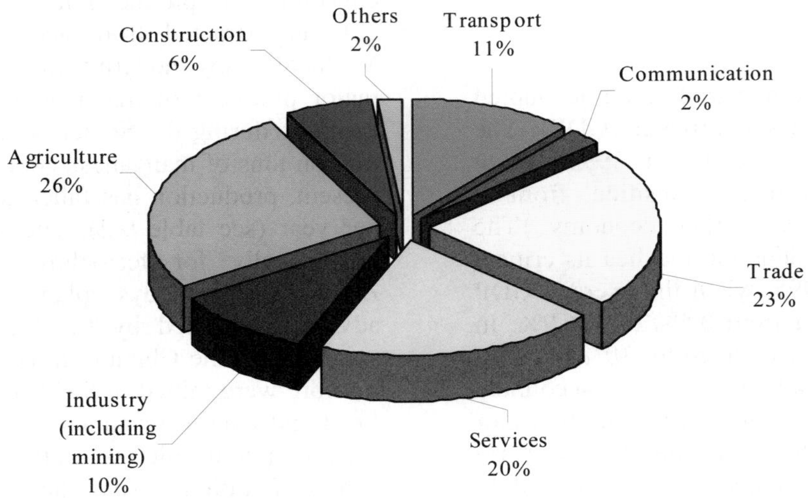

Source: Statistical Year Book of Georgia, 2001.

Table 9.1: Mineral reserves and major mining facilities (thousand tons, except when indicated)

Commodity	Major operating entities	Estimated reserves*	Location of main facilities	Status
Manganese, ore (mill. tons)	Chiatura complex	226	Chiatura region	Small scale operation
Copper, ore	Madneuli complex	97,970	Bolnisi region	Operating
Gold (kg)	Quartzite joint-venture	48,247	Madneuli deposit	Operating
Lead-zinc, ore	Kvaisi deposit	2,851	Kvaisi region	Out of operation
Arsenic, ore	Lukhumi deposit	150	Upper Racha region	Out of operation
	Tsana deposit	335	Lower Svanetiya region	Out of operation
Barite	Chordi deposit	1,862	Onis raioni	Out of operation
Bentonite	Gumbri and Askana deposits	10,006	Gumbri and Askana regions	Small scale operation
Diatomite	Kisatibi deposit	7,808	Kisatibi region	Out of operation
Coal (mill. tons)	Tkvarcheli, Tkibuli-Shaori and Akhltsikhe deposits	473	Tkvarcheli, Tkibuli and Akhltsikhe regions	Small scale operation
Petroleum, crude (mill. tons)	About 60 wells accounting for 98% of output	11	Mainly in Supsa, Mirzaani and Teleti regions	Operating

Sources : Department of Mineral Resources and Mining Protection, Ministry of Environmental and Natural Resources Protection; Mining Industry of Georgia in a Free Market Environment, Eds. Tvalchrelidze A. and Nishikawa Y., 2002; and Levine R. Mineral Industry of Georgia, 2000.

Note : *Mineral reserves were estimated using the Soviet methodology, which is not comparable with western methods.

Figure 9.2: **Map of principal deposits of metallic minerals**

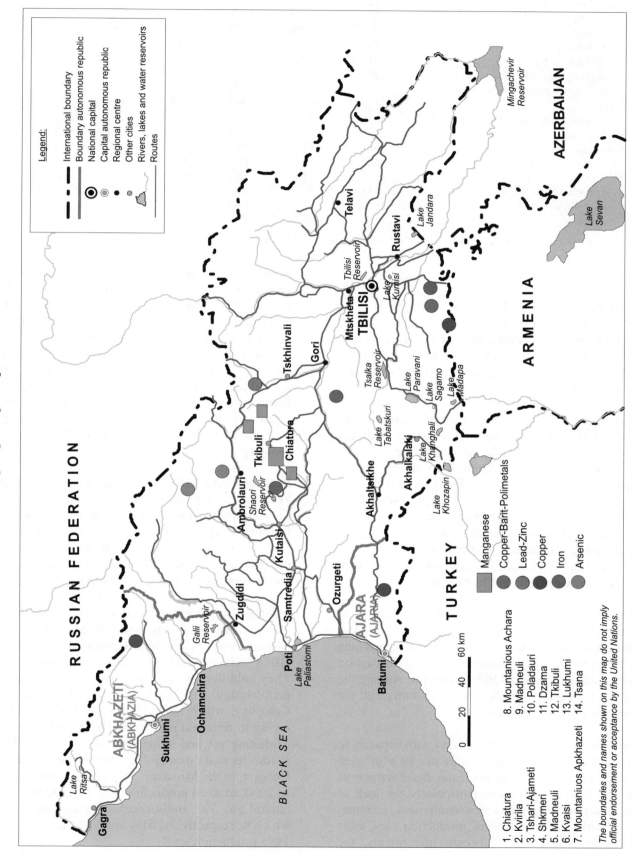

The boundaries and names shown on this map do not imply
official endorsement or acceptance by the United Nations.

Table 9.2: Production of selected mineral and industrial commodities

Commodity	1995	1996	1997	1998	1999	2000
Coal, thousand tons	42.6	22.5	4.6	14.7	12.0	7.3
Petroleum, thousand tons						
Crude:	42.7	127.9	133.8	119.2	91.3	109.5
Refined:	38.7	18.7	30.4	40.1	59.1	31.7
Natural gas, million m^3	3.3	3.3	..	..	..	79.5
Manganese, thousand tons	41.9	101.9	14.2	16.0	54.9	63.1
Copper, concentrate, thousand tons	..	5.1	4.1	6.0	7.2	8.0
Gold, kg	..	500.0	700.0	700.0	2,043.0	2,924.0
Construction materials, thousand m^3	141.9	179.1	211.8	446.2	267.9	281.0
Cement, thousand tons	59.0	85.0	94.1	198.6	341.4	347.7
Bread and bakery products, thousand tons	296.4	262.3	198.7	172.5	113.6	111.3
Wine, thousand decalitres	3,669.6	2,282.6	3,121.3	2,303.8	1,939.3	1,816.1
Beer, thousand decalitres	652.9	475.8	785.0	971.3	1,257.6	2,345.0
Synthetic ammonia, thousand tons	65.6	93.2	102.1	77.5	126.6	136.2
Steel, thousand tons	88.4	82.7	103.2	56.4	7.0	0.1
Trucks, units	209.0	95.0	82.0	39.0	38.0	44.0

Sources: Statistical Year Book of Georgia, 2001; and Levine R. and Wallace G. Mineral Industry of Georgia, 2001.

Industrial activities

After the collapse of the Soviet Union, most large industrial enterprises in Georgia stopped functioning or disintegrated into small ones. Industrial output is currently divided as follows: manufacturing (54.71%), energy (38.71%), and mining (6.58%).

More than half of the industrial facilities are concentrated in three cities and their surroundings: Tbilisi, Rustavi and Kutaisi. These areas have traditionally employed about two thirds of the industrial work force and produced more than 66% of the country's industrial output. Nowadays, Georgia's industry is in a precarious state, and has to deal with severe energy shortages, obsolete techniques, inefficient equipment, and lack of investment. Consequently, most enterprises were closed or are operating at low capacity.

Within the city of Tbilisi alone there are chemical plants (e.g. rubber goods, polymeric vessel, pharmaceutical production), aircraft and machine manufacturing, production of construction materials, and food and light industries. Among the largest enterprises are the Aircraft Factory and the Georgia Coca-Cola Bottlers.

Georgia has a steel mill in Rustavi with capacity to produce 1.5 million metric tons per year of steel and other products. The plant has faced numerous problems in recent years, particularly the lack of raw material supply and new equipment, resulting in a sharp decline in steel production (see table 9.2). Recently, due to foreign investments, the Rustavi Metallurgical Plant has restarted operations, but at a low capacity (3-4%). The Rustavi JSC "Azoti" is the largest chemical plant in Georgia. This plant accounted for 80% of all production of the subsector in 1990, and for 99.9% in 2000. It is currently operating at 30% of its capacity, producing mainly fertilizers for agriculture. There is also a cement plant in Rustavi founded in 1956. It produces cement from limestone and clays using the "wet" technology. This plant is currently operating at 20-25% of its capacity.

In Kutaisi, the JSC Kutaisi Automobile Plant, the Zestafoni Ferroalloys Plant and the JSC Chiaturamanganese are the biggest enterprises in the area. They are facing the same problems as the other industrial complexes of the country, although the Zestafoni Ferroalloys Plant was less affected and is currently working at 50% of its capacity.

Most of the petroleum companies operating in Georgia are joint ventures formed with foreign partners, such as Frontera Resources, Ioris Valley, GBOC-Ninotsminda, Anadarko and GeoGeroil. They hold licences to explore and exploit potential petroleum fields. Saknavtobi is the State Oil Company, which has currently reduced operations owing to financial problems. These companies are exploiting oil and some natural gas from 15 oil fields located mostly in eastern and western Georgia, in the Mirzaani, Teleti and Supsa regions. In 2000, total oil production was 109,500 tons, and natural gas 79.5 million cubic metres (table 9.2), which is, respectively, 61% and 96% more than the 1995 production level.

Large parts of State enterprises were privatized or transformed into joint-stock companies. In 2000, 87.5% of privatized enterprises were small companies and 12.5% were large and medium-size companies (table 9.3). Most small and medium-size private enterprises were developed in the food and light industry subsectors, which account for almost 80% of all manufacturing enterprises, as for example the "Kazbegi" beer production, the "Martin Bauer" tea processing and the "Isani-Kartu" shoe manufacturing plants. The privatization of large enterprises, however, progresses at a slow pace, mainly owing to problems related to their ownership, previous debts, legal transparency and lack of internal restructuring (see also chapter 2 on economic instruments, financing and privatization).

9.2 Environmental pressures on nature

Pollution from mining activities

Most Georgian mineral deposits are exploited using the opencast method, which leads to the degradation of fertile topsoil and the pollution of surface water. Moreover, exploitation equipment and processing technologies are outdated, contributing to the unsustainable use of the country's mineral resources. It is estimated that an area of 11,300 hectares is currently degraded due to mining. The management of old and new tailings from mining and processing of metal and non-metal ores, notably manganese, copper and coal, are also environmental issues. If tailings are not properly managed, they become sources of dust, soil, surface water and groundwater pollution by heavy metals and other toxic substances used for extracting ores. Some tailing deposits are located in active seismic zones, such as those from coal and arsenic mining, where local communities and the environment are exposed to a serious risk of accident. In Soviet times, mining waste accounted for 70% of total accumulated waste in Georgia, corresponding to 45.2 million tons.

At the Madneuli open-pit copper mine, acid mine drainage pollutes the nearest river system with copper, lead and zinc (see box 9.1). In addition, seepage from tailing deposits can contaminate soils and groundwater with heavy metals and other harmful substances (e.g. cyanide used for gold extraction). This poses a serious threat to human health, since groundwater is frequently used as a source of drinking water in Georgia. Similar problems exist in the Chiatura manganese mines, where mine waste water containing high amounts of suspended solids is directly discharged into the Kvrila river, which flows to the Rioni river and then to the Black Sea. The Chiaturamanganese company used to treat mine waste water mechanically before 1991; however, an earthquake has damaged the facilities and waste water is no longer treated. In the 1980s, some land was rehabilitated in the Chiatura mining region. Ore exploitation and transport are also sources of air pollution with a typical manganese black dust. Approximately 16,000 tons of arsenic-rich tailings located in Racha (Uravi) have been abandoned without any regard to environmental protection. These tailings are not only sources of soil, surface and groundwater pollution with hazardous arsenic and heavy metals, but they also constitute a threat to the local inhabitants' health, since they are deposited on the bank of the Lukhumi river. Accumulated waste from coal mining and processing amounts to 5 million tons. Coal exploitation in the Tkibuli region is of environmental concern also because of methane emissions from coal layers. These emissions were reduced from 140.7 tons in 1999 to 89.96 tons in 2001, reflecting the decline of the coal mining industry. The coal joint-stock company Tkibulnakhshiri has old and ineffective treatment facilities for coal mining waste water, which are currently out of operation. This waste water containing considerable amounts of suspended solids has been continuously discharged into the Tkibuli river.

Table 9.3: Number of privatized industrial enterprises

	1993	1994	1995	1996	1997	1998	1999	2000
Small enterprises	1,312	1,370	4,699	2,238	1,496	1,928	1,450	883
Large and medium enterprises (transformation to joint-stock companies)	23	554	276	152	92	44	42	126
Total	1,335	1,924	4,975	2,390	1,568	1,972	1,492	1,009

Source: Statistical Year Book of Georgia, 2001.

Box 9.1:   The Madneuli mining and processing complex, Bolnisi region

The Madneuli non-ferrous metal (copper, lead, zinc, barite and gold) deposit was discovered in 1956 and is one of the largest in the Caucasus. It has been exploited since 1975. In 1996 it became a joint-stock company (JSC Madneuli). Although Madneuli produces high-quality copper concentrate, which is exported mainly to Bulgaria, Turkey, the Russian Federation, Yemen and the Islamic Republic of Iran, about 75-80% of its fixed capital asset is obsolete and new technologies for copper exploitation are required. About 12.5 million tons of gold-containing overburden rocks from open-pit operations have accumulated in the Madneuli mine area. In 1994, a Georgian-Australian joint venture – "Quartzite" – was established to extract gold using the "in situ" cyanide leaching method. Seven million tons of materials containing 1.3 g of gold per ton have been already processed.

The mine is located in an agricultural region where about 20,000 to 30,000 people live. Local products, mainly vegetables, are supplied to the inhabitants of Tbilisi and its surroundings. The local environment is very degraded and arable land is becoming useless. The design of the mine and processing operation includes a closed water circuit. However, during the periods that the mine has been shut down, waste water was discharged directly into the river, without pretreatment. Also, open-pit acid water containing heavy metals pollutes the Kura's tributaries. In 1992, the copper content in the Kazretula river was 220 times higher than legal standard and the zinc content was 65 times higher. There is no monitoring of groundwater in strategic places near the tailing dam and the gold extraction operation, which uses a highly toxic sodium cyanide solution. Mining waste heaps are accumulated on more than 240 hectares near the open pit, exposed to wind and rain erosion. They are sources of dust, soil, surface and groundwater pollution. About 31 tons of dust containing heavy metals such as cobalt, chromium, cadmium, nickel, arsenic and others is emitted annually. Environmental rehabilitation of damaged areas is not common in Madneuli. So far, only 42 hectares have been recultivated and some trees have been planted on the walls of the tailing dam to avoid erosion. Owing to its huge volume (20.8 million tons) and area occupied (68.2 hectares), the tailing dam requires a more effective water balance monitoring to prevent accidental spills.

Oil exploration and exploitation have considerably increased in the past three years. However, environmental monitoring of these activities has not been carried out, making it difficult to assess the extent of related environmental problems. Soil contamination by oil products occurs during the exploitation of wells, refining and transport. Some 800 hectares of land are contaminated owing to oil leakage or accidental spills. There are also some abandoned wells that need urgent rehabilitation due to the continuous oil leakage, causing soil and groundwater pollution. Contamination of groundwater from oil extraction techniques that inject oil and gas waste into the wells is also of environmental concern since some sedimentary formations contain fresh, drinking or therapeutic water. The level of air emissions from oil exploitation and primary refining decreased 44% in 2001 compared to 1999. Most equipment is new and highly efficient because of foreign investment in the sector, resulting in a low emission level. But the problem of air pollution due to gas flaring remains. In addition, there is a growing risk of accidental oil spills with the rapid increase in oil exploration and exploitation in the country.

Environmental concerns in industry

During the economic downturn in the years following the break-up of the Soviet Union, the environment became less polluted because of the decline in industrial production. Air and water pollution considerably decreased and there was a general reduction in industrial waste. However, the industrial waste that was generated could not be properly disposed of because there were no special sites for this purpose, and water filters were not maintained.

The management of industrial waste, particularly hazardous waste, is a major environmental issue in Georgia. Currently, huge amounts of industrial waste are stored at industrial sites, dumped at landfills, or buried on sites for hazardous waste disposal ("polygons"). According to the State Agency for Oil and Gas, there are two specific sites for oil waste disposal, located in Rustavi and Sagaredjo. At the Rustavi site, about 6 ha of land are contaminated with oil products, which were partially treated with a bacteriological method and cultivated. According to 1990 data, 18 million tons of industrial waste have accumulated in Georgia (about 28% of total accumulated waste), of which 11.5 million tons are scrap metals from the Rustavi Metallurgical Plant. In addition, there is no waste recycling, which poses a serious problem for some industrial waste such as plastic materials and scrap metals. Consequently, huge amounts of this waste have been stored near their respective facilities. Concentrations of heavy metals and other hazardous substances significantly exceed limits in the upper soil layers of industrial zones. In the Kutaisi industrial area, 800,000 tons of industrial waste containing 40-45% of barium compounds occupy several hectares in the centre of the city. In the area of the Batumi oil refinery, more than

400,000 tons of acid tar have been stored. In Zestafoni, 368,000 tons of slag from ferroalloys production are accumulated (see also chapter 6 on waste management).

Industrial waste-water discharges, with inefficient or no treatment, are significant sources of surface water pollution with phenols, hydrocarbons, copper, manganese, zinc and nitrates, which all exceed permitted levels. Although surface water pollution has decreased in recent years, residual concentrations of heavy metals in bottom sediments are still high. Currently, about 20% of the industrial waste water is pretreated, but the existing treatment facilities are in a precarious state. They do not provide biological treatment, while mechanical treatment is inefficient. In the Batumi refinery, waste water containing more than 500 tons of oil waste was annually discharged into the Black Sea during the 1980s. The refinery's treatment plant for waste water containing oil products, which has been in a poor state for many years, is currently under reconstruction thanks to foreign investment. In the Zestafoni Ferroalloys Plant, total effluents have been reduced, but the mechanical waste-water treatment facility has been operating with very low efficiency. Consequently, significant amounts of toxic substances have been continuously discharged into the Rioni river system (see also chapter 7 on water management).

Industrial sources (excluding the energy sector) accounted for 30% of total air pollution in the 1980s. This figure decreased to less than 10% in 2001 owing to the economic crisis. Emission levels, notably greenhouse gas (GHG) emissions from chemicals, construction materials and food industries, decreased by a factor of 3.1, 3.7 and 3.3, respectively, in 2000 compared to 1990. It is worth noting that the metallurgical sector was the most affected due to the problems faced by the Rustavi Metallurgical Plant, with total GHG emissions reduced 884-fold. In the Zestafoni Ferroalloys Plant, GHG emissions decreased by a factor of only 4.6, indicating a relative viability of this subsector (see also chapter 5 on air management).

9.3 Policy objectives and management

The policy framework in mining and industry

There are no policies or strategies for the sustainable management of mineral resources in Georgia. Basic principles are provided by the 1996 Law on Mineral Resources, but specific mechanisms have not yet been developed. The national environmental policy includes the protection and rational use of mineral resources. Some projects addressing environmental issues in mining, such as the development of regulations for mining waste management and the Ministry of Environment and Natural Resources Protection staff training in assessing environmental impacts from the exploration, exploitation and transport of oil and gas resources, are included in the NEAP. However, their implementation has been rather slow. The Mining Promotion Master Plan, developed by the Ministry of Economy, Industry and Trade in cooperation with the Japan International Cooperation Agency (JICA), was finished at the end of 2002. It is a long-term plan to be implemented in 15 years, with three main stages: (i) mining reconstruction, (ii) development, and (iii) growth.

Measures for the reconstruction and development of the Tkibuli coal mines are set in the Programme for the Reconstruction and Development of the Coal Industry in Georgia. This programme was developed by Saknakhshiri (State Coal Company), accepted by the Ministry of Fuel and Energy, and approved by presidential order in August 1997. Some coal mines were closed and one was kept in operation, in accordance with the plan. Other measures foreseen by this plan could not be implemented so far owing to the lack of funds. In 2003, 2.2 million lari (approximately US$ 1.1 million) will be allocated from the State budget as subsidies, mostly for salaries, for the Tkibuli coal mines. Recently, the evaluation of these mines by foreign experts indicated that their exploitation is not profitable due to the complex geology of the deposit and the ore characteristics.

Box 9.2:   The Rustavi JSC "Azoti" Plant

The Rustavi JSC "Azoti" joint-stock company is the largest chemical plant in Georgia, employing 3200 people and with an annual production capacity of 400,000 tons of ammonia. The plant produces nitric acid, which is neutralized by gaseous ammonia to form ammonium nitrate, a nitrogen fertilizer used in agriculture. Also, pure sodium cyanide is produced by processing mercury caustic soda. It is used in the hydrometallurgy of precious metals, notably gold and silver.

Today, the plant is in a difficult situation, operating at 30% of its capacity and affected by the country's severe energy crisis. Its equipment is old and the technology used is obsolete, dating from 1979-1980, when the company started operations. Consequently, the plant is a large energy consumer. In 2000, production decreased by 19.1% compared to 1990, while the energy consumption per unit of product increased, resulting in a decrease in energy efficiency. GHGs (CO_2, CO, SO_2, NO_2, NH_3, NO_x, NH_4NO_3, $NaCN$, HCN) and dust emissions generally increased in the 1990-2000 period, but no more than by 2%. However, emissions of toxic substances exceeded their recommended values by 2-14%. The company has a waste-water treatment plant, which is currently out of operation. In the past five years, the treatment plant has worked at a rate of 30-40%. Although there is a lack of computers and analytical equipment, the company's Division for Environmental Protection monitors the waste-water discharges and air emissions twice a day. In 2002 (January to October), 1,744,618 cubic metres of waste water containing large amounts of NH_4 were discharged in the Gardabani water treatment plant. The Rustavi JSC "Azoti" has developed a plan to modernize production, including the restoration of the nitric acid unit and the superheating of steam, and to increase the processing pressure at the ammonia synthesis unit. All these measures will increase energy efficiency and environmental protection, and are also important from the economic point of view. The costs of the planned measures are estimated at US$ 2.5 million, and the profit after their implementation is estimated at US$ 3.6 million per year, allowing the reimbursement of all costs in 5.3 months. However, lack of funds is hampering the implementation of this plan.

The main policy document for the development of industry is the Indicative Plan for the Social and Economic Development of Georgia in 2001-2005, which contains one specific section on industry. This document determines the principal aims and tools of the country's economic policy based on the principles of the market economy. Among the planned measures for industrial development, are:

- The development and implementation of support measures for the industrial sector's development and restructuring, by priority branches, and development of a related national programme;
- The improvement of the investment climate and creation of economic incentives to attract investors;
- The promotion of modern management systems at enterprises;
- The support of small enterprise development.

The legislative framework

Georgia has developed a legal framework for the use of its natural resources and environmental protection. The 1996 Law on Mineral Resources is the main legal instrument for the sustainable management of the country's mineral base. It addresses the rational use of minerals during exploration and mining, as well as the environmental requirements related to these activities. The Law also specifies the liability for environmental damage and rehabilitation;

nevertheless, it does not provide the necessary mechanisms to implement it. The oil and gas activities are regulated by the 1999 Law on Oil and Gas, which provides the basis for modern and environmentally sound oil and gas exploration, development and production, including off-shore operations. These regulations were prepared by the State Agency for the Regulation of Oil and Gas Resources, with the assistance of USAID.

The 1996 Law on Environmental Protection includes important provisions such as taxes based on the user-pays and polluter-pays principles, environmental insurance, economic incentives for environmental protection, environmental audit and management, and environmental requirements for privatization. The Law also requires industrial facilities to carry out self-monitoring and develop emergency response plans. Privatized industrial entities are obliged to enforce previous environmental commitments set for the former owner, according to the Law. However, implementation and enforcement of the Law are weak and lack specific mechanisms and regulations.

Other legal instruments used for the environmental management of mining and industry include: the 1999 Law on Ambient Air Protection, the 1994 Law on Soil Protection, the 1996 Law on Environmental Permits, the 1996 Law on State Ecological Expertise, the 1997 Law on Water, the

1998 Law on Hazardous Chemical Substances, and the 1999 Law on Compensation for Damage from Hazardous Substances.

The institutional framework

At present, the management of mining and industry is spread among different agencies. The Ministry of Environment and Natural Resources Protection's Department of Mineral Resources and Mining Protection is responsible for policy development and for issuing licences for mineral exploration and exploitation, except for oil and gas resources. It also controls companies' compliance with the Law on Mineral Resources and the efficient use of ore reserves. The State Agency for the Regulation of Oil and Gas Resources oversees oil and gas companies and issues the related exploration and exploitation licences. The State Department of Geology performs geological surveys and manages the country's geological fund. This Department has a groundwater monitoring network, but this activity as well as mineral exploration and mapping, have not been carried out for many years owing to the lack of funds.

The Ministry of Economy, Industry and Trade is the main institution responsible for the development and implementation of industrial policies in the country. Its Department of Industry is responsible for industry issues, and its Department of Social Affairs has a Division of Environment. Both are actively involved in sustainable industrial development matters, through regulations, policy development and projects. The State Inspection for Technical Supervision is responsible for safety regulations and inspections in mining and industry. It includes a main Department of Mining Inspection, a Division for Metallurgical Enterprise Supervision and a Division for Chemical Enterprise Supervision. Currently, there is no single institution responsible for the promotion of cleaner technologies and environmental management in industry.

The Ministry of Environment and Natural Resources Protection is in charge of environmental management in mining and industry. It issues environmental permits, draws up and implements policies, establishes environmental standards, carries out environmental monitoring, expertise and control, and manages the country's environmental information. The Department of

Emergency Situations of the Ministry of the Interior is responsible for the coordination and contingency plans in the event of industrial accidents, including mining spills.

Regulatory and economic instruments

The Department of Mineral Resources and Mining Protection issues permits for mineral resources use, after approval by the Interdepartmental Licensing Council. Environmental impact assessment (EIA) and State environmental expertise are essential for a permit. However, neither environmental management planning nor a financial insurance system (e.g. bank guarantee) for environmental rehabilitation after mining closure or accidental spills is required.

Permits for oil and gas companies are issued by the State Agency for the Regulation of Oil and Gas Resources. A range of activities require specific permits, such as well drilling, off-shore construction, abandonment, oil and gas waste injection, disposal and management facilities, and gas flaring and venting, according to the 2002 Regulations for Oil and Gas Operations in Georgia. Environmental impact assessment, including environmental protection, spill contingency, waste management and self-monitoring plans, is also necessary for obtaining a permit for oil and gas operations. In addition, environmental insurance is required for a bank guarantee to be used for environmental rehabilitation.

Environmental audits are rare in Georgia, and enterprises are not systematically subject to environmental audits before privatization. As a result, it is difficult to establish and implement formal agreements for environmental rehabilitation of past damage. No system of accreditation for companies performing EIA and environmental audits is yet in place.

Georgia has two main economic instruments to encourage better environmental practices in mining and industry: the tax on the use of natural resources and the tax on pollution with harmful substances, both adopted in the mid-1990s (see chapter 2 on economic instruments, financing and privatization). In general, the enforcement of the polluter-pays and user-pays principles has been weak. There are no economic incentives for investment in cleaner production or for waste recycling and reuse.

Fines are used for violations of the laws on mineral resource use and the environment. However, the revenues collected are not used for funding environmental activities since there are no institutional mechanisms to manage the collection and effective redistribution of those funds.

Environmental management in mining and industrial enterprises

Environmental management systems (EMS) do not constitute an integrated part of the mining industry management in Georgia at the moment and international environmental standards, such as ISO 14000 series and EMAS, are not promoted and diffused. The country does not have a single enterprise that holds an ISO 14000 certificate. Although the Law on Environmental Protection calls for the introduction of EMS and best available technology (BAT) in mining and industry, the lack of financial mechanisms for their implementation is hampering the process. In addition, the staff of the enterprises have no training on such methods and techniques to keep pace with international environmental practices. The petroleum industry, nevertheless, is making efforts to introduce environmental management in its operations, from exploration to conservation of resources, which is expressed through adequate and efficient regulations from the State Agency for the Regulation of Oil and Gas Resources that are now being implemented.

Introduction of cleaner production and international environmental standards

Georgia has done little to improve the framework conditions for the introduction of cleaner production. As economic reforms have been advancing at a slow pace, the impact that market pressure from world export markets exerts on Georgian companies remains weak, in terms of both environmental standards and competitiveness. The general situation is rather unfavourable for the introduction of cleaner production. Low levels of awareness of the economic potential of cleaner production among business decision makers, coupled with resource pricing below market prices and weak regulatory pressures on the environmental performance of companies contribute to this situation. Despite the current problems, a number of cleaner production and environmental management projects in Eastern Europe, the Caucasus and Central Asia have demonstrated that sometimes spectacular gains, both economic and environmental, can be

achieved. Successful demonstration projects were implemented in Estonia, Lithuania, the Russian Federation, Uzbekistan, and many other East European countries. The European Commission (EC) launched a programme in 2001 for developing cleaner production in three countries of Eastern Europe, the Caucasus and Central Asia, including Georgia. The programme has a total budget of €1.5 million. In addition, the Georgian Agency on Climate Change, with support of UNDP/GEF, prepared a detailed document called "Capacity building to assess technology needs, modalities to acquire and absorb them, evaluate and host projects", which analyses potential industrial sectors for the introduction of cleaner technologies with economic profit. In 2003, the Ministry of Environment and Natural Resources Protection will receive 18,000 lari (approximately US$ 9,000) from the State budget to implement a project aimed at introducing ISO 14000 standards in Georgia. So far, the country has no cleaner production projects under way.

9.4 Conclusions and recommendations

During the Soviet period, management was focused on economic growth and rapid industrialization, without proper consideration of environmental issues. Thus, Georgia's industry developed under an energy and resource-intensive regime, resulting in high levels of environmental pollution. The economic crisis reduced environmental pressure from industry. The main environmental problems in industry and mining are related to the use of outdated technologies, low efficiency or lack of pollution controls, and the disposal and treatment of waste accumulated around the facilities. Currently, there are no regulations applied to waste generation, reduction, disposal, storage and recycling. Moreover, the absence of environmental monitoring in Georgia makes it difficult to assess present and past pollution from industrial and mining activities. Waste composition and volume, and the extent of soil, surface and groundwater contamination, and its effects on human health are not known.

Recommendation 9.1:
The Ministry of Environment and Natural Resources Protection, in cooperation with the Ministry of Economy, Industry and Trade, should:
(a) Carry out a complete inventory of mining and industrial hot spots. The inventory should focus on the current state of facilities, equipment and technologies used, pollution prevention and control systems, and waste

management. A risk assessment should urgently be carried out for each mining and industrial hot spot;

(b) Carry out a study of the impacts of harmful mining and industrial emissions, effluents, and accumulated waste, on the surrounding environment and on human health. Priority should be given to hazardous mining tailings, especially those located in tectonic unstable areas. Particular attention has to be paid to the composition and amount of industrial waste, as well as to waste disposal, storage, recycling and reuse.

Recommendation 9.2:

The Ministry of Environment and Natural Resources Protection, in cooperation with the Ministry of Economy, Industry and Trade, should:

(a) Develop a special programme, including a financial mechanism, for the mitigation of priority environmental problems in mining and industry, based on reliable and updated information provided by the inventory (see recommendation 9.1);

(b) Draw up action plans and submit them to international donors in order to raise the necessary funds for their implementation.

Although Georgia has made efforts to integrate environmental objectives into mining and industrial management, progress has been slow. There are no strategies or policies in the mining sector defining concrete mechanisms for improving the situation, and the Law on Mineral Resources lacks modern and effective mining regulations. Reconstruction of the mining sector is, nevertheless, a matter of priority for the country's economic development. Economic recovery will inevitably lead to an increase in harmful emissions, waste-water discharges, and waste generation and accumulation. Moreover, the lack of policies promoting the minimization of waste generation at source, its treatment, recycling and reuse, aggravates the situation. Principles such as BAT, EMS, environmental audits, and environmental insurance, although stated in the Law on Environmental Protection, have not yet been implemented.

Recommendation 9.3:

The Ministry of Environment and Natural Resources Protection should:

(a) Consider developing a strategy to improve the environmental management of mineral resources and introduce better environmental practices in mining;

(b) Update the Law on Mineral Resources and harmonize it with international mining regulations;

(c) Encourage mining and industrial companies to carry out periodic environmental audits in order to evaluate and stimulate their performance and competitiveness;

(d) Develop a strategy for mining and industrial waste minimization, recycling and reuse, particularly for hazardous waste; and

(e) Provide adequate and effective staff training on these issues.

Cleaner production is a preventive environmental strategy aimed at reducing the costs of pollution and waste generation at source by implementing measures that are both environmentally sound and financially viable. The experience of the European Commission with cleaner production projects reveals that, on average, a 20% reduction in waste and emissions is achievable with nil investment. A further 10-20% reduction is possible with relatively small investments with payback periods of less than one to three years. In this process, Government's role and donor support are essential. At the same time, enterprises and their managers must make a commitment to improving their environmental performance continuously. With time, the process should be self-sustaining, driven by the commitment and interest of enterprises, and supported by an enabling policy and institutional framework. Current opportunities for cleaner production in Georgia appear to be greatest in the food and export-oriented industrial sectors. However, cleaner production policies are not developed in Georgia, and related education and training are non-existent.

Recommendation 9.4:

The Ministry of Environment and Natural Resources Protection in cooperation with the Ministry of Economy, Industry and Trade should:

(a) Set goals, establish policies and provide target assistance to promote the introduction of cleaner production. Support for cleaner production should be clearly focused on those sectors that are best disposed to implement and multiply such measures (e.g. food and export-oriented industries);

(b) As a first step, develop some demonstration projects, linked to a broad dissemination strategy, and implement them with financing acquired through international cooperation programmes and other sources.

Most industrial sectors need safety regulations, since the current ones are based on old Soviet directives that require updating. The State Inspection for Technical Supervision has developed new safety requirements according to international standards for the gas sector. However, safety regulations for other hazardous industrial sectors (e.g. chemical industry) have not been developed yet due to the lack of funds for this purpose. The "Azoti" nitrogen fertilizer plant is an example of an industrial risk spot. It is located in the city of Rustavi, an urban area with about 150,000 habitants. The plant produces ammonium nitrate and sodium cyanide, which are highly toxic. Their processing requires the application of effective safety and risk measures, which are currently not developed in Georgia. In the event of an industrial accident, the consequences for the local population and the environment would be catastrophic.

Recommendation 9.5:
The Ministry of Environment and Natural Resources Protection in conjunction with the State Inspection for Technical Supervision and the Department of Emergency Situations of the Ministry of the Interior should:

(a) *Introduce safety measures for hazardous industrial activities in accordance with the UNECE Convention on the Transboundary Effects of Industrial Accidents and the European Union's SEVESO II Directive in order to prevent industrial accidents, which may have severe consequences for the local population and the environment;*

(b) *Develop awareness and preparedness plans at a local level in industrialized regions to specify the roles of local institutions and the community for a prompt accident response, such as the UNEP Awareness and Preparedness for Emergencies at the Local Level (APPELL); and*

(c) *Urgently develop or update, as appropriate, emergency plans at high-risk industrial sites.*

Chapter 10

ENERGY AND ENVIRONMENT

10.1 Overview of energy production and consumption

Prior to 1991, Georgia, Armenia and Azerbaijan were integral parts of the Trans-Caucasian Interconnected Power System. After the collapse of the Soviet Union, Georgia entered into an energy crisis that still continues. The imported fuel and electricity that were 'free' under the interconnected power system now had to be paid for. Prices of gas and imported electricity increased suddenly to world market levels. In addition, the seasonal differences of Georgia's hydropower generation, which had previously been balanced with imported energy, could no longer meet the higher demand in winter with domestic thermal power. Huge arrears in payments for imported gas and electricity led to Georgia's supply being cut off.

Energy production

The installed capacity in Georgia is 4,700 MW, of which 2,700 MW was generated by hydropower plants and the balance by thermal power plants. In January 2002, only 1,700 MW of this capacity was used. The lack of fuel supply and maintenance of the thermal power plants led to their almost complete abandonment. Consequently, the share of hydropower in total energy generation increased from 53% in 1990 to 83% in 1996. In 1999 it fell back slightly, to 80%. Due to poor maintenance, hydropower plants work at 60% of their capacity. The distribution network is also in very poor condition. Losses in the distribution network are estimated to be 25%, including through illegal connections in the cities. Georgia does not have a nuclear reactor for electricity generating purposes.

Thermal power production

Georgia used to have three thermal power stations, of which one is only partially operational at the moment. The 220-MW Tkvarcheli thermal power station in the Abkhazia region was gas-fired. Due to the poor maintenance and the damage it suffered during the conflict there, the plant is not operational and most probably beyond economic rehabilitation. No information was obtained during the mission on the current environmental situation. The main thermal power plant in Georgia is the 1850-MW Gardabani plant near Tbilisi. The Gardabani station consists of 10 units, which are all in extremely poor condition. Two units are beyond rehabilitation; three units could potentially be rehabilitated, while two units are currently being rehabilitated. Only three units are operational, well below their design capacity. The first eight units date from 1962-1972 and are owned by the joint-stock company Tbilsresi. The two most recent units, each of 300 MW, were constructed between 1990 and 1992 and have been privatized. All units have been designed to use gas as their main fuel. Due to the high gas prices and interrupted gas supplies, some units have been adjusted to use fuel oil.

In the past, centralized heating systems based on imported natural gas were developed in the main cities. Tbilisi has one small combined heat and electricity generating plant, the Tetsi plant. This plant has a design capacity of 18 MW for electricity and 40 to 50 MW for heat, but it is not operational. Two of the three units are expected to be beyond repair. Due to the increased price of imported gas, supplies were stopped and the district heating and gas supply system collapsed completely at the beginning of the 1990s. For example, in Tbilisi, 42 gas-fuelled district boilers existed, but all are now out of operation. According to officials of the Ministry of Environment and Natural Resources Protection, rehabilitation of these boilers is not feasible. Part of the gas supply system is operational again in Tbilisi, but most households are still meeting their heating needs themselves.

Figure 10.1: Total consumption and production of electric energy

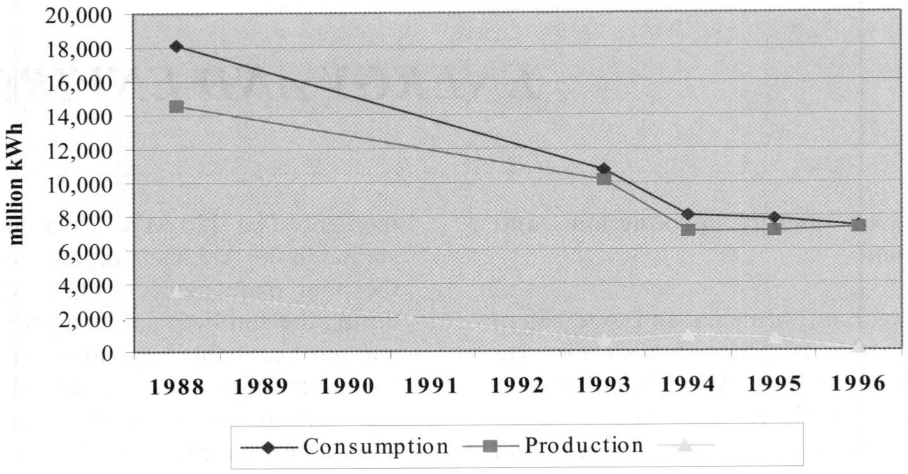

Source: Government of Georgia, 1999.
Note: No data for the years 1989 to 1992, therefore only the downward trend is shown.

Hydropower production

Georgia has a great potential for hydropower and is using approximately 25% of it already. According to Georgia's report to the United Nations Framework Convention on Climate Change, there are 60 hydropower plants with an annual projected output of 10 billion kWh. Currently, the Lajanuri, Khrami I and II, Vardnili, Vartsikhe and Enguri hydropower plants are being rehabilitated with financial assistance from EBRD, Germany and Japan. The 270-metre-high Enguri dam is the largest arch dam in the world. Its reservoir has a capacity of 1.1 billion m^3.

In 2000, the construction of a new hydropower plant (Khadori) started at the Alazani river. The installed capacity will be 24 MW, with an average annual generation of 140 million kWh. The Khadori dam is situated in the troubled Pankisi gorge and is regularly attacked. In 2001 a bridge was blown up, and in 2002 an attack was carried out with a grenade launcher.

It is estimated that there is potential for the construction of another 250 small, medium and big hydropower plants with an expected output of 30 billion kWh. Approximately 80 mini hydropower stations - with a combined capacity of 350 MW - could be constructed within one to two years. In addition to the Khadori hydropower plant, there are plans to develop two large hydropower plants. At the Enguri river, there is the potential to build a 700 MW (1.7 billion kWh) hydropower plant (Khudoni). Proposals for this construction were blocked by NGOs in the early 1990s, but plans have resurfaced, driven by the long-lasting energy crisis. Another large hydropower plant (Namakhvani) could be constructed on the Rioni river.

Wood, gas and kerosene for individual heating

Owing to the collapse of district heating and the unreliability of the electricity supply, many households had to look for substitutes for heating and hot water supply: wood from parks and nearby forests, and kerosene.

Solar, wind and biomass energy, and geothermal waters

Some feasibility and pilot studies have been carried out on the use of wind, biomass and solar energy. The technical potential for these renewable sources appears to be large, e.g., wind energy could generate 1 trillion kWh. The financial feasibility, however, is low, as even in many Western countries these energy sources are still subsidized to be competitive with fossil fuels.

An exception to this might be the application of geothermal waters for hot water supply and heating. Georgia is rich in geothermal waters and there are already a great number of wells, some of them as deep as 4000 m. It is estimated that 1.5 million persons could potentially be supplied with hot water and heating from geothermal waters (see box 10.1).

Box 10.1:   Geothermal waters for heating and hot water supply

The Global Environment Fund (GEF) and the German Bank for Reconstruction (KfW) are assisting Georgia in the development of geothermal waters for the supply of heating and hot water in Tbilisi. The project is part of a larger GEF project focusing on the removal of barriers to the increased use of renewable energy for local energy supply. The project identified 13 barriers in three categories: capacity and institution building, specific institutional and financial barriers in the power sector, and specific institutional and financial barriers in the heating sector. To overcome some of the financial barriers, a revolving renewable energy fund will be established to provide credit on favourable conditions. In Georgia, 156 geothermal wells were identified with a combined flow rate of 6,386 m^3/h and a thermal capacity of 402 MW. One of the most promising sites is situated in Tbilisi. The pilot project is aiming to supply approximately 20,000 residents of the Saburtalo district with hot water from the geothermal well. Its overall cost amounts to $12.85 million and the GHG reduction potential is estimated to be 0.5 Mt of CO_2 over 20 years.

Source: Global Environment Fund.

Energy consumption

Between 1990 and 1996 the share of industry in total electricity consumption decreased from 48% to only 12%, while that of domestic consumption increased from 16% to 52%. These trends can be explained by the complete collapse of the industrial sector after the break-up of the Soviet Union and Georgia's independence. During that same period, the district heating systems suffered from a lack of maintenance and interruptions in gas supplies owing to a steep increase in prices and ceased their operations. Households had to look for alternative resources to meet their energy needs, which led to a shift to electricity for heating and cooking. A survey carried out in the Saburtalo district of Tbilisi showed the following composition of sources used for heating and hot water: electric heaters (32%), kerosene (16%), gas heaters and stoves (43%) and fuelwood (9%). Depending on their characteristics (especially the supply of gas for cooking), other districts may have a different distribution. Especially in rural areas, the dominant source for heating and hot water supply is fuelwood (see figure 10.2).

According to the report submitted by Georgia to the World Summit on Sustainable Development in 2002, there are discrepancies between the demand projected by foreign experts and that projected by national experts. It is hard to establish the price elasticity for electricity as Georgia is characterized by a high-level of non-payment for utilities. Affordability and preparedness to pay play a major role in demand forecasts. A real balance between supply and demand has therefore not yet been struck.

Energy efficiency

The efficiency of energy resource use is extremely low. The energy efficiency of some of the power-generating facilities has been evaluated, but the energy efficiency of industrial facilities and households is unknown. In general, the output of these industrial facilities is low compared to their design capacity, leading to low energy efficiency. As there are not many large industries that are operational, no major efficiency improvements can be expected. However, since small and medium-sized enterprises and the service sector have been growing, there is room for energy-efficiency improvements in these sectors, as well as in households. Energy-efficiency improvements in countries in transition can often be achieved with little or no investment (win-win projects). Energy efficiency also has an impact on future energy demand – and planning – and is therefore of great importance to Georgia.

10.2   Environmental impacts of the energy sector

Energy production in Georgia has a number of negative environmental impacts, ranging from local air pollution to the depletion of natural resources and irreversible change of ecosystems.

Air pollution

The burning of fossils fuels (fuel oil, gas) in the district heating systems and thermal power stations used to be a major contributor to local particulate-matter (PM) pollution, acid rain and global warming. With the long-lasting economic and energy crisis the emissions of thermal power stations have drastically decreased, as can be seen from table 10.1. Since 1995, a slight increase in greenhouse gas (GHG) emissions can be observed. However, after the collapse of unit 10, one of the four working units of the Gardabani thermal power plant, emissions from this plant have been reduced. No data were available on the emissions of PM.

The use of wood, kerosene and gas for the individual heating needs of households has also led to an increase in indoor air pollution. Houses are constructed for central heating and often lack proper chimneys and air inlets for heaters. In addition, the quality of heaters is often poor. In the winter of 2001/02, around 30 people died of carbon monoxide poisoning, including entire families (see chapter 14 on human health and environment).

Depletion of natural resources

The use of fossil fuels for electricity generation is limited in Georgia, as hydropower is the dominant source. Fossil fuels are mostly imported. With the collapse of the district heating systems in the cities most households became dependent on alternative sources of heating. Currently, wood and kerosene are common fuel sources for heating and cooking. This rather sudden change in the beginning of the 1990s resulted in the illegal felling of trees in streets, parks and green belts. According to the State Department for Statistics, 8.6 million m^3 of wood, wood and animal waste were used in 2001 for energy consumption. In certain streets of Tbilisi, tree stumps illustrate the severity of the energy crisis.

Figure 10.2: Energy consumption in households in 2001

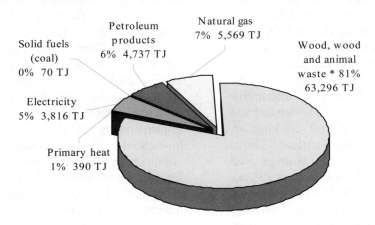

Source: State Department for Statistics, 2002.
* of which 3 TJ animal waste

Table 10.1: Calculated greenhouse gas emissions from energy production

	1980	1985	1990	1995	1997
CO2 (Tg)	28.186	32.688	30.676	2.447	4.470
Methane (Gg) *	103.0	121.0	106.0	6.5	7.2
N20 (Gg)	0.280	0.320	0.293	0.048	0.096
NOx (Gg)	112.71	133.00	124.35	23.84	51.15
CO (Gg)	341.00	363.90	329.00	141.70	297.22
NM VOCs (Gg)	36.69	40.09	37.78	1.16	1.55
SO2 (Gg)	229.03	272.01	247.36	20.24	33.08

Source: Government of Georgia, 1999.
Note:
* >90% derived from fugitive emissions from fuel.

Negative environmental impacts of large hydropower dams

Although hydropower is a favourable source for electricity production compared to thermal generation with coal or gas, there are a number of negative environmental effects associated with – specifically large – hydropower dams. The World Commission on Dams, established on the initiative of the World Bank and the World Conservation Union (IUCN), reviewed the technical, financial and economic performance of dams compared to their planned performance. Based on its investigations, the Commission identified the following negative environmental effects of large dams:

- The loss of forests and wildlife habitat, the loss of species populations and the degradation of upstream catchment areas owing to flooding of the reservoir area;
- The loss of aquatic biodiversity, of upstream and downstream fisheries, and of the services of downstream floodplains, wetlands, and riverine, estuarine and adjacent marine ecosystems; and
- Cumulative impacts on water quality, natural flooding and species composition where a number of dams are sited on the same river.

Many of these effects are specific to the dam's location and characteristics and require a case-by-case assessment. However, based on its review, the World Commission on Dams has concluded that large dams generally have a range of extensive impacts on rivers, watersheds and aquatic ecosystems; these impacts are more negative than positive and, in many cases, have led to irreversible loss of species and ecosystems. In addition, since the environmental and social costs of large dams have been poorly accounted for in economic terms, the true profitability of these schemes remains elusive.

There is no specific information available on the negative environmental impacts of large hydropower dams in Georgia, but it can be assumed that the above-mentioned impacts can also be observed there. In addition, there is little awareness in both the Ministry of Environment and Natural Resources Protection and the Ministry of Fuel and Energy of this issue.

Environmental impacts of pipelines

The environmental impacts of pipelines are mainly related to the risk of an oil or gas leak or spillage, and are location-specific. Planned pipelines in Georgia can potentially affect biodiversity and ecosystems, as they will pass near mineral water sources and a protected area. It is of the utmost importance that the least environmentally sensitive areas are chosen for the pipeline route, and that there is continuous monitoring for leaks and an emergency preparedness plan (see chapter 13 on transport and environment).

10.3 Environmental policy and management in the energy sector

The policy framework

In 1997, the Ministry of Fuel and Energy started with the development of a national energy policy. Technical assistance was provided by the European Union's TACIS programme, USAID and others. However, to date, the Government has not been able to reach a consensus on the strategic directions for the development of the energy sector, and no energy policy exists. This lack of general direction has prevented sufficient investment in and restructuring of the sector. In the past few years a number of simultaneous approaches by both the Government and the donor community in the energy sector can be observed: (i) rehabilitation of small hydropower plants, (ii) rehabilitation of the gas distribution system, and (iii) rehabilitation of large hydropower dams and the gas-fired thermal power plant. The numerous small hydropower plants are being rehabilitated by donors. Rehabilitation costs are relatively low and positive results are obtained within one or two years. The rehabilitation of the gas distribution systems is important to lower the demand for – already scarce – electricity in winter. After the complete collapse of the district heating and gas supply systems in Tbilisi, parts of the city are currently supplied again with natural gas. The third approach is more substantial and involves the large electricity generators. Loans and private investments through privatization have brought in capital for their rehabilitation.

According to a Government document of 1998, the sector's development will be based on eight principles, including the promotion of efficient use and conservation of heat and electricity and the protection of the environment in energy production and use. However, no concrete measurements have followed from this.

The National Environmental Action Plan (NEAP) of 2000 does not mention the electricity-generating sector as a major contributor to environmental problems. Neither the hydropower dams nor the pollution from the thermal power station is identified as a priority. The NEAP does refer to severe shortages in electricity supply and suggests the use of renewable resources for overcoming the energy crisis.

The country's national assessment for the World Summit on Sustainable Development focuses mainly on the energy crisis and energy security, rather than on environmental problems stemming from the energy-generating sector. It is an important self-assessment outlining limitations to Georgia's development, as well as its opportunities. The report also contains a number of important recommendations:

- Ensure training or retraining of managers of energy enterprises;
- Improve and apply heating, hot water supply and ventilation standards and rules in the construction industry with the aim of reducing energy consumption;
- Evaluate the economic efficiency, cost-effectiveness and capacities of low-temperature heating sources;
- Work out and implement phased energy cascade utilization projects;
- Work out the conditions for the allocation of low interest rate credit lines to encourage the adoption of contemporary energy-efficiency technologies.

The legislative framework

The two main regulatory instruments for the Ministry of Environment and Natural Resources Protection are the environmental permit and the State ecological expertise. The construction of hydropower plants with a capacity exceeding 10 MW, thermal power plants and the construction of dams are all listed as category-1 activities in the Law on Environmental Protection and therefore subject to a State ecological expertise in order to obtain an environmental permit. This legislation applies only to activities that started up after the adoption of the Law, in 1996. Consequently, none

of the existing hydropower dams and thermal power stations has been subject to State ecological expertise or has an environmental permit.

Currently, ten hydropower plants have a water abstraction licence from the Ministry of Environment and Natural Resources Protection. The Ministry does not know whether any other plants have been licensed by the regional offices, as no central register of water abstraction licences exists. It is worth noting that, of the ten units of the Gardabani thermal power station, only the two privatized units are in the possession of a water abstraction licence, while the other, State-owned units are not licensed. The abstraction fee is 0.000,000,1 lari/m^3, which is collected by the Ministry of Finance. The Ministry of Environment and Natural Resources Protection does not have any information on the collection rate.

In 1997, the Law on Electric Energy was passed and amended in 1999. It established the responsibilities of the Ministry of Fuel and Energy, and laid down the structure of the energy market. There are no specific instruments allocated to the Ministry of Fuel and Energy for environmental protection.

In 1998, the Presidential Order on the Development of User of Non-traditional Energy Sources gives priority to the use of renewable sources. The aim of this presidential decree is to promote the use of renewable energy sources as one of the primary means of achieving the sustainable development of the energy sector, and it calls for measures to promote the investments needed for to develop these resources.

Economic instruments

Economic instruments are not used in the energy sector. User charges exist for gas and electricity but any regulating effects on behaviour is limited for a number of reasons. There is no free energy market and charges are established by the Georgian National Energy Regulatory Commission. In addition, the population's ability and willingness to pay are very low, limiting the inclusion of environmental taxes in the charges. However, between 1998 and 2001, electricity tariffs for the residents in Tbilisi increased 2.8-fold (from 0.045 to 0.124 lari/kWh). This was the result of the privatization of the Tbilisi distribution company. Investments made in the company also account for the increased tariffs. The increased tariffs were accompanied by stricter enforcement of payment and individual metering, resulting in a higher collection rate and a decrease in consumption. In other regions tariffs do not exceed 0.084 lari/kWh. According to Georgia's report to the World Summit on Sustainable Development, the price of natural gas has not changed significantly in recent years. It has stabilized at around US$ 125/1000m^3 compared to US$ 48/1000 m^3 about ten years ago.

Seventy-five per cent of the distribution company for Tbilisi, Talesi, has been privatized. The privatization has led to a number of major changes, ranging from higher prices to recover better the full costs of electricity and maintenance to increased efforts to collect user charges by cutting off supply. These measures sometimes met with strong resistance, especially the cutting-off of electricity for non-payment.

The institutional framework

The Ministry of Fuel and Energy was established in 1996 and is the competent authority for the energy sector. Most entities for the generation, transmission and distribution have been restructured from State-owned companies to joint-stock companies. The main shareholders are still the State and the employees. The Ministry of Fuel and Energy is responsible for determining and developing energy policy. It is also responsible for the efficiency of the various sources (gas, electricity) used. Environmental responsibilities within the Ministry of Fuel and Energy have been allocated to the Environment Department, which has a staff of three. The allocation of environmental responsibilities in a line ministry is an important prerequisite for sectoral integration. According to the 1997 Law on Electric Energy, the Ministry of Fuel and Energy promotes the environmental protection of all energy activities, and optimally incorporates environmental protection goals in the formulation and implementation of energy programmes.

The Ministry of Environment and Natural Resources Protection is the competent authority for environmental protection. Its main responsibilities, organizational structure and instruments for policy-making are discussed in previous chapters. The Ministry does not have responsibility for the energy sector. Cooperation with the Ministry of Fuel and Energy is limited and informal.

The Georgian National Energy Regulatory Commission is an independent agency responsible for the regulation of tariffs for electric power and natural gas generation, transmission, distribution and import-export licensing.

International energy agreements

United Nations Framework Convention on Climate Change

In 1994 Georgia ratified the United Nations Framework Convention on Climate Change and in 1996 it established its National Climate Change Programme. A special Climate Research Centre was set up in the Department of Hydrometeorology of the Ministry of Environment and Natural Resources Protection. In 1997 a GEF-funded project to help Georgia fulfil its commitments to the United Nations Framework Convention on Climate Change, totalling $350,000, was approved, and a first inventory of greenhouse gas emissions for 1980-1997 was drawn up. As part of the inventory, ten project proposals were prepared, mainly focusing on the use of renewable resources such as wind, solar, geothermal, water and hydropower. Two projects for the rehabilitation of 10 small hydropower plants and the use of geothermal waters for municipal energy supply received funding through GEF (see box 10.1).

Georgia is not listed in annex I to the Convention and is eligible for the Clean Development Mechanism. Although a number of countries have shown interest, no projects have been developed as Georgia lacks the project development capacity (see also chapter 4 on international cooperation).

Energy Charter

Georgia was the first country to sign the Energy Charter in July 1995. The aim of this Charter is to establish a legal framework to promote long-term cooperation in energy, focusing on investment protection, trade in energy materials and products, transit and dispute settlement. Environmental concerns have been incorporated in the treaty through the polluter pays principle. The treaty encourages market-oriented prices reflecting environmental costs and benefits.

Georgia has not ratified the Protocol to the Energy Charter on Energy Efficiency and Related Environmental Aspects. The objectives of the Protocol are threefold: (i) promoting energy-efficiency policies consistent with sustainable development, (ii) creating conditions which induce consumers and producers to use energy as economically, efficiently and environmentally soundly as possible, and (iii) fostering cooperation on energy efficiency. One of the obligations of the Parties to the Protocol is the establishment of an energy-efficiency policy.

10.4 Conclusions and recommendations

Georgia has been facing an enormous energy crisis from which it is only slowly recovering. There is a huge need for investment to counter the years of neglect in the generation, transmission and distribution systems. The energy crisis had some positive environmental effects, such as the decrease in air pollutants and greenhouse gases from thermal power stations and district heating systems. These positive effects, however, were by far outweighed by the negative social consequences for the population and industry, and the shift to indoor air pollution.

Progress is being made with the individual rehabilitation of small hydropower stations. There is no strategy or energy policy prioritizing projects for rehabilitation, and there is little to no interest from the Government in demand management. There are no programmes in energy conservation or efficiency improvements.

International cooperation in energy is important to Georgia for various reasons. Georgia is a Party to the Energy Charter but not to its Protocol on Energy Efficiency and Related Environmental Aspects. The Protocol provides a forum for its Parties to share experience and advice with other countries in transition, as well as with the European Union and members of the Organisation for Economic Co-operation and Development (OECD). In addition, Georgia could benefit from an in-depth energy-efficiency review to assist the Ministry of Fuel and Energy in developing its energy-efficiency policy.

Recommendation 10.1:
The Ministry of Fuel and Energy should draw up a clear strategy for the energy sector, including a strong focus on demand-side management, energy-efficiency and environmental impacts. Accession to the Energy Charter Protocol on Energy Efficiency and Related Environmental Aspects could assist Georgia in developing such a policy, and should be promoted by the Ministry of Fuel and Energy.

In comparison with many other countries, Georgia has one of the 'cleanest' energy sectors, largely due to the collapse of thermal power production, the district heating system and the large share of hydropower in total electricity generation. However, future negative effects can be expected from the planned coal and large hydropower stations unless sufficient measures are taken. The Ministry of Environment and Natural Resources Protection has tools to ensure the integration of environmental concerns in the energy sector, such as the State ecological expertise and environmental permits, but it is not using these to their full potential (see also chapter 1 on policy, legal and institutional framework and sectoral integration). The link between the expertise and the permit is weak, and there is insufficient capacity to manage large projects. The Ministry of Environment and Natural Resources Protection and the Ministry of Fuel and Energy seem to have little awareness and knowledge of the negative environmental impacts of large hydropower dams. The World Commission on Dams has developed a framework for decision-making based on its assessment of several large hydropower dams worldwide. This framework focuses on a number of aspects, including social, financial and environmental, that should be included in the decision-making for large hydropower dams.

Recommendation 10.2:
The Ministry of Environment and Natural Resources Protection, in considering the development of any large hydropower dams should incorporate the recommendations of the World Commission on Dams in its review of the State ecological expertise and the issuance of an environmental permit.

Georgia is a Party to the United Nations Framework Convention on Climate Change and established its National Climate Change Programme in 1996. A special Agency for Climate Change was set up in the Department of Hydrometeorology of the Ministry of Environment and Natural Resources Protection. The first inventory of greenhouse gas emissions for 1980-1997 was drawn up. Ten project proposals were prepared. They focused mainly on the use of renewable resources such as wind, solar, geothermal, water and hydropower. Two of the projects were for the rehabilitation of 10 small hydropower plants and the use of geothermal waters for municipal energy supply. Georgia is not listed in annex 1 and is eligible for the Clean Development Mechanism. A number of countries have shown an interest, but no projects have been developed as Georgia lacks project development capacity (see also chapter 4, on international cooperation).

Recommendation 10.3:
The Ministry of Environment and Natural Resources Protection should develop the capacity to prepare projects under the Clean Development Mechanism of the United Nations Framework Convention on Climate Change.

According to the decree on the Development of the Use of Non-traditional Energy Sources, the Government gives priority to the use of renewable sources such as wind, biomass, solar and geothermal waters. The technical potential for these renewable sources appears to be rather large, e.g. wind energy would generate 1 trillion kWh. It is also estimated that 1.5 million people could be supplied with hot water and heating from geothermal waters.

Recommendation 10.4:
The Ministry of Environment and Natural Resources Protection should review the potential of supporting the establishment of economically viable alternative energy facilities in areas outside the grid.

Chapter 11

AGRICULTURE AND ENVIRONMENT

11.1 Introduction

Geographical areas and climate

Georgia is dominated by the Caucasus Mountains: mountains and hills cover more than half of its territory. The climate is variable but mostly temperate and mild, in the lowlands often humid. A sub-tropical region is found on the Black Sea coast.

Agricultural regions in Georgia are diverse with regard to altitude, relief, soil and climate. Generally climatic conditions for agriculture are favourable. It is common to divide Georgia into the humid west and the dry east. Most of the arable land is found in the lowlands. In the mountains, agricultural land is mainly used as pastures or meadows.

Georgian agriculture has a long history that can be traced back to 5000-6000 BC.

Organization of production, general trends

Until the dissolution of the Soviet Union, Georgia was a major supplier of agricultural products such as vegetables, tea, grapes and wine, citrus and other fruits to other Soviet republics. The crops were cultivated on State or collective farms using industrial farming techniques, but private plots of farm workers were also intensively cultivated.

Following independence in 1991, Georgia's market links with other Soviet republics were cut abruptly. This left the country with an agricultural specialization and products for which there was no market. As a result all major production fell drastically. As a secondary effect crop-processing factories also had to close. Similarly other basic foodstuffs such as grain were no longer delivered from other parts of what had been the Soviet Union. These changes negatively affected the economy and living conditions. In the beginning of the 1990s some people even went hungry.

The structure of production also changed considerably as a result of the serious economic and social crisis in Georgia as well as the privatization of land and production facilities. The intensity of production is now very low, with some agricultural land not being used at all. Agricultural production relies mainly on manual labour, since the material and technical basis for production has deteriorated significantly and is not being renewed.

However, agriculture is still a major source of income even if output has decreased to about 70% of its 1990 level. The official share of agriculture in gross domestic product (GDP) decreased from 33.6% in 1996 to 21.5% in 2000, but its importance for the survival of the population is even more significant today than before. During the 1990s there was a massive reallocation of labour to small-scale farming. Georgians have turned to subsistence farming to survive. About 45% of the population lives in the countryside. Over 55% of the active labour force was employed in agriculture in 2000.

In 1999, 43% of the land or approximately 3 million ha was categorized as agricultural land. Of this land, 26.2% is arable land, 8.9% is under perennial crops and 64.8% are pastures and meadows (see table 11.1).

Table 11.1: Agricultural production

Agricultural area (1000 ha, 2001)	3,020
Arable land (1000 ha, 2001)	793
Perennial crops (1000 ha, 2001)	269
Pasture and meadows (1000 ha, 2001)	1,958
Crop production (ha, 1997)	
Wheat	124,000
Maize	225,000
Vegetables	40,000
Potatoes	33,000
Grapes	94,000
Citrus fruits	9,500
Other fruits	67,000
Tea	40,800
Animal production (heads, 1997)	
Cattle	1,027,000
Cows	551,000
Pigs	330,000
Sheep and goats	584,000

Source: Ministry of Food and Agriculture, 2002.

Privatization of land was initiated in the late 1980s, and much of the agricultural land is now in the hand of private farmers (chapter 12 on spatial planning and land use). The policy is to privatize arable land and to lease the pasture to private farmers. Larger farms are being leased rather than sold off. By 1 April 2000, 25.2% of agricultural land had been transferred into private ownership: 56.9% of this is arable land, 23.9% is under perennial crops and 16.6% is pasture or other grassland. The remaining agricultural land, including the bulk of the pasture, is leased to individual farmers.

The average size of private farms is 0.9 ha per family, which is frequently divided among several plots. As the land market is not working very efficiently (chapter 12 on spatial planning and land use), no significant consolidation of land has been undertaken as a basis for productivity improvements. Land consolidation is necessary to achieve a more efficient and market-oriented agriculture. The situation is difficult but more promising for farmers leasing larger farms, mostly for grain production.

Markets for agricultural outputs and inputs are fully liberalized but often difficult for small farmers to enter. Households also sell fewer of their products because they are used to support members of the extended family and to barter for goods and services.

The lack of capital and credit opportunities, and therefore a low level of mechanization and worn-out machinery, and low levels of agricultural inputs also reduce agricultural productivity. Productivity in both plant and animal production is low.

Processing of agricultural products is a serious bottleneck. Another obstacle to the development of Georgia's agriculture is that the new private farmers do not have access to information or technical advice, for example through extension services.

11.2   Production

Crop production

With a favourable climate and diverse regions, there is a potential for the production of a wide range of crops. During Soviet times Georgia was renowned for its production of wine, tea and fruits including citrus fruits. In particular tea and fruits are no longer as profitable since the exports to other

parts of the former Soviet Union cannot be sustained. For example, the export of lemons and oranges is today difficult because of their unmarketable size and shape, and their low quality in comparison with those from other suppliers. The disruption of transport through Ajaria makes exporting to the Russian Federation even harder.

With production directed towards subsistence, the most important crops today are maize, wheat, vegetables and potato. Grapes, fruits including citrus fruits, tobacco and tea still play an important role for agriculture (table 11.1). An example of an expanding crop is hazelnut.

Animal production

With the collapse of the former economic system and the livestock processing facilities, the general patterns of production and consumption of meat and dairy products have changed significantly. The overall stocks decreased during the first part of the 1990s, in particular for sheep and pigs. Table 11.1 gives data on total animal stocks. Cattle stocks recovered after 1995, and it is likely that the official statistics are underestimates. The average herds of pigs, cattle and sheep are generally very small. Some large poultry farms still survive, but they are in a difficult situation.

Households process milk into butter and cheese using traditional technology, and meat production is dominated by backyard slaughter. Meat and dairy products are still an important part of the Georgian diet, but, owing to limited production, imports are high.

The lack of adequate winter feed and the limited access to financing for stock, winter feed and dairy equipment are major problems in animal production. The lack of winter feed and winter pastures is an important cause of overgrazing in the winter in some regions (see below).

11.3   Environmental concerns in agriculture

Erosion and desertification

The main environmental problem of agriculture is soil erosion. It is a widespread natural phenomenon due to the relief and climate of the country, but it is accelerated by poor land management practices, such as cultivation of land on steep slopes; excessive cutting of forests, shrubs and bushes, including wind shelters; overgrazing; and irrigation washing away topsoil. Wind erosion takes place mainly in the east, while water erosion occurs in eastern as well as western Georgia.

About 250,000 ha of arable land and twice as much pasture and grassland are damaged by water erosion. During recent years it seems that water erosion as well as the related processes of landslides and mudflows have been increasing. The situation is particularly serious in Upper Imereti, Adjchara, Svaneti and in the high-mountain regions.

Increased pressure on the remaining forests (chapter 8 on biodiversity and forest management) by farmers and the general population, compounded by overgrazing close to the villages, intensifies erosion. One reason for overgrazing is that the summer pastures in Dagestan that were used during Soviet times are no longer available. Increasing numbers of grazing cattle also most likely contribute to a worsening situation.

In eastern Georgia the climate is relatively dry, and strong winds during cold periods may cause severe wind erosion. A major reason for what seems to be increasing problems of wind erosion is that the wind shelters that previously protected the fields have been cut down. It is estimated that some 100,000 ha of land has been damaged by wind erosion.

Desertification in eastern Georgia has intensified in the past few years, and is closely related to erosion. Overgrazing, unsustainable logging and the use of unsuitable land as arable land, combined with unusually low levels of precipitation, are causing desertification. About 3,000 ha have been eroded, including in Shiraki, Eldari, Iori, Taribana, Natbeuri, Naomari, Ole and Jeiran-chel valleys, the ridges, plateau and the major part of the south slope of the Kakheti ridge.

Over the past decade only marginal resources have been devoted to monitoring erosion and desertification. This is in contrast to the Soviet period when this and other problems were studied and analysed in depth. The material available today needs updating.

Even if significant efforts have been made to produce anti-erosion programmes by, for example, the Ministry of Food and Agriculture, the programmes have not been implemented due to the lack of funding. Similarly, no special measures have been taken in recent years to combat desertification.

Biodiversity of crop plants and domestic animals

The Caucasus is an important centre of agro-biodiversity. Georgia has a very rich spectrum of crop plants, both in terms of number of crop species and within individual species. The diversity of its fruit trees and grapes is particularly rich. There are also surviving landraces of domestic animals.

During the Soviet period most of the landraces were exchanged for a few introduced varieties, and the landraces were mostly confined to collections for research and future breeding. Today, these collections are under serious threat, mainly for financial reasons. Some efforts are being made to reintroduce old landraces of fruit species for the production of organic products.

Irrigation and drainage

Irrigation and drainage are important for an efficient agriculture, but can also harm the environment. Irrigation is most developed in the eastern, drier parts of the country, and drainage in the west. During the 1990s the irrigation and drainage infrastructure deteriorated seriously. The acreage under irrigation declined from more than 400,000 to 230,000 ha and that under drainage from 130,000 to 65,000 ha.

There is a potential for developing irrigation further in Georgia, but funding restrictions will make this difficult. It is already a tremendous task merely to rehabilitate the available installations. Specific environmental concerns are the extent to which irrigation contributes to soil erosion and eutrophication, and drainage destroys wetlands that are valuable for the preservation of biotopes and biodiversity. Plans for the rehabilitation or development of new irrigation and drainage infrastructure are approved only after an environmental impact assessment.

Donors and international financial institutions have developed projects for the rehabilitation of irrigation and drainage. The Irrigation and Drainage Community Development Project, which was started in 2002, is funded with a loan from the World Bank. The project aims to improve irrigation and drainage. In a first step 18,000 ha of irrigated land and 3,420 ha of drained land will be rehabilitated. An important part of the project is to privatize the infrastructure and to establish "amelioration associations" (see below). An environmental impact assessment has been made and approved for the project.

In eastern Georgia irrigation has caused salinization. Currently, 59,220 ha are severely and 54,340 ha moderately salinized. It is likely that the low quality of irrigation management and infrastructure has added to these problems during the past decade.

In the Kolkheti lowlands the potential conflict between preservation of valuable wetlands and agriculture is obvious. Drainage projects decreased the acreage of wetlands during the Soviet period, but in recent years the drainage system has deteriorated with negative consequences for the farmers. A national park is being established in the central part of the lowlands. In it the wetland biotopes would be protected, while outside its boundaries the drainage infrastructure would be rehabilitated within the framework of the World Bank project (see above).

Use of fertilizers and pesticides

Pesticide use was high in the 1980s, in particular in the citrus, tea and grape plantations. At the end of the 1980s, DDT was found in 90% of the soil samples analysed and in many of the rivers. Contamination of fruits and vegetables was also frequent. As many of the citrus and tea plantations are along the coastline, significant amounts of pesticides as well as nutrients were discharged into the Black Sea.

In the 1990s pesticide use declined sharply, but the use now seems to have stabilized and may even be increasing. According to official statistics only about 1,700 tons of pesticides are imported annually. However, illegal imports, estimated at double this volume, are a serious problem. Pesticides are imported illegally mainly to avoid taxation, and in some cases also because the substances are banned. Another problem is that pesticides destined for destruction are taken from old stocks and used. For example, prohibited (and cheap) mercury substances have recently been used for the treatment of seeds.

The lack of training and the unavailability of advisory services for farmers are obstacles to a good selection and proper use of pesticides. It is also a problem that pesticide sprayers are outdated and do not lend themselves to an even distribution of the active substance. The same problem is valid for spreading of fertilizers. Farmers rarely use any

protection equipment when applying pesticides. The most important issue with regard to pesticide use is to make sure that farmers are applying pesticides with protection clothing in correct doses with efficient sprayers.

As with pesticides, the use of fertilizers is also very low. Essentially only nitrogen fertilizers are used. The levels of run-off of fertilizers and pesticides from the fields are most likely low. However, there are instances where, for example, DDT is still found in run-off from fields. As there is no systematic monitoring, it is not clear how widespread this problem is. It is not possible to conclude whether contamination of persistent pesticides such as DDT and DDE is still a problem.

Pollution from animal production

A few remaining large animal production units, mainly for poultry and egg production, cause severe pollution locally. A significant proportion of the manure produced is discharged without any treatment.

Manure handling in smaller-scale production also contributes to the pollution of water with nutrients and organic substances, probably with significant negative effects on drinking water (chapters 7 on water management and 14 on human health and environment). The producers tend to store manure in the field a considerable time before spreading it, which increases the risk of run-off of nutrients and other substances.

Soil contamination and destruction

In the vicinity of the industrial centre of Rustavi there is significant soil contamination from tin. Additionally, copper and gold mining operations in Kvemo Kartly have polluted surrounding soils. There are some reports of bombings in connection with the conflict in Abkhazia that have caused the degradation of topsoil.

11.4   Policy objectives and management

The policy framework

The policy document for the sector, Concept of Agrarian Policy of Georgia was adopted by presidential decree in 1997. Some items included in the policy are:

- Food security for the population is the main priority and the production of cereals, potatoes, vegetable oil and livestock products are priorities;

- Viticulture, fruit, vegetable and tea production are to be developed for export;
- The production of "ecologically safe" food, especially baby food, should be developed for export;
- Market economic principles should be implemented;
- The privatization of land and the development of a land market should continue;
- The main irrigation infrastructure will remain in the hands of the State while inter-farm distribution will be included in the privatization programme;
- Support should be given to the development of cooperatives among physical persons and legal entities;
- There should be an increase of State investments in irrigation, soil protection, research, selection, breeding, information and plant protection services, development of rural infrastructure and environmental protection.

The lack of funding is a major reason why it has been difficult to implement agricultural policies actively. International support is crucial even for the core budget of the Ministry of Food and Agriculture. International projects in the sector are of major importance for the development of an environmental policy.

The National Environmental Action Plan envisages the development of a national programme for soil protection. This programme would describe the current state and trends in soil degradation in detail; create a picture of natural and anthropogenic processes leading to soil degradation and set out measures for its prevention; and define an investment plan for the prevention of soil erosion.

The Indicative Plan for Social and Economic Development of Georgia produced annually by the Ministry of Economy includes two projects for protecting the soil from erosion and improving soil fertility within the agricultural sector development programme.

The Ministry of Food and Agriculture is preparing a Programme on Soil Protection and Raising the Fertility of Soils for 2003-2010, which can be seen as a response to the NEAP and the Indicative Plan.

A project funded by the Global Environment Fund (GEF)/World Bank, Agricultural Research

Extension and Training (ARET), has a component on improving the handling of manure, anti-erosion measures and biological plant protection on farms in three districts in a river basin running into the Black Sea. Other components of this project aim to improve the links between science and farm production, including the development of extension services. A major objective is to decrease pollution loads in rivers and the Black Sea.

The World Bank Irrigation and Drainage Community Development Project (see above) introduces new policies on responsibility and the longer-term ownership of the irrigation and drainage infrastructure. This project also introduces the concept of "amelioration associations", uniting farmers using joint infrastructure for drainage and irrigation.

An ongoing GEF-funded project addressing, among other things, the problems of desertification, Conservation of Arid and Semi-Arid Ecosystems in the Caucasus, started in December 1999. The project is financed by GEF (US$ 700,000) and managed by the Georgian NGO Noah's Ark Centre for Recovery of Endangered Species. Its duration is 29 months and its objective is to protect arid and semi-arid ecosystems from degradation through the sustainable management of natural resources. Proposals for pasture conservation were worked out, but these have not so far been implemented. To achieve this objective the project intends to identify agricultural practices that favour protection of the ecosystems and key species.

As mentioned in other chapters (e.g. chapter 3), the lack of monitoring data and recent inventories makes it difficult to develop cost-efficient policies and action programmes. This is a matter of concern also for the responsible authorities in the agricultural sector.

The legal framework

The 1996 Law on Environmental Protection has one article on the use of agrochemicals and another on maximum permissible levels of certain chemicals in food products. The main laws governing the use of land are the 1996 Law on Land Registration, the 1996 Law on Agricultural Landownership and the 1994 Law on Soil Protection.

The legal framework for the registration and use of pesticides is developed and implemented in collaboration between the Ministry of Food and

Agriculture, the Ministry of Environment and Natural Resources Protection and the Ministry of Labour, Health and Social Affairs. Important laws are the 1998 Law on Pesticides and Agrochemicals and the 1998 Law on Hazardous Chemical Substances. A list of pesticides registered for use in 1999-2003 has been published by the Ministry of Food and Agriculture, and the Ministry of Health has issued a list of prohibited chemicals. The ratification of the Rotterdam Convention on the Prior Informed Consent Procedure for Certain Hazardous Chemicals and Pesticides in International Trade is a basis for the prohibition of certain persistent pesticides. Additional regulations for the implementation of the legal acts on agrochemicals are being prepared (chapters 4 on international cooperation and 6 on waste, chemicals and contaminated sites).

Even if there is a certain lack of consistency and coordination among the legal acts and ministries involved in regulating the import and use of pesticides, the system is largely in line with procedures in other countries. The ratification of the Rotterdam Convention has a positive impact with regard to the prohibition of certain persistent pesticides. The major problem is that so many of the applied substances are imported illegally.

Draft legislation on "amelioration associations" is being developed. A new draft law, prepared by the Ministry of Food and Agriculture, on the conservation of soil fertility is being discussed by Parliament. This law would be a major step in introducing certain restrictions, such as the maximum number of grazing animals per acreage and the maximum slope for arable land, and in regulating the use of agrochemicals and irrigation.

The institutional framework

The Ministry of Food and Agriculture has the primary responsibility for agricultural policies. Its important departments with regard to environmental issues are the Department of Melioration and Water Resources, the Department of Agroecology, the Agency for Plant Protection and the Agency for Agrochemistry and the Amelioration of Soils. The Ministry of Environment and Natural Resources Protection's involvement in the agricultural sector is mainly related to the registration and use of pesticides, and some issues concerning the use of land resources and erosion protection. Its Department of Land Resources Protection, Waste and Chemical Management is responsible for this work. An Inter-

ministerial Council for Hazardous Chemicals was established in 2002, but it had not met at the time of writing.

The State Department of Geology is responsible for monitoring geological processes, including erosion. Its annual report is supposed to include recommendations for anti-erosion measures. Since the dissolution of the Soviet Union this work has not been funded properly.

Cooperation and coordination between different authorities is not always smooth. For example, the cooperation between the Ministry of Food and Agriculture and the Ministry of Environment and Natural Resources Protection could be improved. There is cooperation on erosion and the registration of pesticides, but the information flow between the Ministries is limited and the regulations issued by the different authorities are not fully streamlined. There are no formal links between the two Ministries with regard to agricultural and environmental policy-making.

In 1999, a national network was established to combat desertification in Georgia. It consists of 27 different governmental and non-governmental organizations and academic institutions and is designed to support the sharing of information and experience between the institutions and to facilitate decision-making on policy issues to combat desertification. Extensive research capacities are found in various institutes of the Academy of Sciences and the Agrarian Academy of Georgia, but the whole system for research and education is underfunded.

The Agrarian University in Tbilisi and its branches have about 7,000 students. Recently, a faculty of agroecology was set up. All students at the university take at least one environmental course, and specialization in environmental issues is reported to be popular.

Donor programmes have supported the establishment of regional training centres in cooperation with local agricultural colleges as well as information centres.

The development of extension services is an important part of the agricultural policy, but the district departments of agriculture and food, subordinated to the Ministry of Food and Agriculture, currently provide only marginal extension services. The Ministry has acknowledged that the development of extension services is crucial in the completely changed structure for production. However, there are several stumbling blocks in their development. First, it is difficult to fund the establishment of the planned new extension service centres, because the State and the farmers are in a difficult financial situation. If the State authorities provided extension services in a centralized structure, the farmers might not have confidence in it. Moreover, attempts by different parts of the Ministry of Food and Agriculture to provide training on separate issues, such as plant protection and soil fertility, are likely to stretch the available meagre resources to the limit.

There are some attempts to address the issue of extension services outside the State sector. The Georgian Farmers Union has an advisory centre in Tbilisi, and the Elkana organization for organic food production has advisers for its members. The Agrarian University has plans to establish "agrobusiness centres".

Environmental awareness of farmers and organic farming

The social and economic crisis largely explains why farmers pay little attention to environmental issues, even though an issue such as erosion is a direct threat to future sustainable farm production. If there are no affordable energy sources other than firewood, even forests planted to protect against erosion will be cut.

In addition to the difficult economic conditions, the lack of extension services and of advice to farmers severely restricts the development of agricultural practices where inputs are used efficiently and safely, and the land and soil used sustainably. Few farmers have any agricultural education or access to advisory services. As a result, their environmental awareness is low, and in view of the difficult day-to-day situation, farmers may not even apply the knowledge and experience that they have.

Considering the economic and social problems in Georgia, the development of organic agriculture with certification of production is not easy. The internal market for organic products is likely to be small, and it is difficult and expensive to set up a credible certification procedure. However, niche markets could probably be developed in the country, and for certain products, such as wine and tea, in other countries.

The biological farming association Elkana (member of the International Federation of Organic Agriculture Movement) promotes organic agriculture. It is funded by different donors and unites about 300 farmers. It provides advisory services and marketing opportunities to its members. Elkana plans to establish certification procedures for organic products in 2003-2004. A draft law on the production and certification of agricultural products is being discussed by Parliament and its adoption would simplify the development of certification procedures.

11.5 Conclusions and recommendations

Agricultural production in Georgia is in difficulty. The structure of production and markets has changed dramatically, and there are essentially no resources available to adapt to the new situation. It is easy to see why environmental issues are not a priority. Therefore, it can be argued that, also from an environmental perspective, it is important at this stage to support the general development of the agricultural sector. The skills and income of the new farmers will need to be improved before any significant environmental objectives are likely to be achieved.

Desertification and erosion are the two most serious environmental issues related to agricultural production. Both are accelerating, which is distressing, since they are essentially irreversible.

With regard to anti-erosion activities, Georgian scientists, agricultural experts and the authorities have significant experience and a high level of awareness. This is demonstrated by the fact that the Ministry of Food and Agriculture has a separate service focusing on issues of soil fertility.

Two obstacles to a successful fight against erosion and desertification are the lack of funding and the lack of awareness of the fact that the restructuring of agriculture and the changes in society call for new approaches. In the planning of efforts it should be remembered that no single institution is able to carry out measures to combat desertification and land degradation successfully: only joint and integrated efforts, based on good information, can promote cost-efficient measures and achieve their targets.

Recommendation 11.1:
The Ministry of Food and Agriculture, in cooperation with the Ministry of Environment and Natural Resources Protection, should re-establish funding for programmes to counteract erosion and desertification as a priority. The programmes

should involve farmers, communities and local authorities. Co-funding and contributions in kind from these stakeholders should be a longer-term objective.

In the current economic climate, it is very difficult to introduce elaborate schemes on environmental protection in the agricultural sector. New or changed practices can be introduced only if they also improve production and living conditions. Energy supply problems are, for example, a mayor cause of destructive logging of forests leading to erosion. The GEF/World Bank project ARET rightly focuses on the demonstration and promotion of "win-win" opportunities, such as using manure for the production of natural gas, that not only decrease eutrophication but also lead to a more efficient use of inputs in agriculture and a better standard of living.

Extension services are a key instrument in the development of efficient agricultural production. There are attempts to develop extension services, but they are hampered by a lack of funding and a general mistrust towards the authorities.

Recommendation 11.2:
The Ministry of Food and Agriculture should, as a priority, develop an action plan to promote the development of extension services that would, inter alia:

- *Strengthen the Ministry's capacity for extension services;*
- *Develop advisory services outside the State sector;*
- *Promote the development of agricultural practices to decrease soil erosion and ensure the safe and efficient use of pesticides and fertilizers;*
- *Promote good irrigation management practices and the introduction of environmentally sound irrigation technologies; and*
- *In the longer term, implement codes of good agricultural practices.*

In the present situation it is difficult to develop and implement coherent policies on agriculture, which would take into account all aspect of agriculture including the environment. The fact that the situation in Georgian agriculture is changing rapidly complicates matters. Many initiatives and projects contribute to its development, but information on experience with these initiatives is not readily available. The strictly sector-oriented approach of the Government sometimes results in

conflicts between authorities. Environment and agriculture is one example where improved communication between the different authorities and stakeholders could contribute to the development of more efficient policies.

The Ministry of Environment and Natural Resources Protection does not have a systematic approach to following the overall development in sectors such as agriculture, and needs to create mechanisms that would give a better basis for the development of future policies in different areas.

Recommendation 11.3:
The Ministry of Environment and Natural Resources Protection, in collaboration with the Ministry of Food and Agriculture, should promote the sharing of information on environmental problems in agriculture among all stakeholders to further understanding of the issue, to inform policy-making, and, over time, as a means of developing national codes of good agricultural practices (see recommendation 11.2).

One effective way of facilitating the sharing of information is annual round tables on the sustainability of Georgian agriculture with the involvement of all stakeholders.

The use of pesticides has plummeted since the 1980s. The regulation of the import and use of pesticides is largely in line with procedures in other countries, but there is a lack of consistency and coordination among the legal acts and ministries involved in regulating the import and use of pesticides. The main problem is that so many of the applied substances are imported illegally.

Recommendation 11.4:
The Ministry of Environment and Natural Resources Protection, in collaboration with the Ministry of Food and Agriculture and the Ministry of Health, should develop an action plan to reduce the illegal import and use of pesticides. This plan should focus on implementation issues more than on the development of new legal acts. The customs authorities and other stakeholders should be involved in the discussions.

A permanent joint working group of the three Ministries, possibly within the framework of the recently established Inter-ministerial Council for Hazardous Chemicals, could in the longer term be an important forum for streamlining the regulations on the import, transport, storage and use of pesticides and other agrochemicals.

Organic farming will not become a major source of production in Georgia in the immediate future. However, the development of organic farming is important for exploring opportunities and developing experience in moving towards a sustainable agricultural production. Market niches for organic products could also boost the income of individual producers.

The main stumbling block is the need to establish a labelling system for certified products. A legal act on environmental labelling of foods has been drafted. The adoption of this law would significantly cut the cost of developing labelling for organic products.

Recommendation 11.5:
(a) The Ministry of Food and Agriculture should promote the development of organic farming. Support should primarily be directed towards developing regulations, capacity building and the establishment and development of organizations for organic farming;
(b) The Ministry of Food and Agriculture, together with the Ministry of Environment and Natural Resources Protection, should promote the ecological labelling of food products, in particular those intended for export;
(c) The Ministry of Food and Agriculture should urge Parliament to adopt the law on the production and certification of agricultural products.

The Caucasus is one of the world's centres for biodiversity, which is also reflected in the wide range of landraces of crop plants and domestic animals that have been selected during the long history of agriculture in the region. Old landraces are not used any more, but collections of, for instance, fruit and grape varieties that were established under Soviet times are under serious threat, mainly for financial reasons.

There are attempts under way to support the conservation of traditional fruit varieties, but unless more is done, there is a risk that important biodiversity will be lost forever.

Recommendation 11.6:
The Ministry of Food and Agriculture together with the Ministry of Environment and Natural Resources Protection should initiate discussions with donors and international organizations to establish projects that would guarantee the future conservation of landraces of crop plants and domestic animals. The promotion of conservation of landraces should be included in the draft national strategy and action plan for biodiversity.

There is significant soil contamination in a number of areas associated with industrial, including mining, pollution, old military installations and possibly bombings in connection with the conflict in Abkhazia. It is important that a full inventory of contaminated sites should be drawn up and a programme of land recovery and recultivation developed and implemented (see recommendations 6.1, 6.3 and 6.6 and 9.1).

Chapter 12

SPATIAL PLANNING AND LAND USE

12.1 The framework for spatial planning and land use

Geography and land resources

Georgia is situated in south-eastern Europe, bordering on the Black Sea. Its land boundaries total 1,461 km: 164 km with Armenia, 322 km with Azerbaijan, 723 km with the Russian Federation and 252 km with Turkey. It has a 310-km-long coastline. Its land area totals 69,490 km^2. The terrain is largely mountainous, with the Great Caucasus Mountains in the north and the Lesser Caucasus Mountains in the south. In eastern Georgia the rivers all join the river Mtkvari, forming the Caspian basin, while the rivers of western Georgia, of which the Rioni and the Enguri are the biggest, run into the Black Sea basin. Georgia's landscape is extremely diverse. Nearly 40% of all the world's landscape types are represented in the Caucasus.

Almost half of Georgia's land area is under agricultural use, much of the remainder is forest (41% of the total area). However, given the mountainous nature of the country, most agricultural land is for pasture or hay. The amount of arable land is limited to about one quarter of agricultural land.

Demography, urbanization and socio-economic characteristics related to the environment

Georgia has a population of 4,945,000 (2001), down from 5,416,850 in 1995, of which about 56% are urban dwellers, while 44% live in rural areas. The capital, Tbilisi, has a population of 1,272,000. Recently, the growth rate has been gradually declining and environmental pressures have resulted more from population movements than from population growth. For the past 10 years, migration from the country and a stream of refugees from conflict areas have played a major role in population dynamics. If previous internal migration were slow (village to town to regional centre to capital), nowadays migration to the capital

is direct. Refugees from conflict zones, 33% of whom have come to the capital, have contributed to this development. The ethnic structure in Georgia has changed and in general become more mono-ethnic. Tbilisi has strengthened its position as the major centre for employment, education and culture. More than half the urban population lives in the four main cities (Tbilisi, Kutaisi, Rustavi and Batumi).

In Georgia, 66% of households live in individual houses, 90% of which are owner-occupied. Only 2% of households live in rental housing. Since 1991, housing construction has fallen sharply (about sixfold). However, since 1999, a certain growth in housing construction has been recorded, primarily in private construction and mainly for internal refurbishing, interior improvements and design. The majority of buildings are in a deplorable state. Over the past decade, minimal repair work was carried out, and about 21% of the housing stock, located mainly in old, historical areas, is in need of repairs. Some 13.3% should be demolished in view of their condition. Instances of housing collapsing are quite frequent, and many families are left without shelter. According to estimates, approximately 400 houses were destroyed and several thousand buildings were damaged in Tbilisi as a result of the earthquake of 25 April 2002.

At the moment, environmental concerns are largely overshadowed by more pressing problems of poverty and insecurity. For the majority of the population in Georgia there was an extremely rapid deterioration of relatively high living standards after the disintegration of the Soviet Union. Vulnerability in Georgia primarily hinges on the economic situation. Inequality, corruption and poverty have increased dramatically in recent years. While casinos are opening in the capital city, approximately half the population (50-55%) is living below the official poverty line. Old-age pensions are a very meagre US$ 6 per month. Improvement of the environment will depend to a great extent on the awareness and commitment of the people, which in turn depends on an improvement of the general economic situation, higher standards of living, anti-corruption measures and increased funding for social programmes.

Administrative structure

Georgia is a republic (see also chapter 1 on policy, legal and institutional framework and sectoral integration). It is divided into eleven administrative units (headed by a governor designated by the President), including two autonomous republics (Ajaria and Abkhazia), and 67 districts (*rayons*). The units were established as a follow-up to a presidential decree in 1995, but this structure is only provisional since it was not approved by the Parliament. The districts established during the Soviet time do not fit the new system, but they continue to exist. At the district level local self-government is exercised through representative and executive bodies of the Government. Each district has a *sakrebulo* (local parliament) and a *gamgebeli* (head of district administration). Both are elected. The question of self-government at district (*rayon*) and municipal levels is being vehemently debated in Georgia. Up to now, municipalities have not functioned as democratic self-governing local authorities. Their powers and obligations are not clearly defined with regard to the State/regional governor and to self-government at the *rayon* level. The fact that the question of regional and local self-government has not been finally resolved in Georgia further weakens the role of regional authorities and the municipalities in land use and spatial development. This weakness is aggravated by the poor financial situation of municipalities and their lack of landownership.

12.2 Privatization of land in rural areas

Starting in January 1992, the Government privatized approximately 25% of the agricultural land, as an urgent measure in response to poverty and hunger. Citizens who were directly involved in farming had the right to receive up to 1.25 ha per family. People who lived in rural areas but were not involved in farming (e.g. working in education, public health) were entitled to 0.75 ha; and people from urban areas could obtain 0.25 ha. Land already owned by individuals prior to this land distribution was included in the 1.25 ha and so the land parcels that were distributed were often smaller than the fixed amount. These quotas did not mean that the land was provided in one parcel. On the contrary, each family was given four to five land parcels in different locations. This has led to the fragmentation of privatized land throughout Georgia. In some areas land distribution was complicated by the inability of the government to control the process and the lack of rules and regulations. As a result of the land reform, 1 million families – i.e. an estimated 4 million Georgians - became owners of small land parcels, with an average of 0.9 ha per household.

The territory of Georgia covers 6,949,000 ha, of which 3,020,000 ha (44%) is agricultural land. The remaining area (57%) is covered by forests and urban settlements. Some 942,000 ha of State-owned land was transferred into private ownership free of charge, and 762,000 ha of privatized land is suitable for agriculture, which amounts to about 25% of the country's total farmland. Now 2,256,000 ha of agricultural land (75%) remains in State ownership, of which 940,000 ha (31%) are currently leased.

Figure 12.1: Ownership of agricultural land

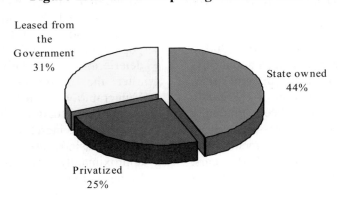

Source: FAO. Strategy for the Land consolidation and improved land management in Georgia. Pre-feasibility study. 2001.

Most of the land that was privatized lies in the vicinity of settlements and in Georgia's more important agro-ecological zones. Most land designated as arable or used for perennials was privatized. The remaining State-owned land is mainly in remote, often mountainous areas, where there is a clear dominance of pasture. Most of the seed production, breeding, testing and other experimental farmland is not yet privatized.

Sought-after land still under State ownership is largely leased under long-term contracts. Often this land has been leased in large blocks (following the former kolkhoz boundaries) to individuals or legal entities. Although the fact that 44% of land is State-owned might at first glance indicate that land is available, the "valuable" land in the vicinity of villages is either privatized or leased. Consequently, not much reserve land is available in the agriculturally important areas. Furthermore, over 60% of the country is mountainous, which is reflected in the large area designated as pasture.

The first stage of land reform as described above took place without a legislative framework and coincided with political and economic crises, civil war and rising crime. Only in March 1996 did the Parliament approve the Law on Agricultural Landownership. Basically, the Law legitimized all the previous acts aimed at the privatization of land in the country. Since then a number of efforts to register land and set up a land cadastre have been successful. This includes the Law on Land Registration of November 1996 and the Presidential Order on urgent measures for the initial registration of agricultural landownership rights and issuance of registration certificates to citizens of Georgia. Subsequently, a number of donor-funded projects have made progress with aerial photography, mapping, cadastre software, database development and registration of land titles, thus contributing to the creation of a database on land use and its ownership. These projects as well as the established legal framework have created a sound base for further activities to improve land management.

At present, the preparatory stage has started for the second phase of privatization of the remaining State-owned land. In November 2001 the draft law on the privatization of agricultural land remaining in State ownership was finalized, and it is now being discussed. This law avoids the fragmentation that resulted from the first phase of privatization. It addresses the issue of minimum parcel size (3 ha) and average parcel size (5–10 ha) to be privatized through land auctions. Its other provisions include the consideration of present leasing agreements (priority sales to present leaseholders), a participatory approach to privatization on the lowest local level (the *sakrebulo,* or community) and a number of other features that form part of a more sustainable land management strategy. However, this law is not yet approved, and there is controversy in Georgia about the future strategy for land privatization.

12.3 Privatization of housing and urban land

In Georgia, as in other countries in transition, free privatization of housing was regarded as a quick, populist sign of the new times. The policy and practice were in no way based on an overall vision of urban development or of the future of the housing stock and the housing sector per se.

Urban land was generally State-owned. Housing was privatized without the underlying or adjacent land (although recently land under multi-flat buildings has formally become part of the property). The 1998 Law on the Declaration of Private Ownership of Non-agricultural Land deals mainly with the privatization of land related to privatized commercial and industrial premises. The 1998 Law on the Administration and Disposal of State-owned Non-agricultural Land stipulates that urban land has to be privatized by public tender (in Tbilisi many tenders were organized, but generally there was only one buyer). The 1999 Law on the Privatization of Urban Land is the latest regulation on the privatization of property in urban areas.

The privatization of urban land and property is under the responsibility of three governmental bodies: the State Department for Land Management, the Ministry of Urban Development and Construction and the Ministry of State Property. The municipalities do not own land, but they are directly involved in the ongoing privatization of the State-owned land within their boundaries. As the question of local self-government has not been finally resolved in Georgia, this further weakens the role of municipalities in the active management of land and spatial development in urban areas.

12.4 Impact on the environment

Spatial planning and land use in Georgia are influenced by specific environmental pressures. Soil erosion remains one of the greatest problems. Erosion is particularly acute in mountainous regions. Along with natural processes, the cultivation of land on steep slopes without appropriate terracing, the excessive grazing and the uncontrolled logging of forests, further contributed to its acceleration. Over the past years an active advance of desertification and salinization have been observed in eastern Georgia. An important problem for Georgia is its vulnerability to environmental hazards: landslides, avalanches and mudflows. Geodynamic processes seem to have intensified recently, with the earthquake of 25 April 2002 in Tbilisi being only one example.

Developments in rural areas

The first stage of the land reform was carried out without respect for modern land management practices. There is no spatial planning and division of responsibilities between ministries is unclear. As a result, one third of agricultural land (about 1 million ha) is subject to erosion, of which 378,000 ha are arable land, and 650,000 ha are hayfields and pastures. Some 218,000 ha (7.3% of agricultural land) are saline. Because of inadequate drainage, 109,000 ha (3.6% of agricultural land) are reverting to marshland. Another 175,000 ha (5.9% of agricultural land) are in danger of desertification because of a deficient irrigation system. For the above-mentioned reasons productivity is low and environmental pressures are high. The restoration of productivity and the protection of soils require vast expenditure that farmers alone cannot afford.

According to the UNECE Land Administration Review (HBP/WP.7/2001/9), about 4 million people have received land parcels. This results in an extremely heavy land fragmentation and the loss of more than 20% of productive farmland that now has to be used to build new access roads or establish boundaries, enclosures and fences. Land surrounding former State farms and other industrial complexes has been abandoned and this has led to further fragmentation. The rural physical infrastructure is desolate. It was built for large-scale farming and is totally ineffective for current farming in small-scale structures. The irrigation system, also installed during the period of large-scale farming, is now ill-adjusted to the new land tenure structures. Water management has collapsed and the former water users' associations are no

longer active. Water management should be re-established with new landowners and the existing systems adapted to the new plots.

Developments in urban areas

Neither the legal nor the institutional framework is at present conducive to effective urban land management or sustainable urban development. Owing to the lack of any kind of relevant urban master plan or zoning schemes, the privatization of urban land is not related to the future use of the privatized plots. The privatization price therefore has no connection with the commercial profit potential. Nor do privatization agreements contractually oblige the buyer to participate financially in building the infrastructure (roads, water, sewerage, car parks) needed to support the future development of privatized land. From this viewpoint, the privatization of urban land can be considered an unfair distribution of future economic obligations and benefits between the new private owner (the winner) and the municipality (the loser). One of the examples is the case of land on the administrative borders of five major cities being re-allocated to the Agricultural Land Reform Fund. These plots used to be in the cities' master plans as areas for recreation (in Tbilisi, it was the land around Samgori reservoir). However, the plots were privatized under the privatization programme for agricultural land, and expensive villas and secondary homes were built on this valuable municipal land. This situation, which is not rare and could be repeated at the second stage of land privatization, should be seen as a threat to sustainable urban development. Should the Ministry of Urban Development and Construction be abolished (as expected), it important that the Ministry of Environment and Natural Resources Protection pay due attention to the issues of sustainable urban development.

Proper management of land stock is obstructed by the fact that municipalities do not own the land within their boundaries. The present privatization of State land does not include the transfer of land to the municipalities. Vital urban development requires public sector development projects such as schools, hospitals, technical infrastructure and social housing. Municipal ownership of the necessary land would facilitate quick decisions on these projects and lower costs. In the present situation, municipal ownership can be secured only by a deliberate transfer of the State land to the municipalities. According to the non-governmental Association of Urbanists of Georgia, the donor programmes are aimed mostly at rural land reform, while assistance to urban land management is not sufficient.

In major cities the problems are disorganized traffic and parking, resulting in traffic jams. Environmental pollution caused by municipal services is also a problem. In principle, cities were well-equipped with central heating systems, but such services are currently not operating. Firewood, gas or kerosene stoves are used instead. Municipal services are in very poor condition, and sewerage, water pipes and electricity supply are often out of order, factors which can eventually have catastrophic environmental effects there. In addition, availability of hot water, gas and electricity supply is a major issue that determines the level of dwelling comfort and its value on real estate markets. Urban transport as well as obsolete municipal infrastructure and services in cities and industrial centres are the main sources of pollution.

The major problem related to the built environment is not new construction, but rather the need to modernize and renovate the housing stock which was privatized together with shared rights and obligations for the common elements of the property (roof, stairways, plot of land). However, emerging construction markets are confined to extremely narrow consumer groups (high-income households) and building activities are essentially concentrated on new construction, both residential and commercial. With average incomes very low and the wealthy preferring new construction, the market for housing renovation has not had a chance to develop. The problem is aggravated by the fact that the State transferred overall responsibility for the housing sector to municipalities, which do not have the financial resources and the management skills to maintain the housing stock and its infrastructure. A draft law on housing condominiums has been prepared, but is still under consideration in Parliament.

12.5 Policy objectives and management

The policy framework

After the disintegration of the Soviet Union, the previous system of socio-economic, spatial and environmental planning became irrelevant. The framework Law on Environmental Protection (1996) introduced the basic requirements of the new system of strategic environmental planning. At the same time, an attempt to introduce a new system of socio-economic planning was made in

1997 when the Law on Fundamentals of Indicative Planning of Economic and Social Development was adopted. These laws stated that a new system and policies for spatial and land-use planning should be worked out. Despite several attempts to set objectives, strategies and priorities in this area, these activities were very limited.

Within the USAID-supported project Land Policy Conference for the South Caucasus Region, Georgia will prepare a draft land policy action plan agenda based on papers and documentation with an analysis of critical problems and land policy issues prepared by a group of experts. The final land policy development action plan will be issued at the Conference to be held in Tbilisi in February 2003 with the participation of Georgia, Armenia and Azerbaijan. The Association for the Protection of Landowners' Rights is a grant co-recipient in Georgia. It is expected that regional international cooperation on land administration issues will promote, inter alia, transboundary cooperation on environmental protection and spatial planning.

In May 2001 the UNECE Working Party on Land Administration reviewed Georgia's land reform. The review recommended that "land consolidation should be started as an enforced, legally regulated measure". Land consolidation is seen as a measure to reduce fragmentation by reallocating parcels and rearranging holdings so as to improve environmental aspects of land use and increase agricultural production. A strategy for the reintroduction of spatial planning could be drawn up and reflected in land consolidation procedures. Participatory approaches to community development and local self-government are regarded as an integral part of land consolidation. In November 2001, the Food and Agriculture Organization of the United Nations (FAO), in cooperation with the State Department for Land Management, worked out a pre-feasibility study entitled Strategy for Land Consolidation and Improved Land Management in Georgia. Three preconditions for land consolidation were identified: public awareness, a legislative framework and spatial planning.

Urban development, especially in Tbilisi, is disorganized. For environmental and economic reasons, there is a need for short-term city development plans (5-6 years), zoning, and optimization of urban traffic. City planning units in the municipality of Tbilisi need reorganization to strengthen coordination and transparency. At present, there is a lack of information-sharing even among different departments in the municipality. The Rules of Land Use and Building Regulations of Tbilisi were developed by the Ministry of Urban Development and Construction through its subsidiary body "Habitat-Georgia" and the municipality of Tbilisi, and it has been a legally binding document since 9 August 2001. The introduction of the Regulations was driven by the fact that: (a) existing regulations have no requirements for single parcels and they were not suitable for the new conditions for many other reasons; (b) the new institutional set-up is not in place; and (c) transparent public participation procedures do not exist. The Regulations envisage the preparation of general and detailed zoning maps for Tbilisi within nine months after enforcement of the document. The Regulations also foresee the setting-up of a Tbilisi land-use and building regulation council for (a) policy development and monitoring; (b) public hearings on special permits; (c) the preparation of decisions on approving zoning maps; and (d) organization of public hearings and awareness campaigns. However, since August 2001, no practical actions have been taken to implement the Regulations.

The legislative framework for spatial planning

During the Soviet era, all land was public property and belonged to the "United State Land Fund", which was divided into several categories based on land use: agricultural land, State forestry farms, State land fund and non-agricultural lands (industrial areas, urban areas and resorts). Spatial planning and land use were a part of the central planning system based on strictly centralized territorial and economic planning.

The existing system of spatial planning in Georgia is still based on the outdated Soviet legislative norms and regulations, for example, the 1985 Law on City Zoning. The last time spatial development plans were prepared was in the early 1980s. Since that time, national regional programmes on industrial and residential areas, regional development plans, master plans for cities and other residential areas have been neither revised nor developed. In the early 1990s, the President and the Government regularly issued statutory acts. These decrees demanded either the prolongation of the validity of old plans, their revision or the preparation of new plans (in May 2001, Presidential Decree No. 204 prolonged the validity of all cities' and other settlements' master plans until 31 December 2003). However, all attempts to revise

them or develop new plans have failed due to economic crises, the lack of financial resources, the outdated legal framework and the low priority of this sector in international donor programmes.

The only law regulating spatial planning in any way is the 1999 Law on Comprehensive State Expertise and the Approval of Construction Projects. Its aim is to improve the spatial planning process, to protect the safety and health of the population, and to protect the environment through the comprehensive State expertise of construction projects. According to the Law, the function of comprehensive State expertise is to check if the construction projects meet legislation. The Law stipulates that the Ministry of the Economy conducts the State Technological Expertise of Construction Projects, while the Ministry of Environment and Natural Resources Protection is responsible for the State Ecological Expertise of Construction Projects. According to the Law, documentation for spatial planning (such as master plans for cities) also needs expertise and approval.

Although there is no framework law regulating spatial planning, several attempts were made to draft legislation to mitigate the consequences of uncontrolled territorial development for the environment, human health and cultural heritage and to regulate the spatial planning process through zoning. Among these legal acts are the 1997 Law on Tourism and Resorts, the 1998 Law on Sanitary Protection Zones for Resorts, and the 1999 Law on the Protection of Cultural Heritage. Few laws have provisions for participation of the general public and the private sector in the preparation of zoning plans at the initial stage.

The legislative framework for land administration

The legislation on land administration is more advanced than that on spatial planning – a common situation in many countries in transition. Many new laws have been adopted. One of the reasons is that land administration (primarily the registration of private rights in land and the creation of land markets) is a priority for international donor assistance and therefore has considerable resources. However, even in this area, there are many inconsistencies in legislation, and implementation mechanisms need further attention.

Under the Constitution (art. 21), property is considered inviolable. Universal rights include those of ownership, acquisition, transfer and inheritance, although the Constitution provides that such rights may be restricted in the public interest, provided that due process is exercised and appropriate compensation is paid. The privatization of land, housing and enterprises is governed by a number of laws, decrees and resolutions. In addition to the 1995 Constitution and the 1997 Civil Code, legislation includes:

- The 1996 Law on Agricultural Landownership;
- The 1997 Law on the Privatization of State Property;
- The 1998 Law on the Declaration of Private Ownership of Non-agricultural Land; and
- The 1998 Law on the Administration and Disposal of State-owned Land (1998).

Land registration is governed by the Civil Code and the 1996 Law on Land Registration, which provide that ownership rights are recognized only if registered. The 1999 Law on Land Parcel and Related Real Estate State Registration Fees sets fees for the initial registration and subsequent transactions. Only registered rights can be officially sold, leased or used as collateral. The Presidential Order on Urgent Measures for the Initial Registration of Agricultural Landownership Rights and the Issuance of Registration Certificates (No. 237, 1999) was issued to accelerate and simplify the requirements of the initial registration of agricultural land.

Land valuation is addressed in the 1997 Tax Code, which provides for different base tax rates for agricultural and non-agricultural land. No specific law has yet been framed to address the consolidation of fragmented agricultural parcels and to promote rural development. As for urban areas, draft legislation has been prepared for housing condominiums, urban development, and land-use zoning for Tbilisi (the latter has already been adopted by the municipal council of Tbilisi).

The institutional framework

Land-related matters are currently managed by several State agencies. The State Department for Land Management is responsible for land reform, land transfer and allocation, land cadastre and registration of property rights in land, land statistics, monitoring and control over privatized and leased land, and land valuation. Its head office is responsible for developing State land management policies, designing and implementing programmes, and preparing legislation on land management. Its regional and local offices carry out land registration and cadastre operations. With land registry information, the administration can discover what properties lie within any territory subject to environmental action (e.g. protected spaces, polluted areas, noise corridors). It can address the property owner directly in case of environmental violations (unlawful urban development or land use).

The Ministry of Environment and Natural Resources Protection, through its Department for Waste Management and Land Resource Protection, is responsible for the inventory of degraded and contaminated land, soil erosion, and the assessment of damage from land contamination. It is responsible for landscape planning and related implementation measures.

The Ministry of Food and Agriculture is responsible for agrarian reform. It has to formulate agrarian reform policies to be taken into account by the State Department for Land Management in its implementation of the land reform. The Department of Geodesy and Cartography regulates surveying and mapping activities conducted by State organizations and the private sector. The Ministry of Urban Development and Construction is responsible for housing policy, spatial planning, municipal services and the preparation of building norms and standards. The Bureau of Technical Inventory is subordinate to the Ministry of Urban Development and Construction and has records on urban real estate. The Ministry of Refugees and Accommodation is responsible for drawing up and implementing State policies for internally displaced persons. Other ministries and agencies in the areas of health, sanitary, hydrometeorological services, forestry and transport are also involved in land-related activities.

There is also the State Commission for Land Use and Protection, which was set up in February 1996. All ministries dealing with land participate in its work. Among its principal functions are rational use of land and the creation of conditions for higher agricultural productivity, the administration of State lands, decisions on change in land use, and legislation. Another responsibility is the approval of the borders of cities and other settlements, regional centres, resorts, and the allocation of land for State and public needs. The Commission was established at the time when local self-governance, land-related agencies and the State Department for Land Management were being established. At present, it seems that the Commission in many aspects duplicates the functions assigned to ministries and agencies dealing with land issues and its usefulness could be reconsidered.

A number of non-governmental organizations (NGOs) and associations are important partners for spatial planning and land-use management. The Association for the Protection of Landowners' Rights is a significant adviser for farmers and other landowners. The Integrated Rural Development Centre supports the sustainable development of rural areas (agricultural efficiency, environmentally friendly agricultural methods, spatial planning in rural areas). The Association of Urbanists of Georgia carries out important work in regard to urban zoning and the protection of Georgia's heritage in urban areas and rural settlements.

12.6   Conclusions and recommendations

A clear territorial-administrative structure and a division of responsibilities between different administrative levels are prerequisites for the effective organization of a spatial planning system and management of the environment. The issue of administrative subdivision of the country and self-government are being hotly debated in Georgia. At the national level, there is a lack of regional and local perspective. Although this raises a number of difficult issues, the Government and Parliament should develop a clear and efficient political and administrative structure in order to secure sustainable development, efficient spatial planning, land use and management. Whilst it is necessary to maintain State and government powers and control over land use and management, transparent and simple administrative structures could contribute significantly to the identification of priority issues, efficient decision-making, and the effective implementation of policy decisions at regional and local levels. Sustainable land use and territorial development require local decisions and implementation.

Recommendation 12.1:
The Parliament (through legislation) should streamline the administrative structure of the country, based on the principle that the division of responsibilities and the rights of the State, the region and the municipality should be clearly set out (overlapping of functions and duplication of efforts must be avoided). The principle of the decentralization of powers should be accepted.

There is virtually no legal basis for spatial planning and physical development. The old master plans dating from the Soviet period are not relevant to today's social-economic issues. Passing laws on spatial planning and physical development should be an urgent priority for the Government and for Parliament. Without such tools and the resultant specific plans, sustainable regional and urban development is not possible. Pressures for new development without a legal and planning framework would seriously threaten the very large cultural and historic values in Georgia's urban and rural environment. At present there are neither the competent personnel nor the economic resources to carry out fast, full-scale master planning for all areas where it is required.

Very often new construction and tender documentation and changes in land use are approved without regard to urban development documentation. In the municipality of Tbilisi, for example, the lack of a common database on city development and frequent changes of the chief architect hinder an orderly urban development process. New fast planning procedures and products, which adequately address the most urgent urban development issues, are essential. Focus should be on both the administrative structure and content of spatial planning and development control.

No one outside of the local authority and Parliament should have power to decide land-use issues. Power to ensure that land use in proposed projects is in accordance with approved land-use plans should rest solely with the local authority's planning department.

Recommendation 12.2:
Relevant bodies should, as a matter of priority:
(a) Prepare a new framework law on spatial planning; in this legislation control of new development should be given political priority. The law should also ensure the implementation of international obligations in granting or allocating land during privatization;
(b) Take steps to identify and register all State land. Standards and relevant procedures should be developed for determining public land needs;
(c) Carry out a physical and legal survey of real property and documentation of cultural and historical heritage and protected zones by establishing an appropriate register. This activity could be carried out within a subregional environmental context in Georgia and its neighbours (Armenia and Azerbaijan).

Recommendation 12.3:
(a) *The Government, in cooperation with the municipalities, should establish a list of geographic areas where a large number of development proposals exist or are expected in the near future; environmental assessment of these geographic areas should be given priority in order to avoid negative impacts on the environment from the privatization of urban property and market development. All municipalities should establish a unified database on city development;*
(b) *The Government of Georgia should pay special attention to the city of Tbilisi, which should streamline its planning and decision-making structure, and base its decision-making on a transparent, user-friendly multipurpose information database on city development; and apply its Rules of Land-use and Building Regulations and provide funding for the preparation of zoning maps.*

The Government has carried out a massive land privatization campaign in rural areas, but a significant amount of land still remains in State ownership. Now the Government proposes to privatize this land, expecting to gain extra revenue for the State budget and increase farm efficiency. However, due to inefficient farming and the lack of markets for farm products, rural land in Georgia has little value and the Government should not expect to raise much income from its sale. The Government should also remember that any sale of land to farmers is likely to decrease investment in agriculture, as farmers would have to use their scarce resources to buy land rather than to invest in developing the farming sector. Given the state of the rural economy, the Government should concentrate on measures to increase the value of land and provide it with stable income through the leasing of land to private individuals and companies. Most of the State-owned land is located in mountainous areas with a significant natural value. Measures should be taken to maintain and protect such areas in the public interest. The key component in the discussions for the second stage of land privatization is also the concept of public needs. Rural land is needed for the creation of transport infrastructure, oil and gas pipelines, control over development of natural reserves and resources.

The existence of several State bodies, as well as municipalities, responsible for different aspects of urban land privatization, the lack of valid urban development plans and the non-involvement of the

municipalities in the privatization processes create particular problems for sustainable urban development. A clear and transparent land privatization policy is essential. It should identify: (i) what land can be privatized and what land should remain in public ownership; (ii) procedures that would cut the red tape and facilitate land transfer. To prevent further damage to infrastructure and the environment any future land privatization should be based solely on land management programmes.

Recommendation 12.4:
The relevant bodies should undertake the following steps in the further privatization of land in rural areas:
• *Carry out land surveys of areas that are to be privatized to obtain an accurate picture of their situation. This could be undertaken by the land management offices;*
• *Implement land-use planning projects based on these surveys;*
• *Register the boundaries of new agricultural units or State reserved lands in the cadastre. At this stage the Government is the owner of these land parcels;*
• *Hire an independent appraiser and establish a market value of the farm unit and then offer it for auction with this market value used as a starting price.*

Recommendation 12.5:
(a) *The Government should clarify and simplify the institutional structure responsible for the privatization of urban land.*
(b) *Before further privatization, the urban areas where development pressures are strong, or are expected to become strong in the short term, should be quickly identified. This concerns in particular the central and historical areas of Tbilisi. In these areas, the Government and the relevant municipalities should give priority to providing quick, simplified development plans before privatization.*
(c) *The Ministry of Environment and Natural Resources Protection and the Ministry of State Property, in cooperation with the biggest municipalities, should draw up a list of areas required for, or to be held in reserve for, public sector development projects, as well as districts of cultural and historical heritage and green areas.*

Improving the performance of the housing sector is an important factor in urban environment. There is a definite need to provide decent housing and social protection for needy households. Many households are also very vulnerable to environmental hazards, the most telling example of which is the series of earthquakes that shook Tbilisi in April 2002. Many lives could be lost unless urgent measures are taken to improve the existing housing stock in Tbilisi and other major cities. At least 1,700 families need relocation. As most people are poor, major improvements in this sector in the short and medium term will not take place without targeted assistance from the Government.

The privatization of housing has been a central element in the Government's privatization policy since 1992. At present approximately 90% of the housing stock is privatized and some 450,000 families live in multi-storey privatized housing. Properly managed and maintained privatized housing is vital to Georgia's short- and medium-term environmental development. Although the Civil Code includes the concept of private ownership of flats in multi-storey buildings and contains some very important regulations for such ownership, e.g. the obligation to create homeowners' associations, Parliament has not yet passed a separate law on the private ownership of multi-flat housing. It is unrealistic to assume that the limited regulations on this type of housing contained in the Civil Code will be sufficient to regulate this very important part of Georgia's housing stock.

Private ownership of multi-flat buildings can operate efficiently only if the owners of the units are themselves aware of, take responsibility for, and are able to manage the rights and obligations deriving from this type of ownership. As this is a new and unknown type of ownership in Georgia, flat owners urgently require information and assistance.

Recommendation 12.6:
The Government should develop a national housing development strategy giving special attention to city development and new housing construction, strictly in accordance with environmental concerns, land-use and zoning plans.

Chapter 13

TRANSPORT AND ENVIRONMENT

13.1 Introduction

According to the Statistical Yearbook Caucasus 2002, the transport and communications sector contributed 11%–14% of GDP in the 1998–2001 period (industry contributed about 17% per year in the same period). Furthermore, the quality of transport affects many sectors of the economy, including agriculture. Currently, the sector is overstaffed and underfunded, suffers from a poor level of maintenance, and produces few reliable statistics. Georgia needs a more efficient transport system, but its overall development has been good, compared to other sectors.

Georgia's strategic geopolitical location links Europe to Asia (east–west) and the Russian Federation to Armenia, Turkey, and the Islamic Republic of Iran (north–south). Georgia is promoting itself as an international transit corridor, focusing initially on the currently more politically stable east–west corridor. The two main components are the East–West Energy Corridor

(the existing Baku–Supsa pipeline and two new pipelines) and the Transport Corridor Europe–Caucasus–Asia (TRACECA) (figure 13.1), which consists of road, rail and port components that require some upgrading.

Georgia expects high economic and social benefits from transit freight and passengers (i.e. TRACECA and East–West Energy Corridor). Such benefits will depend on a stable political situation, a competitive tariff policy, a unified transport-development strategy within Georgia for all modes, coordinated action by the corridor countries, and even coordinated action with other transit corridors. For example, integration with the Danube river transport system would affect the development of Georgia's sea ports and sea fleet). To reap ecological benefits (i.e. sustainable transport), Georgia's Constitution, environmental laws, and international conventions and agreements require that the development of transport, including the transit corridors, should comply with environmental standards.

Figure 13.1:   Map of TRACECA

Transport can affect the environment at the local (smog), regional (acid rain) and global levels (climate change). Its activities can cause significant negative impacts on land use and on the biological, physical and social environment. Transport infrastructure removes land from other activities, such as agriculture, and can fragment or destroy natural habitats. Biological impacts can include damage to flora, fauna and sensitive habitats (e.g. the Black Sea). Physical impacts can include erosion, water pollution from release of oily water during port operations, soil pollution from accidental spills of hydrocarbons during rail accidents and air pollution from vehicle emissions. Social impacts can include land acquisition and compensation issues, damage to community resources such as water supply zones and health impacts. These last, for example, may be higher exposure to HIV/AIDS (especially with large infrastructure projects like a large pipeline project that require work camps and outside workers, higher mortality and morbidity rates as a result of vehicle accidents, and a higher incidence of respiratory diseases as a result of air emissions.

The total number of road accidents and fatalities in 2001 was significantly lower than the 1990 level, but the total number has also shown an increasing trend since 1995. According to the Traffic Police, there are about 11 accidents per 10,000 inhabitants, which is relatively high (England has 1–2 accidents per 10,000 inhabitants). The Traffic Police have identified several accident causes, namely the poor condition of the roads and vehicles (e.g. tire blowouts during driving) and the erratic behaviour of pedestrians. Speeding is thought to be the dominant cause of accidents on the main roads. Without comprehensive accident data analysis however, the relative contribution of each cause to the accident rate cannot be confirmed, and it is not possible to design a good accident prevention programme.

Available data indicate that mobile sources are responsible for an increasing share of total air emissions, from about 70% in 1991 to about 91% in 2001. Mobile sources contributed 31% of the dust, 37% of SO_2, 82% of NO_x, 90% of the non-methane volatile organic compounds (VOC), and 98% of CO in 2001. Transport is also contributing an increasing share of CO_2, from 11% to 31% in the 1990–1997 period. There are no routine data available on other important transport sector emissions, such as ozone (O_3), noise or persistent compounds and heavy metals, such as lead (Pb) and polynuclear aromatic hydrocarbons (PAHs). For a

number of reasons (e.g. age and origin of the vehicles and deficient fuel-control system, vehicle-control system, traffic circulation management and public transport management), vehicles in Georgia generate very dirty emissions.

There could also be some indirect impacts. For example, improved transport infrastructure as planned within TRACECA, for instance, without improved control over the transport of hazardous chemicals (including hazardous waste) or customs procedures could result in significant health and social impacts. Better transport infrastructure (without improvements to the environmental management system) could attract more traffic, including more traffic in illegal substances (e.g. drugs, banned pesticides, hazardous waste), or it could raise speeds, increasing the risk of accidents involving vehicles carrying hazardous materials.

13.2　The Sectors

Rail sector

The rail network is 1565 km, 4% of which is included in the TRACECA rail corridor. Most of the network is electrified; some 67% of rails are single-track lines. Half the rail network is operated by personnel and hence associated with a higher degree of risk, especially on the single-track lines. The other half has semi-automatic or automatic alarm systems. If rail traffic and speed increase, the risk factors will increase proportionally. The rail fleet comprises 244 electric locomotives (67% > 20 years old), 184 switch engine locomotives (relatively new) and 11,000 cargo rolling stock (different ages).

In the past five years, the Transport Police has investigated about one or two rail accidents per year, where two or three wagons (usually containing hydrocarbons) derail and spill their contents. Such accidents usually occur in the bad rail segments, and are reported to the Minister of the Interior.

Road sector

The main road network is about 21,000 km, of which about 1,400 km are main roads, 3,300 km are regional roads and the rest (about 16,000 km) are feeder roads. About 8,000 km are asphalt roads, 10,000 km are gravel roads and 3000 km are earth roads. The density of hard-surface motor roads is about 271 km/1000 km^2.

Five main roads and highways (or 859 km) are used for international transit: (i) Poti–Tbilisi–Red Bridge; (ii) Mtskheta–Kazbegi–Larsi; (iii) Sarpi–Batumi–Samtredia; (iv) Khashuri–Akhaltsikhe–Turkish border; and (v) Tbilisi–Marneuli–Guguti. The often rough topography, the low-capacity highways (often only 7 m wide), the inadequate maintenance regime and poor road condition (Georgia only has about US$ 200/km for road maintenance, whereas Germany's Road Department has US$ 45,000/km), the poor technical standards of vehicles, and other adverse conditions are hindering traffic flow and increasing the accident risk. Because of the limited finances available through donor funds and the Road Fund, there are no large road projects at the moment, only a small number of bridge projects and road-rehabilitation projects (the latter usually involve only resurfacing and hence have limited environmental impacts).

In 1999, there were 320,478 registered vehicles, or 59.5 vehicles per 1000 inhabitants, a relatively low rate of car ownership. Most private vehicles are 10 to 20 years old. Few people can afford to replace or properly maintain their cars at this time. The number of second-hand European cars is increasing, but the vehicle fleet still mainly consists of Soviet-made cars. Soviet models generally consume more fuel and produce more emissions. Most public transport vehicles are also in poor condition.

Aviation

There are four international airports: Tbilisi, Kutaisi, Batumi and Senaki. Traffic at Kutaisi, Batumi and Senaki is with East European, Caucasian and Central Asian States; Tbilisi also has traffic with Europe, Asia and the Middle East. The overall number of passengers decreased by 51% in the 1997–2001 period. In 2001, Tbilisi received 93% of the international passengers.

In 1998, UNDP funded the preparation of a Civil Aviation Master Plan, which identified projects for the modernization and development of air transport in Georgia. Although the Master Plan addresses many topics (e.g. legislation, organization, aerodromes, air traffic management, air navigation faculties and security), it does not specifically address environmental issues (there is no chapter on environmental management). At this time, for instance, aircraft waste is simply mixed with municipal waste.

Security measures are adequate at Tbilisi airport, but insufficient at the airports that may receive only one or two flights per week. The air navigation system was recently upgraded in Tbilisi, improving traffic safety and transit flight capacities through Georgia's air space.

The aircraft in use generally conform to noise regulations, especially during this period of reduced activity. Georgia has two or three chapter II aircraft – models that are being phased out in Europe. Other aircraft conform to the International Civil Aviation Organization's chapter III regulation, i.e. modern noise regulations.

Shipping

Georgia has a 315-km coastline on the Black Sea, two thirds of which lies within the autonomous republic of Abkhazia. Plankton populations and fish stocks have declined and pollutants such as PAHs are said to be accumulating in the mollusks and fish. Alien species were introduced into the Black Sea by the ballast water of ships. The ships and ports pollute the Black Sea through oil spills and waste water.

The shipping fleet comprises 13 tankers of various tonnage. Batumi and Poti Ports are Black Sea ports included in the TRACECA network. Batumi Port, a municipal port, has 11 berths, an overall length of 2.3 km, a general-cargo capacity of 2.3 million tons a year, and a liquid-freight capacity of 8.8 million tons a year. This port is used mainly to export crude, petrol, diesel and light oil. Poti Port, a State port, has 14 mechanized berths, an overall length of 2.8 km, and a 3.6-million-tons-a-year capacity. Dry and liquid bulk cargo, general cargo and containers can be handled, but dry cargo, such as grain, has predominated. The ports are handling increasing amounts of freight. In anticipation of more transit traffic, infrastructure capacity is being added, including container facilities, special terminals for oil and chemicals, and railroad–ferry terminals.

The two ports have ISO 9000 certification, indicating a commitment to continually improving their management. Environmental management facilities, however, are still not adequate. Small oil spills often occur during loading and unloading. The equipment to combat a significant oil spill, if that were to happen, is insufficient (e.g. there is no oil-collecting salvage tug). There are no incinerators to treat ship waste. Private companies collect sewage and solid waste for delivery to the municipalities. Batumi Port collects about 50,000 tons of ballast water per year for processing at its own treatment plant. Special barges transport bilge water to Batumi oil terminal treatment plant. In 1997, 330 tons of bilge water from Batumi Port and 730 tons from Poti Port were treated. All current waste treatment systems are insufficient. Necessary improvements were identified through the World Bank's Integrated Coastal Zone Management (ICZM) project. Some environmental management equipment is on order. Poti Port will install some "best" technology to treat contaminated water in December 2002. Otherwise, the ports are awaiting funds to make such orders.

Pipeline sector

The Baku–Supsa oil pipeline, from Baku on the Caspian Sea to the terminal at Supsa on the Black Sea, began operation in 1999: 45% (370 km of 830 km) of this 530-mm-diameter, 6-million-tons-a-year-capacity pipeline is within Georgia. The Supsa terminal, which is owned by the Georgian Pipeline Company, has four, 40,000-ton capacity reservoirs. The pipeline extends from the terminal to a floating facility – a single buoy mooring, where tankers are loaded with crude oil (about 85,000 tons/week). Incidents affecting the environment are said to have occurred along the Baku–Supsa pipeline, for example severe erosion and leaks where old, non-operational pipelines are still in place.

Two new pipelines may be operating by 2005. The 1760-km Baku–Tbilisi–Ceyhan (BTC) oil pipeline will transport up to 1 million barrels per day (or 50 million tons a year) of crude oil from the Sangachal terminal in Azerbaijan through Georgia to Ceyhan on Turkey's Mediterranean coast. The 690-km Baku–Tbilisi–Erzerum gas pipeline (South Caucasus pipeline, or SCP) will be able to carry 7.3 billion m³ of gas from Sangachal through Georgia to the Turkish border.

The new pipelines are designed to a high technical standard. Their construction will undoubtedly have the usual range of impacts, including water and drainage, erosion, waste management, spill containment, noise and air emissions, which according to the proponent's document would be mitigated adequately. However, the pipelines will require a 44-metre-wide right of way, and this will entail clearing many trees and other vegetation. Although mitigation measures for the clearance operations include transplanting rare and endangered species that are likely to be affected and some replanting after construction, the construction of the pipeline and the operation of the

pipeline may in fact disturb wildlife, such as migrating birds and bear, by fragmenting habitat.

The environmental impact assessments of the two new pipelines were nevertheless controversial, as the pipelines pass near sensitive zones: geodynamic zones, Borjomi mineral water resources, and protected areas (including Ktsia–Tabatskuri Managed Reserve, an IUCN category IV area). The biggest potential threat to the environment is associated with catastrophic (e.g. earthquakes) or unplanned events (e.g. sabotage). If such events were to occur (even though the proponent argues that this is improbable), it could result in a major spill that contaminates significant groundwater, surface water, wetlands, or soil resources, and result in significant impacts on flora, fauna, important wildlife habitats, and drinking-water supplies. The core environmental debate is whether any risk to these precious resources is acceptable, and the environmental perspective leans towards "no".

The main criticisms levelled against the pipeline projects were:

- Alternative routes were not sufficiently analysed;
- The potential risks (geological, such as earthquakes, and hydrogeological, such as areas where groundwater runs at a high volume and speed);
- The security issues (e.g. one alternative route that was preferable environmentally was discounted after only a superficial evaluation of the security risks); and
- Insufficient detail and time schedules were provided for various mitigation measures and environmental management plans (reinstatement plan, monitoring plan).

The Ministry of Environment and Natural Resources Protection approved the pipeline project, with certain conditions in December 2002.

13.3 Current Status and Trends in the Transport Sector

Freight

The volume of freight rose in the 1997–2001 period, from 19.7 million tons to 33.1 million tons. Freight volumes in 2001, however, are still only a fraction (13%) of the 1990 level.

Road freight consists predominantly of exports and imports between Georgia and its neighbours. Rail freight (75% oil products) increased significantly recently, from about 4.7 million tons in 1995 to 13.1 million tons in 2001. Oil transport indices for the Baku–Supsa pipeline have come close to the planned level. Air and shipping freight volumes are insignificant compared to those of rail and road freight.

Most transit freight comes from Azerbaijan (74%) and Armenia (9%). Transit freight from elsewhere has decreased in the past few years, probably due to several factors, including complicated border-crossing procedures, high tariffs compared to other Black Sea ports, illegal activities of the road police, deteriorating safety standards, and low cost-effectiveness – matters that are being addressed to a certain extent under Georgia's responsibilities under the TRACECA project.

Passenger transport and public transport (in Tbilisi)

In 2001, passenger numbers were still only about 35% of the 1990 figure, but they are increasing, from 246 million to 364 million in the 1994–2001 period (figure 13.2). It is the number of bus passengers (now minibus passengers) that is increasing, as the use of electric transport (trolleybus, 272 km; underground, 27 km; and tramway, 36 km) – the more economical and ecological means of transport (producing fewer emissions and less noise than the fuel-combustion

alternatives) – showed a slight negative trend from 1993 to 2001.

Tbilisi municipality is slowly bringing more order to the public transport system. For instance, in 2001, it specified 5 routes for its 18 trams, 19 routes for its 86 trolleybuses, 35 routes for the 162 buses and 223 routes for the 3010 minibuses. It has also limited the number of public vehicles per route. Routes are now allocated every two years. Additional routes are being planned (e.g. a trolleybus route to the suburbs and a bus route to the airport), and new public transport routes are being integrated into the Tbilisi Master Plan. The municipality has developed a five-year programme to increase the number of large buses and trolleybuses (one large bus can replace four or five minibuses). There is some focus on developing more "ecological" transport, for instance five electric routes (20–25 km) are being integrated into the *Tbilisi Special Economic Development Programme*.

Tbilisi municipality is moving in the right direction. However Tbilisi, especially the city centre, was not designed to accommodate the current number of vehicles (4,200–4,500 vehicles/hour in some cases). The river valley prevents a good dispersion of air pollutants and gives the city a linear structure, with a very limited number of main streets. Insufficient organization of traffic increases congestion, worsening air quality. The demand for transport in Tbilisi should be managed, and reduced over time.

Figure 13.2: Passengers carried by general-purpose transport types

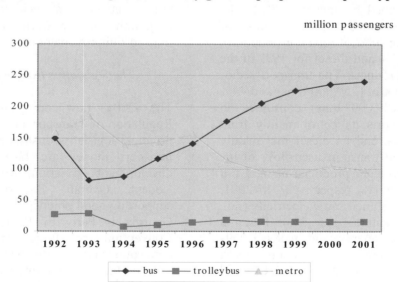

Source: State Department for Statistics. Statistical Yearbook of Georgia, Tbilisi, 2002, and a computer printout, at the time of interview, Nov. 20, 2002.

Transport-demand management is a relatively new focus for sustainable transport experts. One component of such programmes is to improve the transport options. This would include measures to improve the conditions for pedestrians, traffic-calming measures, and improvements to public transport. For example, improvements to the public transport system could include developing an integrated ticketing system and improving the condition and cleanliness of the vehicles and the driving habits of the operators, thus making public transport more attractive to users and potential users.

In addition to improving the transport options, there are three other major components in transport-demand management: market and pricing reforms (e.g. congestion pricing, removing parking subsidies, road pricing), parking and land-use management (e.g. parking charges), and various programmes (e.g. campus transport management programmes). All together, the measures make driving private vehicles less attractive than using public transport. A comprehensive transport-demand management programme (with many simultaneous measures) could reduce vehicle traffic by 20–50% (resulting in significantly less congestion, air pollution and noise and fewer road accidents and decreasing the need to build more infrastructure).

Energy for the transport sector

In 2001, the transport sector accounted for about 15% of the total final consumption of energy, surpassing that consumed by industry (8%). The transport sector consumed 358,000 tons of petroleum products (or 58% of total consumption). Petrol accounts for 62% and diesel for 19% of the imported petroleum products. The transport sector consumed all of the petrol (259,000 tons) and 44% of the diesel fuel (89,000 tons) consumed in Georgia. Georgia imports its petrol mainly from Romania and Bulgaria, and its diesel fuel mainly from Azerbaijan. Road transport used 96% of the transport sector's petroleum products; air and rail transport used 3% and 1%, respectively. In 2001, the transport sector consumed some electricity (rail, 6%; road, 2%) and natural gas (3%). Being a significant consumer of energy, and of fossil fuels in particular, the transport sector accounts for a significant share of dust, CO_2, SO_2, NO_x, VOC, and CO emissions.

13.4   The Decision-making Framework

The policy framework

A *Transport Policy Concept Paper* was prepared by the Ministry of Transport and Communications, its sectoral administrations, the Parliamentary Committee of Economic Sector Development, and other experts; it was approved by Presidential Decree No. 528 in 1997. It addresses the sector's main economic policies (e.g. investments, restructuring, tariffs) and defines the role of the State as securing conditions of sustainable development in the transport system, providing integration into the international transport system, and ensuring the safety of citizens and the safe carriage of goods. The Concept Paper is the basis that guides the development of the transport sector, providing the framework for specific transport policies. It promotes a balanced, multi-modal system of transport, where environmental impacts are to be assessed and monitored, in collaboration with the Ministry of Environment and Natural Resources Protection.

Also noteworthy is the National Environmental Action Plan (2000). It recommends some specific measures to improve traffic-related urban air quality problems, such as increasing the share of public transport, in particular electric transport, strengthening and coordinating the institutions that will implement the ban on leaded petrol, and optimizing and regulating traffic. To improve urban air quality, the Pilot Project in Air Quality Management (a follow-up to the NEAP) identified two strategies: a vehicle and fuel control programme and a traffic circulation and public transport improvement programme.

The legislative framework

The 2001 Law on State Management and Regulation of Transport and Communication is the principal legislative instrument. Laws for different transport modes are also in effect or under development (Aviation, Road, Marine and Rail Codes). Overall, 88 regulatory instruments supporting good practice are in effect. Furthermore, Georgia is Party to 12 road conventions (e.g. Convention on Road Traffic), 18 maritime conventions (e.g. United Nations Convention on the Law of the Sea and International Convention for the Prevention of Pollution from Ships

(MARPOL)), and 8 civil aviation conventions (e.g. Convention on International Civil Aviation). Georgia has also ratified the Basel Convention on the Control of Transboundary Movements of Hazardous Wastes and Their Disposal. To become a transit country, Georgia has to ratify 11 more priority conventions (usually dealing with technical standards, such as the safety of containers). The Ministry of Transport and the Ministry of Foreign Affairs seem fully committed to this.

Georgia also participates in various other agreements. For instance, the 1998 Basic Multilateral Agreement on International Transport for Development of the Europe–the Caucasus–Asia Corridor guides the development of the TRACECA network. (Members include Armenia, Azerbaijan, Bulgaria, Georgia, Kazakhstan, Kyrgyzstan, Mongolia, Republic of Moldova, Romania, Tajikistan, Turkey, Turkmenistan, Uzbekistan, and Ukraine.)

Other important agreements include those associated with pipeline development. The development of pipelines is predominantly regulated by host government agreements. In signing the agreements, the Parties endorsed the environmental, health and safety standards and practices observed by the international petroleum pipeline industry.

Furthermore, the Ministry of Transport and Communications is subject to Georgia's environmental laws, such as the Laws on Environmental Permits and on State Ecological Expertise. Large transport projects require an environmental permit, which is issued based on an environmental assessment. In the 1999–2002 period, at least five transport projects completed the EIA/ecological expertise process, including one bridge project and four projects for Poti Port: oil terminal, universal terminal, ferry complex and chemical loading zone. Two road-rehabilitation projects, one railway line project (Kolkheti–Kulevi route), one bridge project and the pipeline projects are in process.

In sum, a legislative framework may be in place, but implementation still falls short of best practice. Two EIA examples illustrate this. First, the legislation requires that large transport projects should obtain an environmental permit before proceeding, but several port-related projects were approved by presidential decrees before completing the EIA process – significantly weakening the planning-instrument role of EIA. Second, the EIAs

themselves do not follow best practice. For instance, in the case of the Kolkheti–Kulevi railway project, there was no scoping process to develop the terms of reference, alternative routes (to minimize impacts on a Ramsar site) were not sufficiently evaluated, and construction-phase impacts were generally omitted.

Economic instruments for environmental management in the transport sector

Georgia has taxed leaded and unleaded petrol and diesel since 1993. The tax rates as of 1999 are 0.12 lari/kg of leaded petrol, 0.04 lari/kg of unleaded petrol, and 0.035 lari/kg of diesel. The tax difference between leaded and unleaded (67%) is similar to that of many OECD countries. However, it is unclear whether this tax is still relevant since leaded petrol was banned in 2000, and the leaded petrol that is on the market is illegal. Also, as of November 1998, there is a 60% excise tax and a 20% VAT on transport fuels. Unleaded petrol is priced significantly higher than diesel. The above taxes, as implemented, and the price structure do not encourage sustainable transport (i.e. switching to cleaner fuel).

There are three vehicle taxes for the Road Fund: a tax on the import of cars, based on the age and engine capacity of the vehicle; an annual charge (0.25–0.4 lari per horsepower); and a tax on foreign-registered vehicles on entry into the country. The revenue from the three taxes and the general road user charge is quite limited, and can be expected to have only a small indirect environmental benefit, by increasing the total cost of transport (see also chapter 2 on economic instruments, financing and privatization).

Regulations and standards concerning fuel quality

The import of petrol and diesel is subject to obligatory certification. However, with fuel imported from East European, Caucasian and Central Asian countries (usually diesel), the Georgian certificate is based on the certificate from those countries. As a result, very little diesel is tested. For fuel originating elsewhere, the importer submits a sample to a laboratory accredited for such work. The laboratory analysis is carried out according to 1970s Soviet standards. Only the research octane number (RON) and lead content are measured. Few of the fuel-testing laboratories are functioning at this time, and the lab equipment is insufficient or the testing protocols are not enforced. Petrol stations do not properly identify fuel quality. Overall, it is difficult to obtain accurate information on fuel quality.

The various technologies have different fuel-quality requirements. Soviet models run on low-octane petrol; European models run better on higher octane. One way to increase a fuel's octane level is to add lead. Also, many older cars require leaded petrol because the lead lubricates and protects the soft valves. The EU standards require catalytic converters on petrol-powered cars, engines designed for high-octane/<u>unleaded</u> petrol (lead destroys catalytic converters). Georgia is importing increasing numbers of second-hand European cars with catalytic converters and it imports much low-octane petrol, which is at times altered through the addition of lead to obtain higher-octane/leaded petrol.

The legal basis for phasing out lead to 0.013 grams/litre is the 1999 Law on Amendments and Modifications to Some Legislative Acts. The Law does not clearly define the functions of the various executive bodies. Neither does it regulate other hazardous substances, e.g. other aromatic hydrocarbons. This Law as it now stands cannot be implemented. Georgia now aims to follow the Common Policy for Eastern Europe, Caucasian and Central Asian countries, which is to phase out leaded petrol in the 2005–2008 period. A special commission prepared the Strategy (Concept) of the State Programme for Improving Fuel Quality, which was approved in January 2002.

Improving fuel quality and promoting the use of high-quality petrol will require several interrelated interventions, as outlined in the Strategy for Improving Fuel Quality and in other background documents (e.g. Options for Policies and Measures for Implementing Lead Phase-out). These interventions include: changing the Criminal Code and the Administrative Violation Code (i.e. strict sanctions for non-compliance); developing better fuel standards; developing modern refining capacities (to produce lead-free high-octane petrol); implementing better controls at the border (about 60% of the fuel enters the country illegally); improving fuel-testing procedures and equipment; implementing strict inspection of the wholesale and retail distribution network; requiring precise descriptions at petrol stations; increasing public awareness about fuel-quality issues and vehicle fuel requirements; slowly replacing the old car fleet; improving garage services and repairs; improving vehicle testing; banning the import of lead, except for small quantities for scientific research; and developing an appropriate monitoring and control system.

Emission standards

The Cabinet Ministers' Decision No. 634 (1995) on the prevention of exhaust gas pollution from motor vehicles and Presidential Decree No. 258 (1997) on the approval of the State programme on safety of traffic in Georgia provide the framework for vehicle emission standards. These are out-of-date Soviet standards for measuring CO and hydrocarbons in exhaust gas and soot in diesel engines. Note that improving vehicle emissions will require concurrent improvements in fuel quality, the vehicle fleet and the emission standards.

Vehicle inspection programmes and emissions testing

Vehicles are subject to mandatory yearly inspection. Currently, 64 units perform the technical inspections. Each unit has a representative from the Centre of Ecological Control and Technical Service of Motor Vehicles, who checks the CO concentration or soot content against the current emission standards. The inspection produces five documents: the results of the technological test and the emissions test, and receipts for the payment of the car insurance, the road tax, and the certificate label. All five documents are reviewed by the Traffic Police, who then provide and apply the vehicle sticker.

The road tax collected at the time of the inspection does not depend on the age of the vehicle. The emissions tests do not differentiate between Soviet models and European models. Apparently, neither the inspectors nor the repair shops are familiar with modern emission control systems. Catalytic converters are often simply removed. The use of catalytic converters is resisted for a number of reasons, including the added expense of running the emission-control technology and the lack of technical services for those devices. There is an obvious need to further develop the vehicle testing system. Georgia may soon ratify the UNECE Agreement Concerning the Adoption of Uniform Conditions for Periodical Technical Inspections of Wheeled Vehicles and the Reciprocal Recognition of such Inspections, bringing some improvements to the current situation.

The institutional framework

Many institutions are involved in the environmental management of the transport sector.

The Ministry of Environment and Natural Resources Protection is responsible for environmental policy, EIA and environmental permits, including permitting transport infrastructure, research and developing strategies and action plans, such as phasing out the use of leaded petrol, resource management (e.g. air protection) and emissions monitoring. The State Department of Hydrometeorology monitors ambient air quality.

The main objective of the Permanent Secretariat of the Intergovernmental Commission TRACECA is to solve the problems and eliminate the obstacles within the TRACECA route (e.g. price and tariff policy, customs procedures). It aims to contribute to the growth and competitiveness of the transport corridor. It has undertaken some small environmental projects.

The Ministry of Transport and Communications comprises several administrations: road, rail, airport and marine. The Ministry has policy-making, legislative and monitoring functions for the transport sector. It reviews the draft regulations of its administrations against the transport policy. As of 2003, it should have a safety agency to address the ecological and safety aspects of the transport sector.

The Ministry of Transport and Communications has a work plan (Presidential Decree #No. 302) to facilitate the replacement of the car fleet (with a time schedule and identified responsible parties). Work plan tasks include developing recommendations to encourage the import of new cars and economic incentives to encourage vehicle owners to install catalytic converters. The work plan also calls for tenders to: procure fuel-testing equipment, develop facilities to recycle car parts and to produce catalytic converters, and develop a disposal site for old vehicles. Other tasks include developing a new regulation for car servicing, new standards for oil products, training courses for professional drivers, public awareness programmes, and a transport scheme for Tbilisi.

The Road Administration has a Safety Department to monitor traffic safety. The Safety Department is currently developing a list of economic instruments to facilitate the replacement of the car fleet (e.g.

new cars will pay less than older cars for various services). These economic instruments will bring Georgia in line with international practice if they are implemented.

The Rail Administration's Council for Technical, Scientific and Information Issues has a Division for Environmental Protection. This one-year-old Division has a director (who previously worked for the Ministry of Environment and Natural Resources Protection) with three staff. More staff are now needed, given the international focus and the need to increase monitoring. The Division completed an inventory of rail assets (e.g. buildings, garages) and subsequently identified the following environmental priorities: cleaning-up Batumi station, building noise barriers along high-noise rail segments, and reinforcing rail segments where the rail line passes as close as 2 m from the Black Sea at high tide. To solve this issue, the Rail Administration is collaborating with the Service for the Protection of the Coast (Ministry of Urban Development and Construction).

Previously, the Airport Administration had an environmental officer, but 20 staff were dismissed during restructuring, including the environmental officer. Now environmental duties are shared between the Airport Service and the Aircraft and Engine Service.

The Marine Administration's headquarters is in Batumi; there is also a small representative office in Tbilisi. The State Marine Safety Inspection Department deals with navigational safety issues and the Maritime Rescue Coordination Centre coordinates rescue operations and oil spills. All Georgian ports are subordinate to the Marine Administration, and each port has a department to deal with environmental issues. All parties are trying to comply with the Black Sea Convention.

The State Department for Roads is responsible for planning and implementing road projects. Since independence, its budget has been severely limited, and it now implements only a few small projects each year. It does not have environmental expertise in-house.

The Ministry of the Interior is responsible for car registration and licensing, permitting the 64 vehicle-inspection units, issuing driver's licences and permitting driving schools. The Transport Police is responsible for investigating aviation, shipping and rail accidents. The Traffic Police investigates road accidents and enforces traffic regulations. The Ministry of the Interior is both a regulator and inspector (e.g. it permits the vehicle-inspection units) and a law enforcer through its Traffic Police. Its dual role could lead to a conflict of interests.

The Ministry of Fuel and Energy is responsible for energy policy and for regulating fuel quality. Its Supervising Department of Energy and Fuel Quality, established four years ago, will be responsible for fuel quality testing in the future, in collaboration with the State Department of Standardization, Metrology and Certification. The latter will draw up the fuel standards.

Local governments, including large municipalities such as Tbilisi, control their own public transport. The municipality fixes some fares and provides free public transport to some vulnerable groups, such as refugees and blind people. Tbilisi has an Urban Transport Service, which sets the public transport routes. It also monitors the contracts of the companies involved: 7 bus enterprises and 64 minibus enterprises. Electric transport (trolleybuses, trams and underground) is managed by one enterprise under the municipality.

Other important decision makers are British Petroleum and the donor community. British Petroleum designed the two new pipelines. It hired consultants to complete their EIAs. The Ministry of Environment and Natural Resources Protection hired experts from the Netherlands to review the EIAs and to help prepare permit conditions.

The donor community has funded various projects with a transport-and-environment component, including the Energy Transit Institution Building project (to establish a sustainable oil transport system), the Integrated Coastal Zone Management (ICZM) project (to establish a national oil spill contingency plan), the TACIS Black Sea project (EIA training), the regional TRACECA project (to develop the transport corridor) and the rehabilitation of the Port of Poti and the Transcaucasian Railway. Assistance was also provided to develop a concept paper on the State Programme for Improving Fuel Quality and a related action plan to implement changes to the Criminal Code and the Administrative Violation Code. Small energy efficiency projects, including the installation of new rectifiers at two metro stations and an energy audit of the Tbilisi Metro, were also supported. Other proposals for energy efficiency projects are awaiting funding (e.g. a pilot project to convert some taxis and minibuses to

natural gas; a feasibility study for recovering used motor oil).

13.5 Conclusions and Recommendations

The transport sector clearly provides social and economic benefits to the people of Georgia, contributing 14% of GDP in 2001. Transport, however, including roads, rails, ports, aviation and pipelines, is associated with actual and potential environmental impacts. Currently, freight volumes and passenger volumes are slowly recovering their pre-independence levels, and the construction of two new pipelines is about to begin. With freight and passenger volumes still at reduced levels, Georgia has found it an opportune time to improve the environmental management system for transport, as evidenced in its Transport Policy Concept Paper (which supports sustainable transport) and various other initiatives, such as fuel quality improvement initiatives.

The Government strongly supports the development of Georgia's transit potential. The attention is on the future economic benefits; less attention has been given to the potential serious environmental impacts associated with porous borders (e.g. potential increase in illegal trade) and larger volumes of hazardous chemicals being transported on Georgian territory (inadequate framework to manage imports and exports and the transport of dangerous materials at this time). The Law on Environmental Permits (art. 4k) subjects the implementation of infrastructure plans, projects and programmes and, more specifically, transport infrastructure development programmes to EIA.

Recommendation 13.1:
The Ministry of Environment and Natural Resources Protection should initiate a study to be undertaken and supported by the TRACECA project, on the transit corridor development programme to assess the impact of integrating Georgia (and the other member countries) into the international transport system. The study should identify alternative routes, alternative technologies and mitigation measures.

Leaded petrol was banned in Georgia in 2000; however, a significant amount of leaded fuel remains in the market, presumably illegally. At the same time, the differentiated tax rate for leaded and unleaded petrol, introduced in 1993, remains in effect. The tax difference (67%) is similar to that of many OECD countries. Since 1998, there has also been a 60% excise tax and a 20% VAT on transport fuels. Unleaded petrol is priced significantly higher than diesel. These taxes, as implemented, and the price structure do not encourage sustainable transport (i.e. switching to cleaner fuel).

Recommendation 13.2:
The Government should set up a programme to implement the ban on leaded petrol, taking into account the needs of the existing car fleet.

A *Strategy (Concept) of the State Programme for Improving Fuel Quality* was approved in January 2002. The Ministry of Transport has a work plan (Decree No. 302) to improve vehicle quality. The documents clearly outline many of the inter-related steps needed to begin the process of improving fuel quality and vehicle quality in Georgia.

Recommendation 13.3:
The Ministry of Transport and Communications should ensure that the approved work plan is implemented, as outlined in Decree No. 302, and that progress is strictly monitored and reviewed.

Tbilisi has severe air quality problems. Furthermore, its specific geography does not allow the operation of a large number of vehicles. Other parties, as referred to above, are working on fuel and vehicle quality (i.e. technological issues), but little attention has been given to one very important component of a sustainable transport system: demand management. Every effort is needed to decrease total demand for transport in general and demand for private transport in particular. The Tbilisi municipality is moving in the right direction with some of its initiatives (e.g. more electric transport), but it lacks a comprehensive transport-demand management programme. Transport-demand management has four components: improvements to the transport options, market and pricing reforms, parking and land-use management, and various site-specific programmes.

Recommendation 13.4:
The Government should support Tbilisi municipality to:
(a) Prepare a transport-demand management plan based on strengthening demand for the most environmentally friendly transport modes and technologies. This plan should identify a battery of measures to encourage a more efficient use of the existing transport system, thereby reducing total demand for transport by private car;
(b) Subsequently implement, to the extent possible, all the transport-demand management measures;
(c) Evaluate progress in managing the demand for transport on a yearly basis, to review accomplishments and to revise and improve subsequent demand-management measures.

Chapter 14

HUMAN HEALTH AND ENVIRONMENT

14.1 Population health status

Population dynamics

The population of Georgia was estimated to be 4.95 million in 2000, down from 5.42 million in 1991. The Georgian population is older than the average Eastern Europe, the Caucasus and Central Asia (EECCA) population, but younger than the average EU population, as shown in table 14.1. The population density in Georgia is relatively high (73.2 inhabitants per km^2), although the percentage of urban population (57.7%) is relatively low. There is a positive natural growth rate in the population, but a negative migration (i.e. "emigration") resulted in decline in the population size in the 1990s. According to the Statistics Department 450,000 to 550,000 people left the

country during the 1990s, mainly ethnic Russians migrating to the Russian Federation.

Life expectancy at birth is 74.66 years (see table 14.2), which is above the average of 67.18 years in Eastern Europe, the Caucasus and Central Asia, but below the EU average of 78.31 years. There was an increasing overall trend in life expectancy between 1981 and 2000, but there was a temporary decline after independence, between 1991 and 1995. Georgia's life-expectancy estimates should be considered with caution, because they are based on incomplete death registration, and unknown changes in the size of the population add to the inaccuracy of the estimates.

A comparison between vital statistics and medical records in 1998 reveals that 22% of live births were not registered by the Civil Registry. Likewise, 20% of all deaths were not registered.

Table 14.1: Population dynamics

	Georgia (2000)	EECCA average (2000)	EU average (1999)
Population (millions)	4.95	288	376.95
Population aged·			
0-14 years (%)	20.43	21.77	16.99
15-64 years (%)	65.99	63.09	66.94
> 65 years (%)	13.58	11.14	16.07
Area. km^2	70000	..	..
Population density per km2	63.6	..	..
Births per 1000 population	10.5	11.02	10.69
Deaths per 1000 population	9.27	13.04	9.92
Natural growth rate per 1000 population	1.23	..	0.77

Source: WHO Health for All Data Base, 2001.

Table 14.2: Selected population health indicators

	Georgia (2000)	EECCA average (2000)	EU average (1999)
Life expectancy	74.66	67.18	78.31
Standardized death rate for all causes of death per 100,000 population	884.38	1362.95	681.45
Infant mortality per 1000 live births	12.21	16.27	4.94
Maternal mortality per 100,000 live births	49.18	37.29	5.05

Source: WHO Health for All Data Base, 2001.

Mortality rates

Standardized mortality rates in Georgia from all main causes of death are lower than the average rates in Eastern Europe, the Caucasus and Central Asia, and for malignant neoplasms, injuries and poisoning, diseases of the respiratory organs and digestive systems lower than the EU averages.

The structure of mortality illustrates that the proportional mortality from cardiovascular diseases in Georgia is predominant and substantially greater than in the rest of the UNECE region. Proportional mortality from malignant neoplasms and diseases of the respiratory system is relatively low in Georgia, well below that in the UNECE region.

A comparison of the causes of death mentioned in the death certificate and information in medical records revealed that in 37% of the records for 1996-97 there was an error in the main cause of death; in 1998 the figure was 24%.

Morbidity rates

There was a general decline in hospitalization in the 1990s, which is likely to reflect changes in access to and provision of health care rather than in incidence rates. In 1993 there were 1,106.59 hospitalizations per 100,000 persons due to respiratory system diseases, whereas in 2000 there were 697.31. Similarly, there were 534.14 hospitalizations per 100,000 persons due to infectious parasitic diseases in 1993 against 335.75 in 2000.

The incidence of tuberculosis in the early 1990s was 30 per 100,000 persons, but there has been a steep increase in the number of reported cases in spite of the decline in access to health care. The incidence of tuberculosis peaked in 1996 at 161.21 cases per 100,000 persons and was 105.25 cases per 100,000 persons in 2000. There has also been a steep increase in the incidence of malaria, from 0.02 cases per 100,000 persons in 1990 to 5.50 cases per 100,000 persons in 2000.

The incidence of hepatitis A declined from 143.20 cases per 100,000 persons in 1991 to 51.02 in 1999. It is difficult to judge the effect of changes in access to health care and use of diagnostics in the 1990s.

14.2 Health risks related to environmental factors

Ambient air: Population exposure and health effects

In 2002 the Ministry of Environment and Natural Resources Protection and a private company conducted a comprehensive assessment of sources, emissions and levels of air pollution in Tbilisi, and assessed population exposure and the health effects of these levels. This project used existing monitoring data, and measured PM_{10}, NO_2, ozone and benzene using passive samplers. Emission data indicate that industrial emissions in Tbilisi are very low, and emissions from traffic are the dominant source.

According to stationary air pollution monitoring in 1999, the annual average concentration of particles was 200-400 $\mu g/m^3$, substantially down from 200-900 $\mu g/m^3$ in the early 1990s. The daily averages of PM_{10} measured in 2002 in the city centre ranged from 24 to 58 $\mu g/m^3$. In 1999 the annual SO_2 average based on stationary monitoring was 180 $\mu g/m^3$. The concentrations were not measured in the early 1990s. The diffusion tube measurements of SO_2 in 2002 were substantially lower, with two-week averages from 3 to 10 $\mu g/m^3$. The annual average concentration of NO_2 was 40-50 $\mu g/m^3$ in 1991 and remained similar in 1999. In two-week diffusion tube measurements in 39 locations of the city, the average concentrations varied from 15 to 86 $\mu g/m^3$, and, using dispersion models and geographic information systems (GIS), 164,722 people (12%) in Tbilisi were estimated to be exposed to levels above the EU standard of 40 $\mu g/m^3$. The two-week averages of benzene varied from 14 to 32 $\mu g/m^3$ and of ozone from 41 to 113 $\mu g/m^3$.

In July-August, however, air emissions combined with the geographic and climatic conditions in the city often lead to photochemical smog episodes. Usually in January, weather and pollution conditions lead to typical winter smog episodes. During these periods the air pollution concentrations may be substantially higher than the levels mentioned above.

Current concentrations of PM_{10}, NO_2, ozone and benzene are likely to exceed current EU and WHO limit values. Levels of ozone and benzene are particularly high. SO_2 concentrations are generally low and not likely to exceed the EU and WHO limits.

The estimated overall annual impact of short-term exposure to particles, SO_2, NO_2 and O_3 included 450 hospital admissions due to respiratory diseases. The impact of long-term exposure to particles included 8,500 years of life lost. Table 14.3 shows the estimated impact of air pollution in Tbilisi in 2002 and the estimated annual reduction (minimum-maximum) that would be achieved by meeting EU limit values in 2005 (PM_{10} 40 $\mu g/m^3$, stage 1) and 2010 (PM_{10} 20 $\mu g/m^3$, stage 2).

Lead in petrol is currently a serious problem in Georgia. By law the maximum level of lead in petrol is 0.013 grams per litre. In practice, lead concentrations are on average substantially higher.

A major problem is the illegal import of low-octane petrol, which is then upgraded with lead additives to increase the octane level.

The major health effects of exposure to lead are an increased risk of hypertension and coronary problems in adults and a reduction in neuropsychological development in children, measured as IQ capacity. The GEO-2110 Country Programme for Phasing Out of Lead in Gasoline in Georgia estimated benefits from reducing lead in petrol from the current average level of 0.050 grams per litre to 0.013 grams, as stipulated by the law in force at present. The benefits included a reduction in hypertension in 200,000 adults, a reduced risk for 600 non-fatal heart attacks and 600 cardiovascular deaths per year, and an improvement of 3,200,000 IQ points in children.

Table 14.3: Estimated impact of air pollution in Tbilisi in 2002 and estimated annual reduction (minimum-maximum) achieved if EU limit values are met in 2005 (stage 1) and 2010 (stage 2)

Main cause	Effect	Estimated total impact in 2002	Reduction in occurrence (minimum-maximum)	
			PM10 at stage 1	PM10 at stage 2
PM_{10}	Respiratory disease hospital admissions (number)	86	0-74	30-80
PM_{10}	Acute mortality (number)	170	0-140	58-150
O_3	Respiratory disease hospital admissions (number)	290	..	..
O_3	Acute mortality (number)	490	..	..
PM_{10}	Congestive heart failure (number)	110	0-92	38-100
PM_{10}	Cerebrovascular hospital admissions (number)	210	0-180	73-200
PM_{10}	Years of life lost due to death	8,500	0-7,300	3,000-7,900
Benzene	Acute myeloid leukaemia (number)	3	2	2
SO_2	Acute mortality (number)	41	0-29	0-29
SO_2	Respiratory disease hospital admissions (number)	12	0-8	0-8
NO_2	Acute mortality (number)	150	0-71	0-71
NO_2	Respiratory disease hospital admissions (number)	62	0-30	0-30
PM_{10}	Restricted activity days	830,000	0-710,000	290,000-770,000
PM_{10}	Ischaemic heart disease	100	0-87	36-95
PM_{10}	Chronic bronchitis - adults (number)	2,000	0-1,700	710-1,900
PM_{10}	Chronic bronchitis - children (number)			
O_3	Asthma attacks	12,000	Nq	Nq
O_3	Minor restricted activity days	650,000	Nq	Nq
CO	Congestive heart failure (number)	340	170 (minimum)	170 (minimum)
CO	Acute mortality (number)	7,500	3,500 (minimum)	3,500 (minimum)
CO	Ischaemic heart disease (number)	270	140 (minimum)	140 (minimum)

Sources: The Ministry of Environment and Natural Resource Protection, and AEA Technology, 2002.

Indoor environment

Two factors have influenced indoor environmental conditions in homes and other buildings over the past decade. The cost of all types of energy has surged, and this has led to changes in heating sources and to more thermal insulation in construction. There has also been a shift to synthetic building materials that emit volatile organic compounds. The consequent decrease in ventilation and increase in chemical emissions have resulted in higher levels of indoor air pollutants. This situation in Georgia is similar to that in Europe and North America following the 1974 energy crisis. Smoking and combustion for cooking and heating are also important potential sources of indoor air pollution. There is little knowledge about the incidence of these or other potential sources of indoor air pollution, such as dampness and mould, and pets.

Decay products of radon constitute an important potential indoor environmental hazard (see ionizing radiation below).

There is little direct information on indoor environmental conditions. The Tbilisi air pollution study measured one-month average indoor NO_2 levels in two central apartments. The average concentrations of 32.3 and 40.5 $\mu g/m^3$ were close to the outdoor concentrations measured in the city centre.

Information on smoking provides indirect information on exposure to environmental tobacco smoke. Smoking is very popular, particularly among men. According to the Chronic Diseases Centre survey in 1999, 60% of the men and 15% of the women aged 40 to 65 are current smokers. The Tobacco Control Counter Centre reported that, in 1997, 30% of 10 to 14-year-old boys and 14% of girls in Tbilisi regularly smoked at least one cigarette per day. This indicates that besides personal smoking, exposure to environmental tobacco smoke is an important public health problem.

Tbilisi Sanepid conducts investigations as a response to complaints about indoor air quality. Problems with poorly vented heating and cooking lead to exposures to high levels of carbon monoxide. Sanepid receives annually 30-50 reports of fatal CO intoxication. A large number of small enterprises are located in residential buildings. Emissions from different processes used there are a common complaint, but control of these diverse

sources is difficult. Asbestos is a common building material in the existing building stock, because there used to be a substantial national production in Kaspi and Rustavi. Also drainage pipelines are commonly made of asbestos. Thus renovation workers as well as inhabitants may be exposed to asbestos, although little is known about the current extent of this problem.

Water leakages from the ageing water distribution and sewage systems add to dampness and mould. Floods in the basements are also common and likely to contribute to mould in homes. There is a need for a national population-based survey to assess the extent of indoor environmental problems in Georgian homes and other buildings.

Food

Microbiological contamination of food products

Food-borne infections are common due to poor hygiene, which, in turn, reflects the main economic problems in Georgia. Perishable food products are sold in open street markets with substandard hygiene conditions. The shortage of tap water and daily interruptions in the water supply in many cities affect the hygiene conditions and increase the risk of food contamination. Interruptions in power supplies may also contribute to spoiling food products that require refrigeration.

Outbreaks of food-borne infectious diseases have been reported throughout Georgia, including in the resorts of Batumi, Borjomi and Kobuleti. According to the National Environmental Health Action Plan (NEHAP), the high risk of food-borne diarrhoeal diseases is an important factor limiting the development of international tourism in Georgia. It is likely that most food-borne infections are not reflected in the official statistics, as presentation rates are likely to be low owing to the high cost of medical treatment that has to be covered by the patients. More detailed information on potential food-borne and water-borne diseases in Georgia is provided in the water quality section, below.

The State Sanitary Inspectorate of the Ministry of Health is responsible for controlling hygiene standards and food safety at food markets, shops and eateries. The Inspectorate also performs scheduled analyses of food samples. According to the Law on the Inspection of Enterprises, unscheduled sanitary inspections of food vendors and manufacturers can be conducted only with the permission of the District Attorney, which can be granted only if sufficient evidence of violations of hygiene norms is presented. These restrictions mean that the Inspectorate focuses on responding to known violations rather than on prevention. The Centre for Disease Control (Ministry of Health) performs epidemiological investigations of outbreaks of infectious diseases.

Chemical contamination of food products

Georgia has an institutional system to ensure the chemical safety of food products. The Ministry of Labour, Health and Social Affairs developed a list of banned chemical substances that cannot be manufactured in Georgia or be imported into the country. It includes specific pesticides and food additives. The State Department of Standardization is responsible for permitting the manufacturing of chemical substances, including pesticides. The Ministry of Food and Agriculture is responsible for monitoring the quality of food products that are produced in Georgia. The State Sanitary Inspectorate also analyses food products, but the data on chemical contamination of food appear to be scarce. The State Sanitary Inspectorate of Borders is responsible for ensuring the safety of food imports.

Chemical food safety monitoring is limited. There are very few measurements of pesticides, heavy metals and organic pollutants. Border control is usually limited to checking documents, since the State Sanitary Inspectorate of Borders has limited laboratory capabilities. According to the NEHAP, the illegal import of banned pesticides remains a potential problem, which may result in the contamination of food produced in Georgia. The quality of imported food products may also be questionable. Improvement of food safety monitoring capabilities can be achieved by establishing an inter-agency chemistry laboratory with modern equipment.

Although there is not enough information to assess the scale of contamination of food products with pesticides and heavy metals, it is likely that the situation has improved during the past decade due to the dramatic decline in pesticide use and in the emissions of organic pollutants and heavy metals by industry. However, the data on the current use of pesticides are likely to be incomplete. It is important to strengthen the capabilities of the responsible agencies to monitor chemical food

safety and enforce existing standards on pesticide application.

Water

Contamination of recreational water bodies and sources of drinking water

The municipalities are major sources of surface water pollution. Municipal sewage accounted for 60% of the total volume of waste water in the early 1990s. Its share has been increasing owing to a decline in manufacturing. Only 5 of the 29 municipal waste-water treatment plants in the country are currently operational, and these provide only mechanical treatment. Biological treatment units are not operational at any of the 22 facilities initially fitted with them. In addition, most waste-water treatment plants are considered to be obsolete and in need of urgent repair (see also chapters 7, on water management and 6, on Waste, chemicals and contaminated sites).

Major rivers, such as the Kura, Alazani and Rioni, are contaminated with municipal waste, resulting in high levels of nitrogen compounds, organic substances and, most importantly, human pathogens. While most water-supply systems use uncontaminated water sources, microbiological contamination of water supplies is a serious risk factor for a number of systems. For example, one of Tbilisi's three water intakes uses surface water from the Aragvi river that is at a high risk of contamination from the failing waste-water system upstream.

Major industries responsible for polluting surface water are mining, metallurgy and the chemical industry. The major pollutants are heavy metals (especially copper, manganese and zinc), phenols and hydrocarbons. Waste-water discharges by industrial sources plummeted during the past decade in line with the decline in industrial output. A growth in industrial output may result in renewed pollution of watercourses, as waste-water treatment facilities at many enterprises are either nonexistent or inefficient (see also chapter 9, on mining, industry and environment).

Agricultural sources contaminate both surface water bodies and shallow aquifers that are used by rural residents for their drinking-water supply. Major chemical pollutants are nitrates and pesticides. Many watercourses are heavily polluted by fertilizers and pesticides, and, in some, permissible levels are exceeded by a factor of 5 to 10. Pollution by pesticides and nitrogen compounds exceeded permissible levels in almost every water body. Contamination of individual wells by nitrates and pesticides has also been reported. However, monitoring of well water for pesticides was discontinued owing to the lack of funding (see also chapter 11, on agriculture and environment).

The major water-supply systems use water sources that are not contaminated by industrial waste, so exposure to industrial pollutants through drinking water is unlikely. However, human exposure may occur through the use of polluted waters for irrigation, and the consumption of contaminated food products and fish. Unfortunately, no data on concentrations of heavy metals or persistent organic compounds in food products or fish are currently collected. So the public health impact of industrial waste-water discharges is difficult to assess. It is likely that it is small relative to the effects of air pollution from transport and microbiological pollution of drinking water. The health effects of chemical pollution of drinking water are likely to be insignificant.

Drinking water quality

The Hygiene Requirements for Surface Water Used for Drinking and Recreational Purposes stipulate maximum allowable concentrations of pollutants at water intakes. The norms are very detailed – they include 1,346 chemical, physical and microbiological parameters, few of which are monitored for want of laboratory capabilities and funds. Drinking water quality standards are stipulated in the Hygiene Requirements for Drinking Water Quality. These standards are also excessively detailed, while monitoring is limited to a short list of basic parameters. (For information on monitoring, see chapter 3, on environmental information and public participation in decision-making.)

Water utilities monitor chemical and microbiological water quality at water treatment plants and in distributions systems. In 2001, 57 municipal water utilities maintained their own water quality laboratories, a steep decline from the late 1980s, when every water-supply system had its own monitoring capabilities. In addition, many laboratories are only partially operational owing to the lack of supplies. Data are stored in paper form, and only summaries are included in regular water quality reports.

The State Sanitary Inspectorate, which is responsible for the chemical and microbiological safety of drinking water, maintains its own monitoring programme at water treatment plants and throughout distribution systems, where samples are taken from fixed sites in accordance with specified schedules. In addition, the Inspectorate takes samples, although less regularly, from individual wells and springs. The Inspectorate also responds to complaints about tap water quality. Although the Inspectorate still maintains 53 laboratories throughout the country, these laboratories are in poor condition. No new equipment has been procured since the early 1990s. Water quality analyses are also limited to a set of basic parameters. Capacities for detecting specific water-borne pathogens such as protozoa and viruses are lacking.

Nevertheless, the Inspectorate has an extensive water monitoring programme, and its data demonstrate that there is a problem of microbiological contamination of wells and spring water used for drinking in many areas with intensive agriculture or a dense population. Water from individual wells is not chlorinated and its consumers may be routinely exposed to water-borne pathogens. In the absence of protection zones, shallow aquifers can be contaminated by sewage and agricultural run-off.

The Inspectorate's data also suggest a high risk of microbiological contamination of tap water in some centralized water-supply systems. According to local specialists, most of the non-compliance results from secondary contamination of water in distribution systems rather than from low microbiological water quality at the treatment plant.

Health effects of microbiological water pollution and microbiological contamination of food products

The shortage of drinking water and its poor quality are important causes of gastrointestinal morbidity and epidemic outbreaks of infectious diseases. According to the State of Environment, Tbilisi 2000 report, high rates of gastrointestinal illness in Tbilisi in 1994–1995 were caused by the secondary contamination of water in the distribution system, specifically interconnections with the sewer system. For a number of outbreaks, causative links with drinking water contamination have been demonstrated. For example, in Poti, interruptions in power supply at pumping stations caused the overflow of waste-water systems and the contamination of surface water. Back siphonage of contaminated water into corroded drinking water pipes that were located in trenches filled with contaminated surface water caused an outbreak of hepatitis A.

Georgia's Centre for Disease Control attributed an outbreak of amoebiasis (*Entamoeba histolytica*) in Tbilisi in June-July 1998 to pollution of surface water sources and inadequate water treatment. The origin of this dramatic outbreak, which caused at least four deaths, is disputed by the utility company and the Sanitary Inspectorate, which believe that it was food-borne. During the outbreak, surrogate indicators of microbiological water quality, such as coliforms, did not exceed the standards. However, these bacteria-based indicators might not be informative, since cysts of *E. histolytica* are more resistant to chlorination. At the time of the outbreak, the city's population was advised to boil drinking water, and water treatment was modified to improve coagulation, increase the doses of chlorine and reduce filtration velocities. The incidence of amoebiasis subsequently declined. However, sporadic cases of *E. histolytica* continued to occur with a total of over 1,500 cases from July 1998 to June 1999. The number of annual cases of *E. histolytica* infections has since declined to 249 cases in 2001; most of these cases were diagnosed in Tbilisi.

Diagnosis and reporting of potentially water-borne and food-borne infectious diseases

Rates of reported infectious diseases in Georgia declined in the first half of the 1990s but climbed again in the second half of the decade. The temporal dynamics of hepatitis A and ill-diagnosed acute gastroenteritis are presented in figures 14.1 and 14.2. The same temporal pattern is characteristic for many infectious and non-infectious diseases, including cancers. This decline can be explained, to a large extent, by the collapse of health care delivery and financing systems. Whereas health care had been free before independence, as the health care financing system began to break down, providers started to require cash payments for all services, including treatment of infectious diseases, which resulted in widespread self-treatment or informal consultations outside established health care institutions. Only during recognized outbreaks, such the outbreak of *E. histolytica* in Tbilisi, are victims treated free of charge.

While it is not possible to determine the exact proportion of background cases of acute gastrointestinal infections and outbreaks that are caused by water pollution, it is likely that the vast majority of water-borne infections remain unreported and many lesser outbreaks remain undetected.

Rates of shigellosis and salmonellosis in Georgia (figure 14.3) appear to be comparable with the rates in Azerbaijan and Armenia. However, the former Soviet republics of Russia, Kazakhstan, Estonia and Latvia have substantially higher reported rates, while Denmark, Sweden and Finland have higher rates of salmonellosis and lower rates of shigellosis.

Figure 14.1: Temporal dynamic of reported cases of Hepatitis A

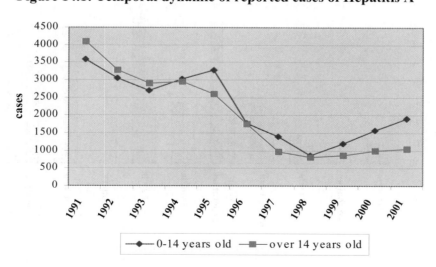

Sources : Centre for Disease Control and National Centre for Health Statistics.

Figure 14.2: Temporal dynamic of reported cases of ill-defined infectious gastroenteritis

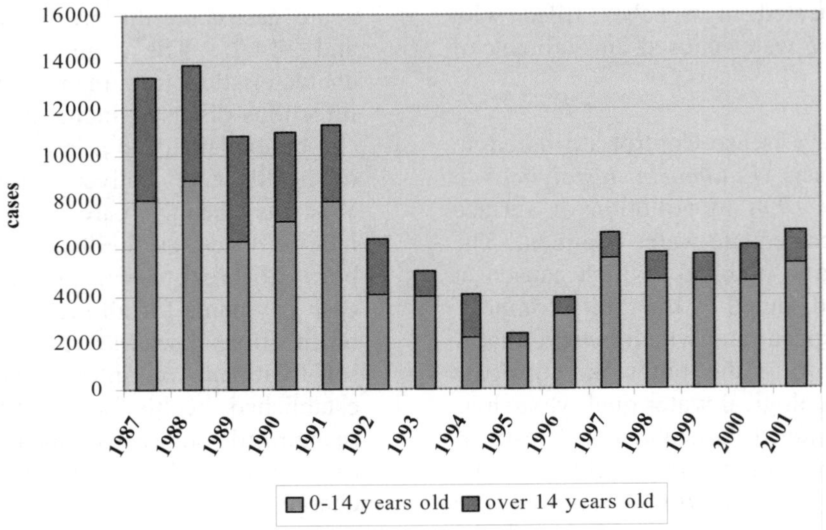

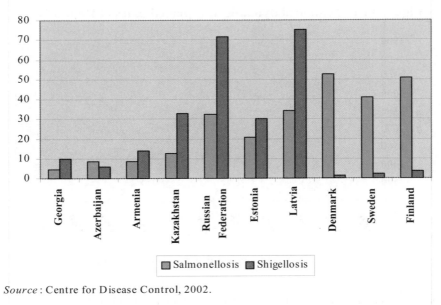

Sources : Centre for Disease Control and National Centre for Health Statistics.

Most reported cases of acute diarrhoeal illness are not diagnosed microbiologically (table 14.4). When the diagnosis is made, it may not be as specific as in developed countries. For example, in 2001, *Shigella sonnei* accounted for 20% of reported shigellosis cases in Georgia and *Shigella flexneri* accounted for 8%, while the other cases were reported mainly as non-specified shigellosis. In developed countries, the majority of shigellosis cases are attributed to *Shigella sonnei* and *Shigella flexneri*.

Waste and soil pollution

The main sources of soil pollution in Georgia are dumping of municipal and toxic waste, use of mineral fertilizers and chemicals in agriculture, industrial activities, oil and gas operations, mining, traffic emissions, and accidental contamination. The contamination can be divided into area (large industrial and agricultural districts), local (e.g. mining, power stations), and linear (transport) (see also chapter 11, on agriculture and environment).

Figure 14.3: Salmonellosis and shigellosis in Georgia and selected countries in 2001, rate per 100,000 population

Source : Centre for Disease Control, 2002.

Table 14.4: Reported cases of potentially water-bone and food-borne infectious diseases in 2001

Diagnosis	All ages		0-14 years old		Children as % of total
	Cases	Rate per 100,000	Cases	Rate per 100,000	
Typhoid	62	1.4	10	1.1	16.1
Salmonellosis	195	4.4	106	11.7	54.4
Shigellosis	436	9.8	264	29.0	60.6
Other confirmed bacterial infections	345	7.8	260	28.6	75.4
Food poisoning	315	7.1	134	14.7	42.5
Amoebiasis (*Entamoeba histolitica*)	249	5.6	61	6.7	24.5
Ill-defined acute gastroenteritis	6,670	149.8	5,367	590.1	80.5
Hepatitis A	2,957	66.4	1,906	209.6	64.5
All potentially food-borne and water-	11,229	252.2	8,108	891.4	72.2

Source: Centre for Disease Control, 2002.

Municipal waste management is compromised both in urban and rural areas due to insufficient organization and limited resources. Most of the existing municipal waste dumpsites are illegal and do not satisfy the international sanitary norms. Approximately 10% of settlements do not have any designated dumpsites, and most sites are in the vicinity of residential areas and often near rivers. The current waste management situation increases the risk of transmission of vector-borne diseases, such as leptospirosis and tularaemia, which are spread through rodents, cats and dogs. For example, Tbilisi has large populations of stray dogs and cats feeding on waste and spreading diseases. There is no special management of hazardous waste, which constitutes a serious potential health risk.

During the Soviet period there were extensive industrial and mining activities in Georgia. Although these have decreased, old landfill sites remained. Based on source information and measurements in the 1980s, heavy metals, including vanadium, cobalt, manganese, copper, molybdenum, nickel, lead, zinc, tin and brome, are major industrial soil pollutants (see also chapter 6, on waste, chemicals and contaminated sites and chapter 9, on mining, industry and environment).

In the 1990s the use of pesticides was also reduced, but illegal trade in pesticides is common. Large amounts of old pesticides and fertilizers have been stored inadequately in rural areas since the early 1990s, and leakage from these storage sites to soil and water constitutes environmental health risks.

Soil pollutants constitute a heterogeneous group of substances with diverse potential health effects. The possible routes of exposure include inhalation of resuspended dust, and ingestion directly or with food and water. Risk assessment requires detailed information on the emission and distribution of pollutants. A risk assessment based on State Department of Hydrometeorology data was recently conducted in the Urals mining region. Current information on soil pollution is insufficient for appropriate risk assessment, and there are no results from epidemiologic studies. Mining tailings contain, among other things, known human carcinogens, such as cadmium and cadmium compounds, chromium and nickel. Some of the heavy metals may have organ-specific effects. For example, long-term exposure to cadmium has effects on kidney tubules, leading to increased excretion of low-molecular-weight proteins. Renal tubular dysfunction may result in nephrolithiasis and osteomalacia.

Ionizing radiation

Contaminated military sites

At independence, former Soviet military bases were left littered with discarded equipment containing radioactive material, such as communications equipment containing radioactive strontium and caesium. There are bases close to Tbilisi, Akhaltsikhe, Akhalkalaki, Kakheti, Kartli, Kutaisi, Senaki, Zestaphoni, Khoni, Poti and Batumi. A number of accidents involving highly radioactive pieces of military hardware have been reported. Individuals who were unaware of the danger, found abandoned radioactive devices, tried to use them and suffered severe radioactive burns.

The accident at the Lilo military training centre near Tbilisi, which occupies a former Soviet military base, was investigated by the International Atomic Energy Agency (IAEA). A number of highly radioactive pieces of discarded equipment containing caesium 137 were retrieved from the base. As a result of radiation exposure nine soldiers suffered severe skin and tissue damage.

Another accident occurred in the village of Matkholi (300 km west of Tbilisi) in July 1998. Some of the villagers had potentially been exposed over a long period to high levels of ionizing radiation from contamination hot spots and the use of contaminated objects at home. IAEA took blood samples to investigate any chromosomal abnormalities. However, this study failed to demonstrate statistically significant exposure-dependent changes in the individuals tested.

On the recommendation of IAEA and with its help, the Georgian authorities initiated a programme to detect radioactive contamination hot spots and retrieve the radioactive sources from abandoned former Soviet military sites. The Nuclear and Radiation Safety Inspectorate of the Ministry of Environment and Natural Resources Protection is responsible for tackling emergencies, including the clean-up of former military bases. It also maintains a registry of radioactive sources in the country and issues licences for radiation-related activities. The Inspectorate employs highly qualified and dedicated specialists, who are implementing a well-organized country-wide clean-up programme. Despite their recent concerted efforts, the problem persists because there are so many potentially contaminated sites. Another problem that needs to be solved urgently is the lack of a permanent storage facility for radioactive waste.

The overall health effect of radioactive contamination from military bases is limited to isolated incidents involving a limited number of individuals.

Health industry

Radiation doses from medical procedures account for 40 to 50% of total population exposure. The high population exposure is due to the use of outdated medical equipment. For example, more than 50% of X-ray units that are currently in use in Tbilisi were manufactured before 1985. Health facilities own over 87% of all registered sources of radiation in the country.

The Chernobyl accident

The region of Georgia along the Black Sea coast, especially Abkhazia, was contaminated by the fallout from the Chernobyl accident. Soil contamination resulted in the radioactive contamination of local food products, especially subtropical crops, such as Georgian tea. Radioactive contamination of food products is not currently monitored.

Natural radiation

Georgia is a country with potentially high radon exposure as there are geological formations with a high uranium content, and many buildings are constructed with local materials. Exposure to radon gas occurs mainly through inhalation of radon gas at home. The contamination of drinking water contributes to exposure mainly through the vaporization of radon. The main potential health effect of exposure to radon is lung cancer. As the effects of exposure to radon and tobacco smoke are synergistic, a very high rate of smoking among the Georgian population may exacerbate the effects of potentially widespread radon exposure.

Although both NEHAP and the National Health Policy include radon exposure surveys, monitoring still has to be initiated. The lack of monitoring equipment is a problem that has to be resolved. Currently, there are practically no data on radon concentrations in Georgian homes.

Noise pollution

The State of the Environment Report in Tbilisi (2000) includes an analysis of the sources, levels and effects of noise pollution. The results may to some extent be generalized to other major cities. Tbilisi is considered a noisy city due to transport. The main roads are narrow and the traffic on these roads is heavy. The population density in the city centre is approximately 25,000 per km². Noise spreads from the centre located in a valley to the city hillsides. The age and poor condition of passenger cars contribute to noise pollution. Recently the number of minibus taxis has increased. Most are in a poor state of repair, and they add to the noise pollution. Traffic jams are very frequent at the crossroads, and intensified by the traffic lights either being out of order or not functioning due to the absence of electricity. The noise arising from air transport is local and spreads only to areas near the airport. (See also chapter 13, on transport and environment.)

The Scientific Research Institute of Environmental Protection is responsible for the monitoring and management of noise, but there is no systematic nationwide monitoring of noise, because of limited resources. Noise is measured as a response to complaints by the public. There are approximately five major complaints that lead to investigations and measurements per year.

From 1999 to 2002, noise was measured in five sites in Tbilisi. The noise level at 7.5 m above the curb ranged from 71dB to 80 dB. Railroad noise 25 m from the track was 65 dB during the day and 63 dB at night. Noise was also measured in 1999-2001 in Rustavi (73-75 dB), Poti (72-74 dB), Telavi (70 dB) and Gori (72 dB). According to European standards, the maximum noise level for urban areas is 65 dB during the day and 55 dB at night.

These sporadic measurements indicate that traffic noise has reached disturbing levels in the major cities, and the levels are expected to increase due to a rising trend in traffic density. Therefore, there is a need to monitor urban noise levels and consider preventive measures against noise in urban planning.

Occupational health

During the 1990s there was a structural shift in occupational exposure as a result of the decline in heavy industry, changes in agricultural practice and the development of small enterprises. In addition, unemployment increased. At the same time there was a decline in occupational health care, and the diagnosis and reporting of occupational disease dramatically decreased. The system of diagnosis and registration of occupational diseases broke down in the 1990s, and the official statistics are therefore not reliable. There is little information on current working conditions, and there is no official monitoring of work exposure and preventive measures are not enforced.

The Institute of Occupational Medicine and Ecology, founded in 1927, has a long tradition in occupational hygiene and medicine. The Institute is responsible for the diagnosis of occupational diseases in the country, but it suffers from a serious lack of funds.

Occupational health care is in a state of crisis, because the old legislative and service systems have ceased to exist. There is no general insurance system for occupational diseases and accidents. Individual employers are liable for compensation if their workers' health is harmed, and compensation therefore depends solely on the financial capacity of the employer.

Natural disasters

Earthquakes, large landslides in mountain regions, and floods and related soil erosion are common natural disasters and may have a substantial direct or indirect public health impact.

During the past decades there have been several earthquakes in the Shida Kartli, Imereti and Racha regions. Hundreds of homes were damaged beyond repair during a recent earthquake in Tbilisi. The mountain landslides are typical in the regions of Ajara, Svaneti, and Racha. Floods have caused soil erosion in the Svaneti, Lechkhumi, Imeriti and Racha regions. Mudflows in Mtiuleti, Racha and Shida Kartli have damaged arable land and reduced their size, and damaged water-supply systems. Earthquakes and floods may also indirectly lead to chemical catastrophes in areas with large chemical reservoirs.

In 2000, there were over 60,000 environmental refugees in Georgia. One third of them, from the Svaneti region and the mountainous regions of Ajara, had lost their homes in the strong earthquakes in 1990 and needed urgent assistance.

14.3 Environmental health policy and management

The policy framework

The National Environmental Action Plan (NEAP) was prepared by the Ministry of Environment and Natural Resources Protection and adopted by presidential decree in 2000. This Plan includes short-term and mid-term goals for environmental protection and institutional development. It provides a detailed analysis of environmental pollution problems in Georgia. Among the priorities it lists are microbiological pollution of drinking water, chemical and microbiological contamination of surface water bodies, ambient air pollution in cities and waste management. The NEAP lists specific projects designed to improve drinking water quality and to reduce discharges into surface water bodies. However, insufficient financing of the proposed measures undermines their timely implementation.

The National Environmental Health Action Plan (NEHAP) was developed in 1998 by the Ministry of Labour, Health and Social Affairs with the assistance of the World Health Organization (WHO). It is currently (December 2002) being reviewed by Georgia's State agencies. Upon completion of the review, the NEHAP will be submitted to the President. Its objectives correspond with those of WHO programmes. To achieve them, the country intends to develop a legal system in accordance with European Union guidelines. The draft NEHAP includes a detailed programme of action to reduce the health effects of environmental pollution. It calls for an assessment of environmental risk factors, the setting of priorities for decision-making and the implementation of measures to reduce the health impact of harmful environmental factors. It also pays significant attention to data collection and analysis to provide information support to environmentally oriented decision-making. An important programme outlined in the NEHAP is the creation of centralized environmental health databases, the expansion of monitoring programmes and the improvement of data quality (see also chapter 3, on information and public participation in decision-making).

The NEHAP also provides detailed programmes to reduce environmental pollution and the population's exposure for each environmental medium (air, water, soil) and source of pollution (transport, industry, energy production, agriculture). All programmes specify State agencies and institutions responsible for their implementation. However, due to complicated organizational structures, unclear and overlapping responsibilities and the lack of a legal framework defining the mechanisms of implementation of State programmes, the specific responsibilities, budgeting procedures and reporting requirements have not yet been specified for many of these agencies.

Georgia's National Health Policy (1999) identifies priorities in health policy and strategy to improve public health. Two sections of this document, Solutions to the Problem of Health Impact of Environmental Exposure and Establishment of an Environment that is Safe for Health, provide a detailed inventory of environmental health problems and list specific measures to be implemented. The Policy lists microbiological pollution of drinking water as a priority and sets the following water-quality-related goals:

- Improve drinking water quality for 60% of the population by 2005 and reduce the burden of water-borne infectious diseases by 90%;
- Increase to 80% the proportion of the population that is supplied with running water;

- Improve water disinfection, first of all in rural supply systems;
- Improve drinking water monitoring;
- Restore water distribution systems;
- Restore waste-water treatment plants;
- Improve the sanitary protection of water sources; and
- Reduce waste-water discharges.

While the National Health Policy includes measures that should be fully supported, the funding mechanisms are not elaborated in this document. Instead, the Policy includes general statements that the Ministry of Finance "should provide unconditional and timely funding for the programmes in their entirety". Given the large number of health improvement programmes outlined in the Policy, this may not be entirely realistic.

Both the NEHAP and the National Health Policy list radon monitoring in indoor air as a priority. They also address the problems of radioactive waste that is currently stored in a temporary storage site. The measures outlined in these documents are summarized below:

- Undertake indoor radon monitoring to detect homes with concentrations exceeding the WHO guideline;
- Undertake remedial measures to reduce indoor radon concentrations;
- Introduce new building norms and regulations to reduce radon concentrations in new housing;
- Solve the problem of radioactive waste storage;
- Reduce doses for personnel and patients in medical facilities by introducing standards and using newer equipment with low-intensity exposure.

The legislative framework

Article 37 of the Constitution guarantees citizens the right to live in a healthy environment. The framework environmental health laws, such as the Law on Water, the Law on Nuclear and Radiation Safety, the Law on Pesticides and Agrochemicals and the Law on Food Products and Cigarettes, provide a general legislative basis for the protection of public health from the effects of environmental pollution. The State agencies responsible for their implementation develop normative acts that outline specific standards and procedures.

The institutional framework

The Ministry of Environment and Natural Resources Protection has broad responsibilities for environmental protection. It sets water management rules and standards, issues licences for water abstraction from any source, sets discharge norms and issues discharge permits. It also controls the emission of pollutants into ambient air and enforces existing emission norms. It determines health-based air pollution indices for each city and estimated pollution charges depending on the overall level of air pollution in a given city.

The Ministry of Labour, Health and Social Affairs is responsible for monitoring drinking water quality, and the control and enforcement of regulations related to drinking water abstraction, treatment and distribution. To some extent, its monitoring replicates the monitoring by water utilities. The Ministry also monitors food safety and responds to complaints about food quality and hygiene standards. It is responsible for controlling hygiene norms in public buildings and industrial enterprises. Another of its responsibilities is controlling the application of norms and regulations governing hazardous waste and radiation safety.

The Ministry of Labour, Health and Social Affairs also sets occupational safety standards and rules. The Institute of Occupational Medicine and Ecology implements research projects for the Ministry, monitors occupational hazards, diagnoses and treats occupational diseases, and performs investigations to determine causes of occupational illness. The activity of this institute is severely limited by the rules restricting inspections of industrial enterprises.

The Ministry of Food and Agriculture jointly with the Ministry of Labour, Health and Social Affairs is responsible for enforcing the Law on Pesticides and Agrochemicals. It is also controls the manufacturing of food products.

14.4   Conclusions and recommendations

According to the general health indices, the health of Georgia's population is better than the average in Eastern Europe, the Caucasus and Central Asia. However, limited access to health care, underdiagnosis of diseases, incomplete registration of births and deaths, as well as difficulties in defining population size, all influence the health statistics, and in some cases the indices may be

overoptimistic. Increases in the incidence of tuberculosis, malaria and some other earlier rare infectious diseases, as well as food and water-borne infectious disease epidemics, indicate problems in water and air quality, and housing.

Ambient air pollution, indoor environmental conditions including radon decay products, water quality problems, and dysfunctional waste management constitute the main environmental hazards with a substantial public health impact.

The NEAP prepared by the Ministry of Environment and Natural Resources Protection and adopted by presidential decree includes short-term and mid-term goals for environmental protection. Achieving these goals will substantially reduce the environmental health hazards to the Georgian population. The NEHAP prepared by the Ministry of Labour, Health and Social Affairs and to be signed by the President also includes a detailed programme of actions to reduce the health effects of environmental pollution. Furthermore, the National Health Policy lists environmental pollutants as priorities to improve public health.

The development of an integrated approach to environmental health management requires close cooperation between the Ministry of Labour, Health and Social Affairs and the Ministry of Environment and Natural Resources Protection. Cooperation is needed in particular in environmental and health monitoring, the sharing of information, environmental and health impact assessment, and the planning of actions.

Relevant and valid information on public health and environmental conditions over time is a prerequisite for rational decision-making in environmental health management. Georgia inherited the health and environmental information systems from the former Soviet Union. The health information system used standardized routine data collection in polyclinics and hospitals, and the reporting was conducted through two or three stages to the national offices. The allocation of human resources and the breadth of surveyed health outcomes were extensive, but lack of quality control limited the efficient use of data. A major weakness was the aggregation and transformation of data, which seriously limited the use of regional data in the assessment of health effects of environmental exposure. The use of health information from this type of system for assessing environmental health effects has recently been evaluated and discussed in detail. There was also extensive standardized monitoring of air, water and soil quality by the State Department of Hydrometeorology.

The health and environmental information systems are in transition. Since 1990, due to the severe economic and social crisis, health and environmental data collection has sharply declined in Georgia. The lack of financial and technical resources and institutional weakness are the major problems. Both the NEAP and the NEHAP emphasize the need for environmental and health information. There are several ongoing or planned projects to improve the collection of relevant data. This data collection should be planned and developed so that the information will facilitate the assessment of the population's exposure to environmental factors as well as the assessment of the environmental health impact.

Recommendation 14.1:
The Ministry of Labour, Health and Social Affairs and the Ministry of Environment and Natural Resources Protection should:
(a) Jointly review the NEAP and NEHAP to ensure their mutual consistency and to set priorities for future action for environmental health management;
(b) Develop health and environmental information systems in close collaboration so that they can be combined to monitor environmental health effects, to assess environmental health impact, and to support decision-making in environmental health policy. The Ministries should support the efforts of the Centre for Health Statistics and the Centre for Disease Control to improve health data quality and continue surveys to identify data quality problems, train personnel, establish computerized databases and implement procedures for data quality control. (See recommendation 3.1.)

The extensive use of lead in petrol constitutes a serious public health problem especially for children, whose intellectual development is compromised by exposure to lead. The existing law (July 1999) requires a total ban of petrol containing more than 0.013 grams of lead per litre, and this should be enforced. (See chapter 13, on transport and environment.)

Recommendation 14.2:
The Ministry of Labour, Health and Social Affairs should monitor blood lead levels in children as an indicator of a reduction in exposure to lead.

Ambient air pollution in urban areas has a substantial public health impact. A recent quantitative assessment of the impact of air pollution in Tbilisi, as well as calculations of the benefits of reducing air pollution to European Union standards, provide strong justification for action. Similar effects are likely also in other urban areas. Transport is currently the main source of air pollution and traffic density is increasing, which results in increasing exposure and health effects. Air pollution levels should be reduced to protect public health (see chapters 5, on air management and 13, on transport and environment).

Recommendation 14.3:
The Ministry of Labour, Health and Social Affairs and the Ministry of Environment and Natural Resources Protection, in collaboration with other ministries, should protect public health by continuing actions to reduce the population's exposure to air pollution, in particular from vehicle exhaust fumes. Air pollution monitoring should be strengthened, and, in view of its relevance to health, PM_{10} should be monitored in the future.

There is sporadic information that several indoor factors are likely to cause adverse health effects. These include combustion products from heating and cooking, smoking indoors, radon decay products, and dampness and mould. In order to develop strategies for improving indoor environmental conditions in homes and other buildings, more objective information is needed on sources, emissions, concentrations and exposure. Smoking regulations and restrictions are essential to ensure improved indoor air quality.

Indoor radon exposure is a potentially serious problem, and radon monitoring should be a priority for radiation protection. Further decision-making should be based on the results of a nationwide survey that will provide information on the indoor radon concentrations in different areas of the country. At the moment, there is no monitoring of radon contamination of drinking water.

Recommendation 14.4:
(a) The Ministry of Labour, Health and Social Affairs should develop a strategy for improving indoor environmental conditions. The first task is to collect information by conducting a representative survey in homes and other buildings. Restriction of smoking indoors to reduce exposure to environmental tobacco smoke is strongly justified for health reasons;

(b) The Ministry of Environment and Natural Resources Protection should conduct a nationwide survey of indoor radon exposure and use its results to develop a strategy to minimize the public health impact.

Microbiological contamination of drinking water is a well-recognized problem in Georgia. Improvement in water treatment can substantially reduce the burden of water-borne diseases. Measures should be focused on prevention of secondary contamination of water in distribution systems and uninterrupted basic water treatment at treatment plants. While continuous chlorination is of paramount importance, uninterrupted physical treatment of surface water (filtration and coagulation) is also necessary for water supply systems that are using surface water sources or poorly protected ground water sources (see recommendation 7.1).

The ability to diagnose infectious diseases should be improved. While it may not be feasible to simultaneously improve laboratory capabilities at all medical facilities across the country, limited resources can be focused on establishment of national and regional diagnostic centres equipped with modern methodologies. Improving the ability to detect these pathogens in food products and water supplies will provide the opportunity not only to determine causes of outbreaks and take timely containment measures but also to conduct regular surveys across the country and work on outbreak prevention.

Monitoring of chemical pollution of water supplies is limited to a few basic parameters and quality control is lacking. Data on the chemical contamination of food products are extremely limited. Many chemical laboratories are underfunded, underequipped and understaffed. The existing limited resources should be pooled to establish an inter-agency chemistry laboratory with modern equipment and well-trained personnel. This central laboratory would enable the Georgian environmental health specialists to address urgent issues of environmental pollution in different parts of the country and provide reliable data for risk assessment and priority-setting. It may also serve as a reference laboratory and a training centre.

Recommendation 14.5:
The Ministry of Labour, Health and Social Affairs should:
(a) Focus resources on the establishment of central and regional laboratories with expanded capabilities to diagnose a wide range of infectious diseases and detect bacterial, viral and protozoan pathogens in water and food samples;
(b) Concentrate resources to establish at least one well-equipped inter-agency laboratory for chemical analyses of environmental samples including water, ambient and indoor air, and soil.

ANNEXES

ANNEX I

SELECTED REGIONAL AND GLOBAL ENVIRONMENTAL AGREEMENTS

Worldwide agreements		Georgia	
Year		**Year**	**Status**
1949	(GENEVA) Convention on Road Traffic		
1951	International Plant Convention		
1954	International Convention for the Prevention of Pollution of the Sea by Oil		
1957	(BRUSSELS) International Convention on Limitation of Liability of Owners of Sea-going Ships		
1958	(GENEVA) Convention on Fishing and Conservation of Living Resources of the High Seas		
1958	Convention on the Continental Shelf		
1958	Convention on the Territorial Sea and the Contiguous Zone		
1958	Convention on the High Seas		
1960	International Convention for the Safety of Life at Sea		
1960	(GENEVA) Convention concerning the Protection of Workers against Ionising Radiations		
1963	(VIENNA) Convention on Civil Liability for Nuclear Damage		
	1997 (VIENNA) Protocol to Amend the 1963 Vienna Convention on Civil Liability for Nuclear Damage		
1963	(MOSCOW) Treaty Banning Nuclear Weapon Tests in the Atmosphere, in Outer Space and under Water		
1969	(BRUSSELS) Convention on Civil Liability for Oil Pollution Damage		
	1976 (LONDON) Protocol		
1969	(BRUSSELS) Convention relating to Intervention on the High Seas in Cases of Oil Pollution Casualties		R
1971	Convention on Wetlands of International Importance Especially as Waterfowl Habitat1977		
1971	(RAMSAR) Convention on Wetlands of International Importance especially as Waterfowl Habitat	1996	R
	1982 (PARIS) Amendment		
	1987 (REGINA) Amendments		
1971	(GENEVA) Convention on Protection against Hazards from Benzene (ILO 136)		
1971	(BRUSSELS) Convention on the Establishment of an International Fund for Compensation for Oil Pollution Damage		R
1971	(LONDON, MOSCOW, WASHINGTON) Treaty on the Prohibition of the Emplacement of Nuclear Weapons and Other Weapons of Mass Destruction on the Sea-bed and the Ocean Floor and in the Subsoil thereof		
1972	(PARIS) Convention on the Protection of the World Cultural and Natural Heritage		R
1972	(LONDON) Convention on the Prevention of Marine Pollution by Dumping of Wastes and Other Matter		
	1978 Amendments (incineration)		
	1980 Amendments (list of substances)		
1972	Convention on the Prohibition of the Development, Production and Stockpiling of Bacteriological (Biological) and Toxin Weapons, and their Destruction		
1972	International Convention on the International Regulations for Preventing Collision at Sea		
1972	(GENEVA) International Convention for Safe Containers		
1973	(WASHINGTON) Convention on International Trade in Endangered Species of Wild Fauna and Flora	1996	R
	1983 (GABORONE) Amendment		

S = signed; **R** = ratified; **D** = denounced.

Worldwide agreements		Georgia	
Year		**Year**	**Status**
1973	(LONDON) Convention for the Prevention of Pollution from Ships (MARPOL)	1995	R
	1978 (LONDON) Protocol (segregated ballast)		
	1978 (LONDON) Annex III on Hazardous Substances carried in packaged form		
	1978 (LONDON) Annex IV on Sewage		
	1978 (LONDON) Annex V on Garbage		
1975	Convention Concerning the Protection of the World Cultural and Natural Heritage		R
1977	(GENEVA) Convention on Protection of Workers against Occupational Hazards from Air Pollution, Noise and Vibration (ILO 148)		
1979	(BONN) Convention on the Conservation of Migratory Species of Wild Animals	2000	R
	1991 (LONDON) Agreement Conservation of Bats in Europe	2001	R
	1992 (NEW YORK) Agreement on the Conservation of Small Cetaceans of the Baltic and North Seas (ASCOBANS)		
	1995 (THE HAGUE) African/Eurasian Migratory Waterbird Agreement (AEWA)	2001	R
	1996 (MONACO) Agreement on the Conservation of Cetaceans of the Black Sea, Mediterranean Sea and Contiguous Atlantic Area (ACCOBAMS)	2001	R
1980	Convention on the Physical Protection of Nuclear Material		
1981	Convention Concerning Occupational Safety and Health and the Working Environment		
1982	(MONTEGO BAY) Convention on the Law of the Sea		R
	1994 (NEW YORK) Agreement Related to the Implementation of Part XI of the Convention		
	1994 (NEW YORK) Agreement for the Implementation of the Provisions of the United Nations Convention on the Law of the Sea of 10 December 1982 relating to the Conservation and Management of Straddling Fish Stocks and Highly Migratory Fish Stocks		
1985	Convention Concerning Occupational Health Services		
	(VIENNA) Convention for the Protection of the Ozone Layer	1996	R
	1987 (MONTREAL) Protocol on Substances that Deplete the Ozone Layer	1996	R
	1990 (LONDON) Amendment to Protocol	2000	R
	1992 (COPENHAGEN) Amendment to Protocol	2000	R
	1997 (MONTREAL) Amendment to Protocol	2000	R
1986	Convention Concerning Safety in the Use of Asbestos		
	(VIENNA) Convention on Early Notification of a Nuclear Accident		
	(VIENNA) Convention on Assistance in the Case of a Nuclear Accident or Radiological Emergency		
1989	(BASEL) Convention on the Control of Transboundary Movements of Hazardous Wastes and their Disposal 1995 Ban Amendment	1999	R
	1999 (BASEL) Protocol on Liability and Compensation		
1990	(LONDON) Convention on Oil Pollution Preparedness, Response and Cooperation		R
1992	(RIO) Convention on Biological Diversity	1994	R
	2000 (CARTAGENA) Protocol on Biosafety		
1992	(NEW YORK) Framework Convention on Climate Change	1994	R
	1997 (KYOTO) Protocol		R
1993	Convention on the Prohibition of the Development, Production, Stockpiling and Use of Chemical Weapons and on Their Destruction		
1994	(VIENNA) Convention on Nuclear Safety		
1994	(PARIS) Convention to Combat Desertification	1999	R
1997	(VIENNA) Joint Convention on the Safety of Spent Fuel Management and on the Safety of Radioactive Waste Management		
1997	(VIENNA) Convention on Supplementary Compensation for Nuclear Damage		
1998	(ROTTERDAM) Convention on the Prior Informed Consent Procedure for Certain Hazardous Chemicals and Pesticides in International Trade		

S = signed; **R** = ratified; **D** = denounced.

Selected bilateral and multilateral agreements *(continued)*

Regional and subregional agreements		Georgia	
Year		**Year**	**Status**
1950	(PARIS) International Convention for the Protection of Birds		
1951	Convention for the Establishment of the European and Mediterranean Plant Protection Organisation		
1957	(GENEVA) European Agreement - International Carriage of Dangerous Goods by Road (ADR) European Agreement Concerning the International Carriage of Dangerous Goods by Road (ADR) Annex A Provisions Concerning Dangerous Substances and Articles Annex B Provisions Concerning Transport Equipment and Transport Operations		
1958	(GENEVA) Agreement - Adoption of Uniform Conditions of Approval and Reciprocal Recognition of Approval for Motor Vehicle Equipment and Parts.		
1958	Convention Concerning Fishing in the Water of the Danube		
1968	(PARIS) European Convention - Protection of Animals during International Transport 1979 (STRASBOURG) Additional Protocol		
1969	(LONDON) European Convention - Protection of the Archeological Heritage		
1969	(LONDON) European Convention - Protection of the Architectural Heritage		
1973	(GDANSK) Convention on fishing and conservation of the living resources in the Baltic Sea and the Belts 1982 (WARSAW) Amendments		
1974	Yugoslav-Italian Agreement on the Protection of the Waters of the Adriatic Sea and Coastal Areas Against Pollution		
1974	(Helsinki) Convention on the Protection of the Marine Environment of the Baltic Sea Area		
1976	European Convention for the Protection of Animals Kept for Farming Purposes		
1976	Protocol for the Prevention of Pollution of the Mediterranean Sea by Dumping from Ships and Aircrafts		
1976	Protocol Concerning Co-operation in Combating Pollution of Mediterranean Sea by oil and Other Harmful Substances in Cases of Emergency		
1976	Convention for the Protection of the Mediterranean Sea against Pollution		
1979	(BERN) Convention on the Conservation of European Wildlife and Natural Habitats		
1979	(GENEVA) Convention on Long-range Transboundary Air Pollution 1984 (GENEVA) Protocol - Financing of Co-operative Programme (EMEP) 1985 (HELSINKI) Protocol - Reduction of Sulphur Emissions by 30% 1988 (SOFIA) Protocol - Control of Emissions of Nitrogen Oxides 1991 (GENEVA) Protocol - Volatile Organic Compounds 1994 (OSLO) Protocol - Further Reduction of Sulphur Emissions 1998 (AARHUS) Protocol on Heavy Metals 1998 (AARHUS) Protocol on Persistent Organic Pollutants 1999 (GOTHENBURG) Protocol to Abate Acidification, Eutrophication and Ground-level Ozone		1999	R

S = signed;   **R** = ratified;   **D** = denounced.

Selected bilateral and multilateral agreements *(continued)*

Year	Regional and subregional agreements	Georgia Year	Status
1980	Protocol for the Protection of the Mediterranean Sea against Pollution from Land-based Sources		
1982	Protocol Concerning Mediterranean Specially Protected Areas		
1986	Agreement for the Environmental Protection from Pollution of the Tisza River and Tributaries		
1991	(ESPOO) Convention on Environmental Impact Assessment in a Transboundary Context		
1992	(HELSINKI) Convention on the Protection and Use of Transboundary Waters and International Lakes 1999 (LONDON) Protocol on Water and Health	1999	S
1992	(HELSINKI) Convention on the Transboundary Effects of Industrial Accidents		
1992	(HELSINKI) Convention on the Protection of the Marine Environment of the Baltic Sea Area, 1992		
1992	(PARIS) Convention for the Protection of the Marine Environment of the North-East Atlantic		
1993	(OSLO and LUGANO) Convention - Civil Liability for Damage from Activities Dangerous for the Environment		
1994	(LISBON) Energy Charter Treaty 1994 (LISBON) Protocol on Energy Efficiency and Related Aspects		
1996	Treaty between the Federal Government of FRY and Government of the Russian Federation on Cooperation on Environmental Protection		
1996	Treaty between the Federal Government of FRY and Government of the Russian Federation on Cooperation on Preventing Industrial Hazards, Natural Disasters and Remediation of their Consequences		
1998	(AARHUS) Convention on Access to Information, Public Participation in Decision-making and Access to Justice in Environmental Matters	2000	R
1999	Agreement for the Establishment of a General Fisheries Council for the Mediterranean		

S = signed;   R = ratified;   D = denounced.

ANNEX II
SELECTED ECONOMIC AND
ENVIRONMENTAL DATA

Georgia: Selected economic data

	1995	2000
TOTAL AREA (1 000 km^2)	69.7	69.7
POPULATION		
Total population, (1 000 000 inh.)	5.4	5.0
% change (1995-2000)	..	..
Population density, (inh./km^2)	..	..
GROSS DOMESTIC PRODUCT		
GDP, **(million lari)**	3,693	6,016
% change (1995-2000)	..	..
per capita, (US$ 1000/cap.)	..	..
INDUSTRY		
Value added in industry (mill. lari)	523.8	963.0
Industrial production - % change (1995-2000)	..	..
AGRICULTURE		
Value added in agriculture (mill. lari)	1,851.0	2,650.0
ENERGY SUPPLY		
Total supply, (Mtoe)	n/a in national statistic	
% change (1995-2000)		
Energy intensity, (Toe/US$ 1000)		
% change (1995-2000)		
Structure of energy supply, (%)		
Solid fuels		
Oil		
Gas		
Nuclear		
Hydro,etc.		
ROAD TRANSPORT		
Road traffic volumes	130 mln.t/km	420 mln.t/km
-billion veh.-km	..	..
- % change (1995-2000)	..	..
- per capita (1 000 veh.-km/cap.)	..	..
Road vehicle stock,	..	..
- 10 000 vehicles	..	..
- % change (1995-2000)	..	..
- per capita (veh./100 inh.)	..	..

Source: UNECE and National Statistics

.. = not available.   - = nil or negligible.

Georgia: Selected environmental data

	1995	2000
LAND		
Total area (1 000 km^2)	69,700	69,700
Major protected areas (% of total area)	4.1	4.2
Nitrogenous fertilizer use (t/km^2 arable land)	6,000	..
FOREST		
Forest area (% of land area)	..	39.6
Use of forest resources (harvest/growth)	..	..
Tropical wood imports (US$/cap.)	..	..
THREATENED SPECIES		
Mammals (% of species known)	..	..
Birds (% of species known)	..	..
Fish (% of species known)	..	..
WATER		
Water withdrawal (million m3/year)	2,000	2,010
Fish catches (% of world catches)	..	..
Public waste water treatment (% of population served)	0.8	0.3
AIR		
Emissions of sulphur oxides (kg/cap.)	3.9	1.2
" (kg/US$ 1000 GDP)	..	..
Emissions of nitrogen oxides (kg/cap.)	4.5	5.6
" (kg/US$ 1000 GDP)	..	..
Emissions of carbon dioxide (t/cap.)	1.0	0.6
" (ton/US$ 1000 GDP)	..	..
WASTE GENERATED		
Industrial waste (kg/US$ 1000 GDP)	..	..
Municipal waste (kg/cap.)	..	..
Nuclear waste (ton/Mtoe of TPES)	no waste generation	
NOISE		
Population exposed to leq > 65 dB (A) (million inh.)	..	..

Source: UNECE and National Statistics

.. = not available.   - = nil or negligible.

SOURCES

Personal authors

1. Abramidze, S. et al. The radiological accident in Tbilisi. IAEA-CN-70/90. TECDOC-1045: Safety of Radiation Sources and Security of Radioactive Materials. September 1998.
2. Bernabé, S. A profile of the labour market in Georgia. A report for the UNDP, State Committee for Statistics in Tbilisi and the ILO. 2002.
3. Beruchachvili, N. Diversity of Georgia's Landscapes and Geographical Analysis of landscape Diversity of the World. In: Biological and Landscape Diversity of Georgia, Proceedings. WWF and The World Bank. 2000.
4. Beruchachvili, N. Georgia's Biodiversity against a Global Background. In: Biological and Landscape Diversity of Georgia, Proceedings. WWF and The World Bank. 2000.
5. Grim, C.E. et al. Prevalence of cardiovascular risk factors in the Republic of Georgia. J Hum Hypertens, 13, 243-247. 1999.
6. Gujaraidze, K. Environmental planning in Georgia. Land use planning and land resource management. Lund University, Sweden, Masters thesis. 2001.
7. Jaakkola, J.J. et al. Use of health information systems in the Russian federation in the assessment of environmental health effects. Environmental health perspectives 2000 Jul;108 (7): 589-594.
8. Kreidl, P. et al. Investigation of an outbreak on amoebiasis in Georgia. Eurosurveillance Monthly, 1999; 4 (10).
9. Levine, R. and Wallace, G. The Mineral Industry of Georgia. 2001.
10. Levine, R. The Mineral Industry of Georgia. 2000.
11. Libert, B. The environmental heritage of Soviet agriculture. CAB International, 1995.
12. Metreveli, K. Forest and Forest Products Country Profile - Georgia. Final version of the report for Georgian Forests Development project (World Bank). 2002.
13. Mirtskhoulava, Ts. Soil Erosion in Georgia, Tbilisi.
14. Samet, J. M. and Eradze, G. R. Radon and lung cancer risk: taking stock at the millennium. Environmental Health Perspectives 2000 Aug. 108 (4).
15. Tvalchrelidze, A. and Nishikawa Y. Eds. Mining Industry of Georgia in a Free Market Environment. 2002.
16. Voisin, P. et al. Suspicion of radiological accident in Georgia: the role of the IPSN.

Material from Georgia

17. AEA Technology plc. Technical Assistance with Development of an Air Quality Management plan and Health Effect Study for Tbilisi – Interim Report, May 2002.
18. Country Report: Georgia. Energy Efficiency and Renewable Energy Resources. 2001.
19. Country Report: Georgia. Review. Energy Efficiency and Renewable Energy Resources. Part II. Draft. 2001.
20. Georgia Online. Tbilisi Tourist Guide 2001.
21. Georgia. Law of Georgia on Environmental Protection. Tbilisi, December 1996.
22. Georgian Center for Environmental Research. National Policies and Strategies.
23. Joint River Management Programme. Project number SCR-E/111231/C/SV/WW Project Synopsis.
24. Ministry of Economy, Industry and Trade. Indicative Plan for the Social and Economic Development of Georgia in 2001-2005.
25. Ministry of Environment and Energy, and DANCEE. OECD EAP Task Force Secretariat. Environmental Expenditures, Environmental Financing Strategies and Use of Economic Instruments in NIS Countries. Environmental financing Strategy: Georgia. Draft COWI version. April 2000.
26. Ministry of Environment of Georgia. Improvement of Urban Air Quality by Reducing Emissions from Transport in Tbilisi. 1998.
27. Ministry of Environment of Georgia. Inception Report. London Protocol Implementation in Georgia.
28. Ministry of Environment of Georgia. National Agency on Climate Change. Bulletin of the National Agency on Climate Change No 10 (e). Tbilisi, 2001.
29. Ministry of Environment of Georgia. National Environmental Action Plan Programme (NEAP). Georgia. Draft 1. English version. Tbilisi, April 2000.
30. Ministry of Environment. Improvement of Urban Air Quality by Reducing Emissions by Transport in Tbilisi. Pilot Project in Air Quality Management. 1998
31. Ministry of Environment. National Environmental Action Plan. Tbilisi, June 2000.
32. Ministry of Labour, Health and Social Affairs of Georgia. National Program on Environment and Health. The First National Conference. March 28, 2001. Tbilisi 2001.
33. Ministry of Labour, Health and Social Affairs of Georgia. National Environmental Hygiene Action Plan for Georgia (NEHAP). Tbilisi, 2001.
34. State Statistical Department of Georgia. Statistical Book. The Industry of Georgia at the End of XX Century and at the Beginning of XXI Century. (in Georgian). 2002.
35. State Statistical Department of Georgia. Statistical Year Book of Georgia, 2001.

Regional and international institutions

36. EC TACIS and The World Bank. Environmental Resources Management, "Irrigation and Drainage Community Development Project".
37. Friends of the Earth. The Greens Movement of Georgia. Annual Report 2001.
38. GEF. Draft Project Brief. Georgia – Promoting the Use of Renewable Energy Resources for Local Energy Supply. 1999.
39. GEF/World Bank Project. Project Description. Agricultural Research, Extension and Training. Tblisi, 2000.
40. Integrated Coastal Management Project (GICMP). Review of Livelihood Security Georgia.
41. NETCEN. Technical Assistance of an Air Quality Management Plan and Health Effect. Study for Tbilisi – Final Report. August 2002.
42. OECD. Towards Sustainable Development. Environmental Indicators. 1998.
43. PA Consulting Group and USAID. Regulations for Oil and Gas Operations in Georgia. 2002.
44. REC Caucasus. Newsletter. August 2001.
45. REC Caucasus. Newsletter. February 2001.
46. REC Caucasus. Newsletter. May 2001.
47. UNDP Country Office in Georgia. A centre for Sustainable Human Development. Partnership to Fight Poverty.
48. UNDP. Global Environment Facility; Government of Georgia. Removing Barriers to Energy Efficiency in Municipal Heat and Hot Water Supply in Georgia. Final Report. Tbilisi, 2000.
49. UNDP. Human Development Report. Georgia 2000. Georgia 2000.
50. UNDP. Rio +10. Georgia. National Assessment Report for Sustainable Development. Prepared for the World Summit for Sustainable Development held in Johannesburg, South Africa. 2002.
51. UNDP/GED. Georgia's Initial Communication Under the United Nations Framework Convention on Climate Change. Tbilisi, 1999.
52. UNDP/GEF and Ministry of Environment and Natural Resources Protection. National Agency on Climate Change. Capacity building to assess technology needs, modalities to acquire and absorb them, evaluate and host projects. II phase of Georgia's enabling activities. Tbilisi, 2002.
53. UNDP/UNOPS Project "GEO-2110 Country Programme for Phasing Out of Leaded Gasoline in Georgia": Volume 2. Options for politics and measures for implementing lead phase out in Georgia.
54. UNECE. Environmental Performance Reviews. Armenia. 2000.
55. UNECE. Environmental Performance Reviews. Uzbekistan. 2001.
56. UNEP GRID-Tbilisi. Caucasus Environmental Outlook (2000).
57. UNEP. Caucasus Environment Outlook (CEO) 2002. Tbilisi 2002.
58. UNEP. State of the Environment – Georgia, 1996.
59. UNEP. The State of the Environment Report in Tbilisi (2000).
60. UNEP-GRID. Tbilisi Environmental Atlas, Tbilisi, 1999.
61. United Nations. Johannesburg Summit 2002. Georgia Country Profile.
62. WWF. Biodiversity of the Caucasus Ecoregion. 2001.

Internet addresses:

Ministries and government institutions

63. Georgian government: http://www.parliament.ge/GENERAL/C_D/countrydata.html
64. Georgian government: http://www.parliament.ge/ECONOMICS/
65. Georgian government: http://www.parliament.ge/GOVERNANCE/GOV/
66. Georgian government: http://www.parliament.ge/GOVERNANCE/GOV/ministr.html
67. Ministry of Education: http://www.parliament.ge/GOVERNANCE/GOV/education.html
68. Ministry of Environment: http://www.parliament.ge/GOVERNANCE/GOV/enviro/Parliament/Ministry.htm
69. Ministry of Foreign Affairs: http://www.mfa.gov.ge/english/index.shtml
70. Ministry of Post and Telecommunication: http://www.iberiapac.ge/mincom/
71. Ministry of State Property Management: http://web.sanet.ge/mospm/
72. Ministry of Transport: http://www.iberiapac.ge/mintrans/
73. National Report on Biodiversity: http://www.parliament.ge/GOVERNANCE/GOV/enviro/biodiversity/bio/bio1.htm
74. The Environment Fund for Georgia: http://www.efg.org/html/about_efg.html
75. The Library of the Congress: http://lcweb2.loc.gov/frd/cs/getoc.html - ge0014
76. The State Chancellery: http://www.parliament.ge/GOVERNANCE/GOV/kanc.html
77. Marine Environment Protection in Georgia: http://www.parliament.ge/gov/enviro/manual/marine.htm

Other internet sites

78.	Basel Convention:	http://www.basel.int/pub/nationreport.html
79.	CENN (Caucasus Environmental NGO Network)	http://www.cenn.org/
80.	CIA	http://www.cia.gov/cia/publications/factbook/geos/gg.html
81.	EBRD	http://www.ebrd.com/english/index.htm
82.	eLaw	http://www.elaw.org/resources/text.asp?ID=266
83.	eLaw:	http://www.elaw.org/search/results.asp?words=georgia
84.	Encarta	http://encarta.msn.com/encnet/refpages/RefArticle.aspx?refid=761556415
85.	Energy Information Administration (USA):	http://www.eia.doe.gov/emeu/cabs/georgia.html
86.	EU	http://europa.eu.int/comm/external_relations/georgia/intro/data.htm
87.	Eurasianet.org	http://www.eurasianet.org/resource/georgia/index.shtml
88.	GEF: Country profiles	http://gefweb.org/Projects/GEF_country_Profiles/gef_country_profiles.html
89.	GEF: Project list	http://www.gefonline.org/home.cfm
90.	Governments on the Web	http://www.gksoft.com/govt/en/ge.html
91.	Grid Arendal	http://www.grida.no
92.	Grid Tbilisi	http://www.grida.no/enrin/htmls/georgia/caucasus/
93.	Heidelberg University	http://www.rzuser.uni-heidelberg.de/~ci4/georgien/georgien/georgienlage.htm
94.	International Atomic Energy Agency	http://www.iaea.or.at/worldatom/Press/P_release/2002/prn0208.shtml
95.	Nuclear Threat Initiative (NTI)	http://www.nti.org/db/nisprofs/georgia/overview.htm
96.	The Library network; WB and IMF	http://jolis.worldbankimflib.org/Pathfinders/Countries/GE/geprivatize.htm
97.	The World Bank:	
	http://lnweb18.worldbank.org/eca/georgia.nsf/ECADocByUnid/AD6A575F2B8DD7DBC4256BD60045DBA3?Opendocument	
98.	U.S. State Dept.	http://www.state.gov/www/background_notes/georgia_9811_bgn.html
99.	UN Monthly Bulletin of Statistics	http://esa.un.org/unsd/mbs/mbsresult.asp?cid=268&wp=1&ps=20
100.	UN Sustainable development,	http://www.un.org/esa/agenda21/natlinfo/countr/georgia/index.htm
101.	UNEP	http://www.unep.net/profile/index.cfm
102.	UNEP Chemicals:	http://www.chem.unep.ch/pops/POPs_Inc/proceedings/stpetbrg/FINAL%20REPORT.htm
103.	US State Department	http://www.state.gov/r/pa/ei/bgn/5253.htm - econ
104.	USAID	http://www.usaid.gov/pubs/bj2001/ee/ge/
105.	Wise	http://www.antenna.nl/wise/435/4299.html